D0364681
13 MAY 1997
-4. NOV. 1988
-1. DEC. 1988
1 3 MAY 2005
28. JAN. 1989
CANCELLED
-5. FEB. 1993

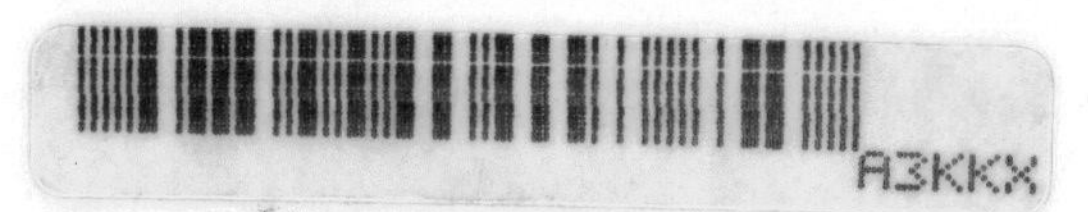
A3KKX

THE TREASURE OF OUR TONGUE

LINCOLN BARNETT

THE TREASURE OF OUR TONGUE

THE STORY OF ENGLISH FROM ITS OBSCURE BEGINNINGS TO ITS PRESENT EMINENCE AS THE MOST WIDELY SPOKEN LANGUAGE

LONDON
SECKER & WARBURG

First published in England 1966 by
Martin Secker & Warburg Limited
14 Carlisle Street, Soho Square, W.1

Sections of this book appeared originally as follows: Condensed versions of Chapters 1, 2, 3, and 5 and a small part of Chapter 4 in Life International, *portions of Chapters 1 and 2 in a short article in* Life, *and Chapter 6 in somewhat different form in* Horizon.
The lines from "Hello Poem" by Robert Sward appearing on pages 191–2 are quoted by permission of The Transatlantic Review.

Printed in Great Britain by
Western Printing Services Ltd., Bristol

THIS BOOK IS DEDICATED

WITH GRATITUDE AND AFFECTION

To F. Fraser Bond

WHO TAUGHT ME—AND SO MANY OTHERS—

TO HONOUR AND CHERISH

THE TREASURE OF OUR TONGUE

ACKNOWLEDGEMENTS

In 1959 my friend Cal Whipple, who is listed on the masthead of *Life* Magazine as A. B. C. Whipple, Editor, International Editions, conceived the idea of a series of articles on the English Language. So far as I know, he was the first person to note and call attention to the phenomenal spread of English around the world following World War II and its adoption as the official or second language of most of the new nations that came into being with the dissolution of the colonial empires. Mr. Whipple asked me to write the series and assigned Betsy Peirce Prince to assist me in the undertaking. Mrs. Prince brought to the assignment her qualifications both as an experienced *Life* researcher and as a linguist commanding fluency in three languages and a working knowledge of several others. The nucleus of this book took form in a series of articles that appeared in *Life International* in 1961 and 1962. The final chapter appeared in part in *Horizon*, July 1963. I wish to acknowledge my debt both to Mr. Whipple for his original conception and to Mrs. Prince whose contribution may be estimated by a glance at the selective bibliography at the end of the book. I might add that a comprehensive bibliography of writings on the English language from the invention of printing down to 1922 was reissued recently (from the original compiled at Harvard four decades ago) in eight volumes.

I should like to thank Dr. I. A. Richards and Dr. Christine Gibson of Language Research, Inc., Cambridge, Mass., and Mr. Datus C. Smith, Jr., president of Franklin Book Programs, Inc., a non-profit organization for international book publishing development, for their interest and assistance in the preparation of Chapters 1 and 2. I am grateful also to Mr. William Harlan Hale, who made valuable suggestions with respect to Chapter 6. In addition to those who lend personal assistance to an author, there are others who affect his work by what they have written and whose contribution cannot be adequately acknowledged merely by including a title or titles in a bibliography. For this reason I should like to emphasize the catalytic importance to me of the writings of Jacques Barzun, Weston LaBarre, Dwight Macdonald, Otto Jespersen, Eric Partridge, Mario Pei, Simeon Potter, and most especially the indispensable work of Alfred C. Baugh.

Finally, I submit my grateful thanks to Mr. Harold Strauss, editor-in-chief of Alfred A. Knopf, Inc., both for his patience and his impatience.

CONTENTS

I

THE LINGUISTIC WONDER OF THE MODERN WORLD

And who in time knows whither we may vent
The treasure of our tongue? To what strange shores
This gain of our best glory shall be sent,
To enrich unknowing nations with our stores?
What worlds in the yet unformed Occident
May come refined with the accents that are ours?

SAMUEL DANIEL (1562–1619)
English poet and historian

The simple answer to Samuel Daniel's multiple question is that the treasure of our tongue has been transported around the world. Strange shores and far-off nations have been enriched with the verbal stores, if not necessarily refined by the accents, that are ours. For, unbelievable as it might have seemed to a contemporary of Shakespeare, English has become the most widely spoken language on earth. Today 300 million people—nearly one in ten—employ English as their primary language; and 600 million—nearly one in five—can be reached by it in some degree.

Few events in man's turbulent history compare in scope or significance with this global linguistic conquest. When Daniel wrote his prophetic lines, he expressed a poet's vision conceived in the bright morning of the expanding British Empire. At the time of the Norman Conquest in 1066, English had no more than 1·5 million speakers. In the ensuing five centuries it evolved slowly into the rich, flexible medium of the Elizabethan poets who, while cherishing their language, never dreamed it might become a universal tongue. In 1582 Richard Mulcaster, the most famous English educator of his day, headmaster of the Merchant Taylors' School in London and later high master at

St. Paul's, remarked: "The English tongue is of small reach, stretching no further than this island of ours, nay not there over all." Portia, in *The Merchant of Venice*, said regretfully of the young English Baron Falconbridge: "You know I say nothing to him, for he understands not me, nor I him: he hath neither Latin, French nor Italian." As recently as the eighteenth century, English was still outranked by French, Latin (for scholarship), German, Spanish, Russian, and Italian; and European academicians deplored the fact that English writers wrote only in English.

Today English is written, spoken, broadcast, and understood on every continent, and it can claim a wider geographical range than any other tongue. There are few civilized areas where it has any competition as the lingua franca—the international language of commerce, diplomacy, science, and scholarship. Its speakers cover one quarter of the globe, ranging from the fair-skinned people of the British Isles through every gradation of colour and race the world around. It is spoken by Christians, Jews, Moslems, Buddhists, Hindus, and adherents of every major religious faith on earth.

The dominance of any language, however, rests not only on statistical superiority and geographical sweep, but on cultural prestige and the status of the people who use it. Voltaire expressed this notion when he observed: "The first among languages is that which possesses the largest number of excellent works." Of the nearly four thousand languages spoken by mankind on this planet today, only a dozen have international or cultural significance. As a primary language, Chinese can claim more speakers than English—an estimated 700 million. It can also boast a more ancient heritage than English and an imposing cultural tradition descending from Confucius and Lao-tse through twenty-five centuries down to the present time. But its alphabet and calligraphy present enormous difficulties. And so far as the spoken language is concerned, its four main regional varieties—each divided into numerous sub-dialects—are mutually unintelligible save to the educated ear. The differences between spoken Mandarin and spoken Cantonese, for example, are as formidable as those between Danish and Dutch. So, the use of Chinese is largely confined to those born to the tongue, and living for the most part in China or Taiwan.

After Chinese and English, the other great languages of the world are, in descending order of the number of speakers who employ them as a *primary* tongue: Spanish with 140 million speakers; Russian with 130 million; German with 100 million; Japanese, 95 million; Arabic, 80 million; Bengali, Indonesian, and Portuguese, 75 million each; Urdu (spoken in Pakistan and parts of India), 70 million; French and Hindi, 65 million each; and Italian, 55 million.

Of these, French has been paramount in the Western world for centuries. It has been the international language of diplomacy since the reign of Louis XIV. It has been the language of culture, of the educated classes, of the aristocracy of all European nations from the Urals to the British Isles. But with the erosion of the French Empire in the last two decades, it has lost ground on every continent. Although its cultural prestige is undimmed and can never wane so long as its literary legacy is preserved for posterity to enjoy, French is no longer the principal language of diplomacy and trade. Even in such erstwhile French dominions as Laos, Vietnam, and Lebanon, English is now a competing tongue. It is noteworthy that in the United Nations, 53 member states now regularly receive transcripts of speeches and proceedings in English, as against 27 which request drafts in French.

Culturally, as well as from the standpoint of geographical radius and numerical status, Spanish ranks near the apex of the linguistic hierarchy. It has hegemony through Central and South America (save for Portuguese-speaking Brazil), and the numbers of its adherents are multiplying swiftly with the swelling populations of the Latin-American states. But it shows no signs at present of overflowing its existing domain. German and Italian are also largely encompassed by their respective national boundaries—although the former was the leading language of science until the Nazi extermination of intellect, and the latter is still mandatory in the higher realms of music and art. Arabic, despite its vast territorial range from Casablanca to Baghdad, and notwithstanding the current hot fires of Arab nationalism, has disadvantages both in speech and writing that will probably preclude its passing very far beyond the limits of the Moslem world.

So far as Russian is concerned, its 130 million speakers are resident mostly within the Soviet Union, whose enormous spatial confines and total population of 224,700,000 also accommodate 148 other languages. Although Russian is the medium for some of the world's greatest literature—the works of Tolstoy, Dostoevsky, Turgenev, Gogol, Chekhov, Pushkin, Pasternak—and although the political and scientific dynamism of the Soviet Union presents the greatest challenge which the English-speaking nations face today, the Russian language is unlikely to win a linguistic war. It has a specialized alphabet, and its inflected grammar is far more difficult to master than the comparatively simple grammar of English. Like Chinese, Russian is currently limited to its geographical place of origin.

English, however, is spreading around the planet at a constantly accelerating tempo. Virtually every capital city in Asia and Africa (save for former French colonies) has an English-language daily. More than 70 per cent of the world's mail is written and addressed in English. More than 60 per cent of the world's radio programmes are in English. It is noteworthy and ironical that among the leading disseminators of English are the Russians and Chinese in their attempt to woo friends and influence nations in uncommitted regions of the earth. The Russians use English for their propaganda broadcasts to the Far East. On African channels formerly dominated by programmes from Cairo in Arabic and Swahili, listeners in Kenya, Malawi, and Zanzibar now receive clear loud broadcasts from Peiping Radio in China—all in English. Freight shipments of heavy machinery and other commodities from Russia to the Near East are stamped "Made in U.S.S.R."—in English. In many cities Russian cultural offices compete with British and American centres in advertising English courses. And of the 30 million books which the Russians annually distribute to former British colonies in Africa and Asia, a large proportion are in English—among them technical books, novels, and children's books, including *Goldilocks and the Three Bears*, by Leo Tolstoy (actual author: Robert Southey).

English is also the language of international aviation, spoken by pilots and airport control-tower operators on all the airways of the world. Besides its status as the official air language of NATO, it is increasingly employed by pilots of many countries on local flights within their own national boundaries. The West

German Luftwaffe and even the flyers of East Germany use it. And the French, though ever jealous of their proud and beautiful language, find English far more efficient for air-ground communication. It takes less time, for example, to say *jet* than *avion à réaction*, or to talk of *flaps* rather than *volets de flexions*. And there are other areas of mankind's diverse activities within which English now reigns virtually supreme. It is the international language of sport in every country where people play *futbol* or *beisbol*. It is the international language of jazz, whose followers in all lands know the difference between *le bebop* and *buki-buki* (boogie-woogie) and can do the Twist. And it is the language of international youth—of teenagers everywhere who wear *blue djins* and *pulova* sweaters, chew *gomma americana* (specifically bubble gum), smoke *Looky Strooky* cigarettes (as in Russia), and enjoy hot dogs and Coke (or, as in Japan, *Koka-Kora*, and its rival *Pepusi-kora*).

It is in the realm of statesmanship, however, that English has attained the status of a universal tongue to a degree never faintly approached by Latin in the heyday of the Roman Empire or by French in the eighteenth and nineteenth centuries. Of the various new sovereign states created since World War II, many have formally adopted English either as their official language or the recognized second language of the land. At the Bandung Conference of 1955, which represented 1·4 billion people from twenty-nine Asian and African countries (including China), the proceedings were conducted entirely in English—not for any love of England or the United States, but because it was the only means by which the multi-lingual delegates could communicate with one another. More recently, when Egypt and Indonesia drew up a cultural treaty, it was specified that the definitive version of the agreement between these two Moslem countries, neither one an ardent lover of the Western world, would be the English-language copy. By the same token, when a trade delegation from Ceylon journeyed to the Soviet Union for a conference, their Russian hosts, who met them in Kabul, Afghanistan, greeted them in English. And when the Dalai Lama fled down from his Tibetan highlands to seek sanctuary in India, he was welcomed by Prime Minister Nehru on the northern frontier.

"How are you?" Nehru asked in English.

"Very nice," the Dalai Lama replied with perfect lucidity (though he was doubtless unaware that the word *nice* has a whole spectrum of meanings of which the original one was "foolish").

The most spectacular advances made by English are in the so-called underdeveloped areas of the world. The polyglot populations of Asia and Africa find it much easier to learn English than to try to comprehend the speech of their nearest neighbours. For, contrary to popular supposition, languages evolve in the direction of simplicity. English, being a highly evolved, cosmopolitan, sophisticated language, has been refined and revised, planed down and polished through centuries of use, so that today it is far less complicated than any primitive tongue. Some of the most difficult languages in the world are spoken by some of the world's most backward people—e.g. the Australian aborigines, the Eskimos, the Hottentots, and the Yahgan Indians of Tierra del Fuego. In West Africa alone, some 60 million tribesmen speak more than 400 different languages; hence, wherever European influence has left its mark, Africans talk to each other in English or French when they leave their local language district—which in some towns may mean across the street.[1] Ghana has proclaimed English its official language and requires English instruction from primary school on. In East Africa, whose tribes have communicated for centuries in Swahili, a linguistic hybrid woven by Arab slavers a thousand years ago out of a mixture of Arabic and Bantu idiom, even rabid nationalists today favour English over Swahili as the common tongue.

English continues to be the lingua franca of the Middle East, despite the political ferment of Islam. From Cairo to Teheran, no traveller who speaks it is ever at a loss in finding lodging, food, or transport. Most Arab radio stations have English programmes; and English-language newspapers, books, and magazines are sold in every major city. Despite recent attempts to employ Arabic more generally in education, most universities in Islam quietly concluded during 1963–4 that English had to be retained as the language both of instruction and of textbooks.

[1] At a meeting of the foreign ministers of the Organization of African Unity early in 1964, the Egyptian delegate began an address in Arabic. From all sides of the hall came cries of "Speak English!" or "*Parlez français!*"

Even at conservative El Azhar University in Cairo, ancient and orthodox seat of Moslem higher learning, English is compulsory at all levels (as well as in the secondary schools which feed El Azhar). Cairo's *Egyptian Gazette*, addressing Arab nationalists, declared recently: "English is not the property of capitalist Americans, but of all the world."

The swift and astonishing spread of English around the globe has not taken place without opposition here and there. The French in particular, ever protective of their cultural heritage, have endeavoured to hold the linguistic lines in their former colonies in Asia and Africa; while in metropolitan France, the Office du Vocabulaire Français continually exhorts newspapers and magazines to avoid the *snobisme* of using English words where French equivalents exist. Unfortunately, succinct French equivalents do not always exist, at least for such vivid contemporary terms as *call girl*, *snack bar*, *supermarket*, *missile gap*, *gadget*, *gunman*, *parking*, *mixer*, *teenager*, *jukebox*, *job*, *flash*, *smash*, and *boom*. Alarmed at the contamination of his native tongue by such vulgar neologisms, René Etiemble, a professor of comparative literature at the Sorbonne, launched a counterattack at the end of 1963 in the form of a best-selling book *Parlez-Vous Franglais?* in which he estimated that at least five thousand common Anglo-American words and thirty thousand technical terms had entered the French vernacular in the last decade. "If we do not take care now," he warned, "in forty years' time the French language will have ceased to exist." Proposing that fines be imposed on *Américanolatres*, Etiemble declared: "The French language is a treasure. To violate it is a crime. Persons were shot during the war for treason. They should be punished for degrading the language." The august Académie française at once backed up Etiemble's campaign by announcing that its dictionary commission would start preparing a blacklist of "foreign words" that are *impropres à la langue*.

A few years earlier in Belgium, a bilingual country where rivalry between French and Flemish has long been a fact of national life, French-speaking Walloons were outraged when Henri Fayat, then Minister of Foreign Trade, addressed the 1958 Council of Europe Assembly in English. "A deliberate insult!" French-language newspapers expostulated. "A political gesture meant to snub a large section of the Belgian population!"

But the Dutch-speaking Flemings, long jealous of French linguistic dominance, had not the slightest objection to the advent of English as Belgium's third and common tongue.

Like the French, the Spaniards are reluctant to let their ancient, romantic language suffer the incursions of a foreign idiom. Of all European countries, Spain has been the least receptive to English, partly because of its geographical isolation, partly because Spaniards historically profess little love for the homeland of Sir Francis Drake. In the spring of 1964 the Royal Spanish Academy at Madrid, not to be outdone by the Académie française, initiated a campaign to defend the Spanish tongue from bastardization by Anglo-American idioms disseminated by the press, radio, television, and the cinema—especially Hollywood films that had been dubbed in Mexico. Many of the objectionable expressions derived, like those which aroused the ire of French purists, from the ever-enlarging glossaries of science, aviation, sports, and jazz, and were borrowed intact. Some, however, acquired a distinctly Spanish accent: e.g. *gangsterismo*, *columnista*, *cocktel* (for cocktail party), and *perrito caliente* (hot dog).

Even in Latin America, where English is now virtually mandatory for business and professional men, purists recurrently plead for the preservation of Spanish as "the most beautiful, majestic and sonorous language in the world". Argentina's Perón tried briefly (and unsuccessfully) to ban Hollywood movies in his country unless Spanish titles were superimposed; today in Buenos Aires, enrolment in English-language schools is increasing at the rate of more than 10 per cent a year. In Peru more recently, the Ministry of Education ordered certain schools in Lima—the Abraham Lincoln High School, the John Dewey High School, the William Prescott High School, and others—to change their names. The order was obeyed; but the names soon reappeared, for they indicated that the schools specialized in English, a commodity in enormous demand.

Throughout Latin America, English is spoken and understood almost everywhere save in the remote hinterland. Wealthy families from Mexico to Chile who formerly sent their teenage children abroad to school in France and Switzerland now tend to enrol them in secondary schools and colleges in England and the United States. In Portuguese-speaking Brazil especially,

English is acknowledged as a necessity for anyone who seeks economic advancement, and as such it is a required course in primary and secondary schools. "Portuguese is a tomb," a Brazilian educator said not long ago. "It is good only in Brazil and Portugal." (In Portugal too, English has made spectacular progress, joining French as a second tongue.) Most of the countries in the Caribbean area are bilingual; American programmes appear on television nightly; airport signs and menus are printed both in English and Spanish; many schools and colleges teach at least half their classes in English. And on the island of Hispaniola, uneasily shared by French-speaking Haiti and the Spanish-speaking Dominican Republic, government officials of the two countries use English for mutual interchange when circumstances make it necessary for them to talk to each other at all.

Perhaps the most notable victory of the English language over nationalistic resistance was recently won in India. In an effort to expunge relics of the British Raj, the Central Government had proclaimed in 1950 that the official language of India would henceforth be Hindi (the vernacular of northern India), and that the transition from English must be complete by 1965. Although this pleased the Hindu populations in the north, the reaction was quite different in the rest of the vast subcontinent, which encompasses 845 distinct languages and dialects. The Bengali-speakers in the east did not like the decree; and in the south the millions of speakers of Tamil and related Dravidian languages protested that fifteen years was too brief an interval in which to adopt a tongue as alien to them as any in the Occidental world. For more than a century English has been the common tongue; and although not more than 3 per cent of India's population of 461,300,000 employ it with any degree of fluency, they represent the ruling 3 per cent—administrators, judges, legislators, and other educated groups. Moreover, the leading newspapers of India (as of Pakistan) are English-language dailies. If English were expunged, they pointed out, there would be no way for all the peoples of the huge land to communicate with one another. Months of argument ensued, marred recurrently by bloody riots. At the University of Lucknow, which switched at once from English to Hindi, levels of learning went into an alarming decline. Faculty members evolved a kind of Anglo-Hindi jargon, inventing hybrid words for technical terms in an attempt to comply with the government edict. The result was Babel.[1]

Finally the so-called "Save Hindi" campaign was called off. The announcement, significantly, was published in English. In Parliament, Prime Minister Nehru declared that for an indefinite period English would continue as an "associate official language". While Hindi-speaking legislators listened in silence and others cheered, Nehru termed English "the major window for us to the outside world".

"We dare not close that window," he said. "And if we do, it will spell peril to our future."

The issue flared again in 1965 when, in accordance with the language act, the fifteen-year period of transition came to an end. Within days of the proclamation on January 26 that Hindi would now permanently become the sole official language of India, students rioted in Madras, Mysore, Kerala and Bengal; two young men burned themselves to death in protest; trains were derailed; nearly one hundred demonstrators were killed by police fire; Hindi books were burned and cinemas showing Hindi films were raided; two cabinet ministers resigned, and the government of Prime Minister Shastri was shaken by an intense and mounting crisis. Finally, after four weeks of disorder, Shastri announced to the Indian Parliament that an agreement had been reached with the chief ministers of all the states that, although Hindi would remain the official language of India, English would continue to be the associate official language as long as the non-Hindi speaking people of India desired it.

In Nehru's words, "We dare not close that window", lies one explanation for the virtually unopposed diffusion of English around the globe. For not only in Asia and Africa, but in Europe, crisscrossed by linguistic frontiers and dissected by deep-rooted cultural loyalties, people of all classes now look to English as a

[1] Similar efforts to make Urdu the language of education in West Pakistan met with no greater success. In a speech at Karachi on May 12, 1964, Pakistan's President Mohammed Ayub Khan said: "I doubt very much if we have reached a stage where we could afford to abandon English and make Urdu the medium of instruction for various sciences."

window, a magic casement opening on every horizon of loquacious men. Smaller countries, whose national languages are encompassed by narrow boundaries, have been the most receptive, because experience has taught them that Anglo-Saxons seldom trouble to master the speech of other lands. When Eisenhower visited Norway some years ago in his role as commander-in-chief of NATO, he remarked: "I have the impression that every second Norwegian speaks the English language." Today in Norway—as in Sweden, Denmark, Finland, the Netherlands, Austria, Portugal, Greece, Turkey, and Japan—English is taught in all schools and colleges, usually as a required subject, but otherwise as the most popular choice among other elective language courses.

In West Germany, schools require six to nine years of English. The obligation meets with no emotional resistance, for unlike the French the Germans feel no sense of linguistic betrayal in studying English; they are eager to learn, and experience little difficulty in the process since English is more a Teutonic than a Romance language. "To a Frenchman," a Swiss journalist observed recently, "his language is a sacrosanct cultural endowment, almost a state of mind. If a German wants to enlarge his intellectual horizons he will take up another language. A Frenchman will read more French."

Even behind the Iron Curtain, English is expanding its enclaves without opposition. In East Germany (where Russian used to be, but is no longer, a compulsory subject), English now holds first place among optional language courses in secondary schools, with twelve applicants for every available departmental vacancy. English classes are equally in demand in Poland. In Yugoslavia, English replaced Russian as the country's second language several years ago. In 1960, for example, Yugoslav publishers issued 86 books in English, 57 in French, 49 in German, and only 31 in Russian. Within the Soviet Union itself, schools offer English from the ages of ten and eleven on; and in some of the larger cities, it is the one compulsory language in the curriculum. One of the best-sellers in the bookshops of Moscow is an English grammar.

The teaching of language in schools, however, represents only one of many channels through which the torrent of English is inundating all lands. A tremendously important source is the cinema—American and British movies are shown the world over. Other tributary freshets include radio and television, recordings of popular songs, English-language publications, adult education courses, language centres, mobile libraries and exchange fellowships sponsored by government agencies and private foundations; and, perhaps most important of all, the incomputable numbers of informal encounters that occur every hour of the day among businessmen, professional men, politicians, scientists, technicians, students, and just plain tourists linked together on a shrinking planet by the swift instrumentalities of the jet age.

Although the flood tide of English dates only from the end of World War II, its incipient stage actually began more than three centuries ago, when British adventurers first carried their speech to the far places of the earth, erecting the initial bastions of empire. In the wake of the conquerors came traders, and after them missionaries—who still exercise a potent force in Africa and Asia. But the major catalyst in the English-language explosion was war—especially the two great conflicts of this century. "War is perhaps the most rapidly effectual excitant of language," a British etymologist has observed. The occupation troops that moved into defeated countries after World War I and on incomparably greater scale after World War II did more to spread English (particularly American English) than any other agency of dissemination. From the hundreds of thousands of soldiers and their dependents deployed throughout both hemispheres, English words and phrases filtered down to every level of the diverse populations in every nation and zone. No longer was English speech the limited possession of the educated, the wealthy, and the peripatetic social élite. It became the economically valuable property of all, from shopkeepers and salesgirls, bellboys and bartenders, down to barefoot urchins in the streets of Tokyo and Teheran, Berlin and Baghdad, who swiftly learned to chirp, "Hey Joe, gimme gum", or "Hey Joe, wanna some fun?"

The popular desire to learn English has increased each year as America's international interests and commercial commitments continue to radiate in widening circles across the seas. The desire has been met by a vast complex of organizations, both national and international, British and American, public and private. The United States Information Agency (USIA) maintains 239 cultural centres in 106 countries, ranging from small circulating libraries that offer English books and magazines to elaborate establishments like Amerika House in Berlin, which provides programmes of lectures, concerts, dances, and language instruction to as many as 1,800 visitors a day. During the last few years an average of 30 million persons have annually used the facilities of USIA centres around the world. Of these more than one million have attended English-language seminars each year, among them 5,000 local teachers whose combined classes represented more than two million pupils. Another United States agency in the field is AID—the Agency for International Development—which offers English lessons for technical-aid projects, and transports foreign businessmen and technicians to the United States, where they are taught English as a prelude to courses in industrial management, engineering, and the like.

The work of these agencies is complemented by the British Council, which was founded in 1934 to promote a wider knowledge of the United Kingdom and the English language abroad and to develop closer cultural relations with other nations. It now maintains staffs in about eighty countries, and in many its primary objective is the encouragement of English-language teaching, either through its own centres or in cooperation with the educational systems of the countries concerned. Particular emphasis is placed on the training of local teachers, and to this end special courses and summer schools were held in some thirty-five countries during 1963 and 1964. Prior to 1970 the Council, which is increasingly becoming the principal agency for the recruitment of English teachers overseas at all levels, plans to have some sixty additional experts serving in key teaching posts under the Aid to Commonwealth English scheme. Meanwhile many young people who have enlisted in the American Peace Corps or the British Voluntary Service Overseas are teaching English to people in the underdeveloped countries of both hemispheres.

It is possible today to hear and learn English via radio in every nation on earth. The BBC alone broadcasts some 177 lessons weekly; the transcript of their series, *English by Radio*, is published with local language explanations in ninety countries.

In addition, with the collaboration of the British Council, the BBC recently prepared a series of thirty-nine beginners' lessons for television, which have been shown with great success in many lands. The B.B.C. also runs lessons for technical students requiring a knowledge of English for specialized fields. Over and above formal teaching, programmes of music with news and comment in English are broadcast throughout the world and around the clock by the B.B.C. Overseas Broadcasting Services, by the Voice of America, and by the radio of the United States Armed Forces.

Along with the government agencies, many private organizations abet the educative process. British and American corporations with overseas affiliates or operating concessions provide English lessons to workers in oil fields, factories, and offices in other lands. The Ford and Rockefeller Foundations have granted millions of dollars to institutions both in foreign countries (the University of Lahore, the Central Institute of English at Hyderabad, the American University in Cairo, Robert College in Istanbul) and in the United States (the University of Michigan, the University of Texas, U.C.L.A., Columbia) which specialize in teaching English to foreign students. Organizations such as English Language Services, Inc., and Language Research, Inc., combine instruction with experimental studies aimed at the improvement of teaching techniques. Meanwhile, all around the globe, English lessons are proffered for varying fees by innumerable private teachers, by international language schools (like Berlitz), and by various home study systems (like Linguaphone), which employ a combination of phonographic recordings and the printed word.

Of vastly greater import than the scale and momentum of the English irruption from its wellsprings in the West is the fact that it came in response to a worldwide and seemingly insatiable demand. The agencies of dissemination are not engaged in force-feeding. Nor, as often implied in Congress and in the press, is the teaching of English merely a propaganda tactic in the Cold War or, worse, an expensive and visionary attempt to promote international understanding through the medium—generally deprecated by the tough-minded—of cultural interchange. No government agency created the demand for English; it was there. In the absence of the demand, no plethora of appropriations, no intensity of missionary zeal could induce millions of people to undertake the arduous chore of learning a foreign language. The eagerness with which these people, sundered from one another by all the great linguistic divisions of mankind, are now dedicating themselves to that chore stems from the realization that English is a gateway to opportunity in every land. For it is the language in which man can best communicate with his fellowman in a small, crowded, and interdependent world.

The universal hunger for English is manifested daily in all countries where it is now being taught. Some recent situations and episodes:

- In Baghdad, during the violent upheaval of 1958, the United States Embassy and the Consulate were forced to close, but the USIA language school remained open by request of the Iraqi government. The reason for the exception was that Iraqi officials were attending the school themselves.
- In Finland, where English classes are hopelessly overcrowded, a number of private corporations participate in what is known as the Teacher-Secretary Plan. They engage British secretaries to handle international correspondence during office hours and to give English lessons to staff employees and others at night.
- In Kabul, when English courses were announced, Afghans queued up in a driving snowstorm to wait their turn to enrol.
- In Tunisia, President Bourguiba deemed English so important for his newly created republic that he asked the United States government for aid in establishing a school. The Bourguiba School of Language at the University of Tunisia is now flourishing, under the joint auspices of the State Department, the USIA, and AID.
- In Teheran, no less than 122 private language schools give lessons in English to thousands of adults, at an average fee of 20 cents an hour. Their services are officially endorsed by the Iranian government with the slogan: "If you don't know English, you know nothing."
- In Peru, villagers and townspeople in many small communities foregather daily at noon in squares and plazas for English lessons via loudspeaker.
- In Japan, an American librarian in a town on the island

of Nagoya agreed to spend a little time conversing in English informally with a casual acquaintance. The next day the pupil returned with a friend. The day after that he returned with several friends. Within a few days the informal group had expanded into a full-fledged class, then into two classes, then three, then four. At this point the harried librarian called USIA headquarters in Washington to protest that she was not a professional teacher and to plead for reinforcements.

How can this worldwide and apparently insatiable demand for English be explained? None of the external factors—business motivations, the extended military and economic influence of the English-speaking people, circumglobal pathways of communication and travel—can adequately account for the phenomenon. The essential catalyst lies in the internal anatomy of the language itself.

Ever since the events at Babel, when, according to Genesis, "the Lord did there confound the language of all the earth", man has lamented his linguistic fragmentation; and he has endeavoured from time to time to construct an ideal supranational language as a medium of intellectual exchange for all lands. None of these synthetic languages—Esperanto, Gloro, Ido, Interlingua, Langue Bleue, Novial, Nulange, Volapuk, or any other of perhaps thirty such inventions—has ever won enough speakers to satisfy the zeal of their proponents. Today, through the accidents of history and entirely under its own momentum, English has become the fulfilment of this philological dream. Dr. Samuel Johnson would have rejoiced to witness its spread. For he cherished the treasure of his tongue. "Wondrous the English language," he once exclaimed, "language of live men!"

2

A HORNET'S NEST OF FALSE SIMPLICITY

I like to be beholden to the great metropolitan English speech, the sea which receives tributaries from every region under heaven.

RALPH WALDO EMERSON (1803–82)

The current, extraordinary spread of the English language around the world would never have begun, despite all the forces of history and all the facilities for its propagation, if English were a difficult language to learn. To the advanced practitioner—the poet, novelist, essayist—it poses great difficulties by virtue of its lush vocabulary of more than half a million words and the flexibility with which they can be employed. The very freedom of verbal choice and arrangement which enables the rhetorician to express a multiplicity of ideas and to articulate subtle refinements of thought may also lure him into labyrinths of syntax less likely to entrap those who move about in more rigidly constructed languages.

Rhetoric is one thing, however, and plain talk is another; it is in the latter realm that English excels. It excels by reason of its basically simple rudiments—a hard core of perhaps one thousand energetic words which fill all the needs of ordinary communication, a few tolerant rules governing their use, and a logical underlying skeletal structure—which can be taught and learned more quickly than is possible in any other language spoken on earth today. For example, during World War II when foreign flyers were brought to the United States for training, it was found that a good working knowledge of English could be imparted in about sixty hours of concentrated instruction.

These assets, which make English so useful as an international language, derive from its history and its cosmopolitan antecedents. For in the course of centuries of development (which will be detailed in a later chapter), it has been periodically enriched and invigorated by elements of many other tongues. As Dr. Johnson observed, "Languages are the pedigrees of nations." Whatever the original accents of the British Isles may have been, as laid down by the earliest Celts, they were altered and revised by repeated waves of invaders that crossed the Channel and the North Sea in the first millennium A.D.—the Romans, Angles, Saxons, Jutes, Vikings, and finally the Normans. Today English is classified as a member of the Teutonic linguistic family, which also includes German, Dutch, and the Scandinavian languages. Yet more than half of its vocabulary is of Latin origin, implanted either directly during the four centuries of the Roman occupation and the permanent Norman conquest or indirectly by eclectic borrowings in later epochs from modern French, Spanish, Italian, and Portuguese.

Because of its variegated background, the English vocabulary presents a familiar countenance to students born to other tongues. Through the centuries it has borrowed so profusely from all other languages on earth and has assimilated words so successfully that today only professional scholars are aware of the national origins of many words in daily use. Here, for example, are some common ones taken from languages other than those in the main line of English descent:

FROM ARABIC: *alcohol*, *alcove*, *algebra*, *alkali*, *cipher*, *cork*, *magazine*, *zenith*, *zero;* and the slang phrase, *so long* (from the Arabic *salaam*—and Hebrew *shalom* —"peace").

FROM DUTCH: *bowsprit*, *brandy*, *duck* (cloth), *gin*, *golf*, *mart*, *uproar*, *wagon.*

FROM ITALIAN: *balcony*, *brigade*, *cavalry*, *colonel*, *duet*, *granite*, *infantry*, *miniature*, *model*, *opera*, *piano*, *sonnet*, *umbrella*, *volcano.*

FROM PERSIAN: *check*, *chequers*, *chess*, *divan*, *jasmine*, *khaki*, *lemon*, *lilac*, *paradise*, *shawl*, *spinach.*

FROM GREEK: *acrobat*, *adamant*, *anthology*, *barometer*, *Bible*, *catastrophe*, *cheer*, *cyclone*, *elastic*, *idiot*, *magic*, *tactics*, *tantalize*, *hoi polloi* (the many).

FROM SPANISH: *alligator*, *canyon*, *cargo*, *mosquito*, *ranch*, *rodeo*, *sherry*, *stampede*, *stevedore*, *vanilla*, *pickaninny* (American slang from *pequeño niño*, small child).

FROM AMERICAN INDIAN: *chipmunk*, *chocolate*, *hominy*, *moccasin*, *moose*, *opossum*, *persimmon*, *potato*, *raccoon*, *skunk*, *tomato*, *wigwam*.

The diversified, cosmopolitan ancestry of the words in the English lexicon has been a major asset in the diffusion of the language as an international tongue. Of equal value is the simplicity of the grammatical conventions that govern their use. Foremost among these is the beautifully logical, straightforward, common-sense, down-to-earth, natural, and wholesome attitude of the English language toward sex. In the Romance languages, all nouns are arbitrarily either masculine or feminine. (In French, for example, *la ville*, city, and *la lune*, moon, are feminine; but *le village*, village, and *le soleil*, sun, are masculine.) In German there are three genders, even more arbitrarily disposed. (The word *Sonne*, sun, is feminine; *Mond*, moon, is masculine; and *Mädchen*, girl, and *Weib*, woman, are neuter.) To British or American students of foreign languages such distinctions seem not only to impose an additional task of memorizing gender as well as meaning, but make no sense in a world where there are men and women, fathers and mothers, uncles and aunts, brothers and sisters, boys and girls, males and females of every species—and things.

This healthy approach toward nouns in English eliminates the necessity of corresponding indications of gender in articles, prepositions, adjectives, and verbs. Take, for example, a simple French sentence: *La plume noire du vieux monsieur est perdue* (The black pen of the old gentleman is lost). The arbitrary femininity of the pen is relentlessly reiterated in the article, *la*, the adjective, *noire*, and the participle, *perdue*. There is no question, no possible shadow of doubt, that pens are female objects. But had the old gentleman lost his pencil instead of his pen, then the sentence would read: *Le crayon noir du vieux monsieur est perdu*, thus establishing the maleness of pencils through every auxiliary word. And if the loss of either implement had been suffered by an old lady instead of an old gentleman, the possessive phrase would become *de la vieille dame*, involving a strikingly different form of the adjective meaning "old," and a metamorphosis of the masculine particle *du* (of the) into the feminine *de la*.

Gender is only one of the many brier patches eliminated by common usage through centuries of hacking and pruning in the tangled thickets of grammar. The inflexions that complicate most other languages have almost entirely disappeared from English. Nouns change only to denote possessive or plural forms, and the changes are extremely simple ones. The possessive case is formed merely by the addition of *'s* (or by the apostrophe alone for some words already ending in *s*). The plural is formed by the addition of *s* or *es* (with a very few exceptions such as *child*, *children; deer*, *deer; foot*, *feet; knife*, *knives; mouse*, *mice;* and a few double plurals like *penny*, *pennies*, *pence*, and *brother*, *brothers*, *brethren*).

Pronouns retain some inflections, especially in the first and third persons: *I*, *my*, *me; we*, *our*, *us; he*, *his him; they*, *their*, *them*. But even here erosion has been at work. The second person, *you*, is both singular and plural, both subject and object. *Ye* has disappeared entirely, and *thou* and *thee* hold their own only among the Quakers. The relative pronoun *whom* is still mandatory in formal writing and in the conversation of all who cherish traditional usage, but it has given way to *who* in colloquial speech and in time will doubtless follow other inflected forms into linguistic oblivion.

Adjectives and adverbs completely ignore the words they modify. They change only to denote comparison, and there are only three degrees: *bright*, *brighter*, *brightest; brightly*, *more brightly*, *most brightly*.

Finally verbs—source of the severest headaches among students—have lost most of their tortuous variations. In classical Greek, for example, a verb may progress through as many as 500 inflexions to indicate complex interactions of tense, mood, voice, person, and number. All modern, living languages have reduced these complexities. But English has gone farther than any other Western language in the process of evolutionary simplification. A conjugation of the English verb *to love* clearly reveals this development, when compared with conjugations of its French and Latin equivalents, *aimer* and *amare:*

I love	J'aime	amo
You love	Tu aimes	amas
He loves	Il aime	amat
She loves	Elle aime	amat
We love	Nous aimons	amamus
You love	Vous aimez	amatis
They love	Ils aiment	amant
They love	Elles aiment	amant

Thus, where Latin requires six personal endings, and French five, English asks only one—the attachment of an *s* to the third person singular. And in the past tense—*I loved, you loved, he loved, she loved, we loved, you loved, they loved*—there are no inflections at all.

The absence, or decay, of inflections in English is not an unmitigated blessing to the foreign-born student. Although it vastly reduces the amount of time which he would expend in memorizing verbal mutations in another language, it may also leave him with a sense of being adrift in an uncharted sea of new words without any formal rules of navigation to guide him. It is often difficult in English to distinguish a verb from a noun. For example, one may *slice* cheese or eat a *slice* of cheese; one may *swim* or go for a *swim;* one may *call* a friend on the telephone or receive a telephone *call*, *call* for help, or leave a *call* for seven A.M. Such free interchange of function among the parts of speech, although one of the delights of the English language, also creates a condition which the late Edward Sapir, Sterling Professor of Anthropology and Linguistics at Yale, described as "masked complexity". "Anyone who takes the trouble to examine these [difficulties] carefully," Sapir observed, "will soon see that behind the superficial appearance of simplicity there is concealed a perfect hornet's nest of bizarre and arbitrary usages."

The heart of the hornet's nest lies in the realm of little words. In the vast lexicon of English, thousands of precise, highly specialized, and often elegant words flower side by side with small, easy-to-learn, highly flexible "parts of speech". It is one of the marvellous endowments of English that these two species of words—the specialized and the general—complement, augment, define, and analyse each other. Thus one may *put out a fire* or *extinguish a fire*; *dismount* or *get off*; *ascend* or *go up*. Among linguists, English is commonly known as an "analytic" language, which is to say that the relationships of words in a sentence are indicated by the order in which they appear (rather than by case endings or other mutations of form) and by an extensive use of prepositions and auxiliary verbs.

The special formula of little verb-plus-preposition is the key to a quick grasp of English speech, if not necessarily to a gracious literary style. In 1920 two Cambridge scholars, Dr. I. A. Richards, now of Harvard, and the late C. K. Ogden, discovered while collaborating on *The Meaning of Meaning*, a book about English semantics, that certain small, persistent words tended to turn up again and again in their analyses of other words and idioms. They became convinced that with a limited set of these indispensable, analytical words, any other word could be defined and any reasonably simple concept clearly and adequately expressed. After ten years of lexicological labour, Ogden evolved what is known as Basic English—an elixir, distilled from the ancient wine of our language, of 850 volatile, versatile words that can say just about anything that needs to be said in ordinary, non-technical talk. Basic English proved invaluable in World War II, when speed of instruction was crucial. Today language courses can afford to be a little more leisurely and vocabularies a little more generous.

The critical discovery made by Richards and Ogden was that their stripped-down lexicon required only eighteen verbs—as against four to ten thousand that may be available in the vocabulary of a college-educated man. The eighteen vital verbs are: *be*, *come*, *do*, *get*, *give*, *go*, *have*, *keep*, *let*, *make*, *may*, *put*, *say*, *see*, *seem*, *send*, *take*, and *will*. The ability of these verbs to do the work of all the others stems from their gift of being able to enter into an astonishing number of mergers with prepositions. Thus a combination like *give out* can fulfil the essential purposes of *announce*, *award*, *bequeath*, *bestow*, *dispense*, *distribute*, *emit*, *expend*, *exude*, *grant*, *proclaim*. And even more spectacularly, *give up* can cover the pivotal meanings of *abandon*, *abdicate*, *abjure*, *cease*, *cede*, *desert*, *desist*, *discontinue*, *forgo*, *forsake*, *relinquish*, *renounce*, *resign*, *sacrifice*, *stop*, *succumb*, *surrender*, *vacate*, *withdraw*, and *yield*.

It is evident that the little words of English constitute a kind of inner voice—a language within a language—capable of understudying most of the flashier ornaments of *The Oxford English Dictionary* and *Webster's New International Dictionary, Unabridged*. They can be of enormous value to the English novitiate because they cover so much ground; each one substitutes for hundreds of bigger, if subtler, words; and they are simple to spell and pronounce. But their simplicity is deceptive. They can be used in so many ways that their very versatility sometimes creates confusion in the mind of the learner. This is the "masked complexity" which the foreign student may discover when he looks more closely at the apparently innocuous alliance of little verbs and little prepositions.

Contemplate, for example, the little word *up*. What is it? Most of the time it behaves like a preposition, indicating direction (*He lives up the street*). But it can also masquerade as an adverb (*It's time to get up*); a noun (*Every life has its ups and downs*); a verb (*I'll up you five dollars*); or an adjective (*The sun is up*). In addition to its multiple function in the combination *give up*, it plays a ubiquitous and sometimes superfluous role in a variety of other expressions, such as *add up*, *clean up*, *do up*, *drink up*, *hurry up*, *join up*, *line up*, *lock up*, *look up* (as in a library), *mix up*, *offer up*, *pay up*, *play up*, *ring up*, *set up*, *stop up*, *tie up*, *tidy up*, *wake up*, *wash up*, *work up*, *wrap up*, *up to now*, and *up to you*. To the foreign student it seems paradoxical that the same meaning is conveyed by *His house burned up* and *His house burned down*; *My wife isn't up yet* and *My wife isn't down yet*; *The train slowed up* and *The train slowed down*. Even more bewildering are those situations where utterly unrelated concepts are evoked by one and the same phrase—e.g. *make up*, whose transient meaning depends on whether the context is cosmetics (*She takes an hour to make up her face*); indecision (*I just can't make up my mind*); domesticity (*Let's make up the bed*); forgiveness (*Kiss and make up*); fiction (*I'll make up some kind of a story*); or atonement (*Some day I'll make up for this mistake*).

The puzzles presented by prepositions perplex not only the foreign student but also those born to the English tongue and most particularly those teachers and writers whose obligation it is to employ them correctly. The little words are sticky, fussy, elusive words even for those who have lived and worked with them all their lives. However, the pragmatic glory of English is that it is able to convey meaning even when niceties of grammar go out the window. It matters little, from the standpoint of intelligibility, if a Frenchman, instead of saying, "I have been here for two hours," says, "I am here since two hours"; or if a German, instead of saying "I am going across town to the store," says, "I over the street by the store go." And it is because of the infinite elasticity of the English language that the many varieties of pidgin and patois have evolved, giving rise to such immortal phrases as "*Him big chief paleface*" and "*No tickee, no washeee*", and making possible communication the world around.

The most excruciating difficulties encountered by the serious foreign student who wishes to learn to write English, as well as speak it, involve neither grammar nor syntax but rather the chaotic lack of correlation between its spelling and pronunciation. An English-speaking person can usually tell by looking at a word in Spanish, Finnish, Czech, Slovak, and, to a lesser extent, German and Italian, how it should be pronounced or how it is likely to be pronounced, and vice versa. In English neither is possible, and the inconsistencies are so multifarious and grotesque that foreigners are not alone in deploring them. Most Americans cannot spell correctly, and for even the most cultivated of professional men on both shores of the Atlantic the incoherent character of English orthography is a timeless problem.

Considered purely as a vocal exercise, the pronunciation of English is not too troublesome. The most difficult phoneme (sound unit) for many foreigners is the Anglo-Saxon *th*, whether soft as in *thin*, or hard as in *that*. The aspirated *h*—in words like *he*, *her*, *how*—causes some trouble. So do words ending in several terminal consonants—like *desks*—save to speakers of Scandinavian languages, whence they came. The American *r* (as opposed to the British *r* which is virtually a vowel in words like *here* and *there*) is often a tongue twister for speakers of Romance languages who roll or trill their *r*'s, and for the Chinese who have no analogous *r* sound and approximate it with an *l*. The Japanese, on the other hand, have no *l* sound and approximate it with an *r*. Save for these few consonants, foreign tongues can curl themselves around the phonemes of English with far less difficulty than Anglo-Saxons encounter in attempting to reproduce the accents of other lands. It is only when the novitiate endeavours to discern some trace of conformity between the sound and spelling of English words that he begins to ask himself whether the study of Aka, Bodo, Lahuli, Mishmi, Swatow, Wenchow, Old Kuki, or Rong might not be more to the point.

The favourite scapegoat of critics of English orthography is the vestigial *ough* monstrosity, which can be pronounced in eight different ways, none of them related phonetically to the letters involved—namely, *tough*, *though*, *thought*, *thorough*, *through*, *bough*, *cough*, *hiccough*. Along with *gh*, English spelling clings to other relics of the past—letters, once articulated, which have been silent for centuries and linger on, apparently for no other purpose than to make things difficult for teachers and pupils and to kindle the ire of advocates of spelling reform. Among these are the *g* in *gnaw*, the *k* in *knight* and *know*, the *w* in *write* and *wrong*, and the *l* in *could*, *should*, and *would*.

Much as they have been decried, silent letters present less of a problem than other less blatant eccentricities of our spelling system. In one ambush the foreign student encounters homonyms—words that sound alike but are spelled differently and have different meanings—such as *pair*, *pear*, *pare*; *beat* and *beet*; *meat* and *meet*; *grate* and *great*; *peace* and *piece*; *sew* and *so*; *you* and *ewe*; *there*, *their*, and *they're*. But in another part of the forest he is waylaid by pairs of words, twins of identical spelling, which are pronounced quite differently and serve different grammatical functions: e.g. the verb *read* (present tense) and *read* (past tense); the noun *tear* (in the eye) and *tear* (in the sheet); the verb *lead* and the noun *lead;* the noun *cóntract* and the verb *contráct*. Unhappily there is no rule, no system, no recourse other than sheer, brute memory for any child, be he born in Buckingham Palace or Bangkok, to learn that the vowel sound known as a long *e* can be represented in more than a dozen different combinations in such words as *be*, *bee*, *believe*, *Caesar*, *key*, *leave*, *machine*, *people*, *quay*, *phoenix*, *receive*, *serene*, *suddenly*. And the vagaries of consonants are no less abundant. With characteristic largesse, English provides thirteen separate spellings for the *sh* sound: *shoe*, *sugar*, *issue*, *mansion*, *mission*, *nation*, *suspicion*, *ocean*, *conscious*, *chaperon*, *schist*, *fuchsia*, and *pshaw*.

Dr. Richards and his associates at Harvard's Language

Research centre have in recent years developed new methods of instruction with film that eliminate much of the confusion caused by these dusty relics of the past. Periodically, however, professional and amateur apostles of phonetic consistency and simplified spelling have made attempts to expunge them from the language entirely. The most notable crusader was the late George Bernard Shaw whose will eventually led to a prize of £500 being offered to the inventor of a new alphabet that would most nearly effect a phonetic wedding of sound and symbol. As an example of the lunacy of English spelling, Shaw constructed the word *ghoti*. He pointed out that the *gh* combination is pronounced like *f* in such words as *cough* and *rough;* the vowel *o* is pronounced like a short *i* in the word *women*; and the *ti* combination is pronounced like *sh* in the word *nation*. Hence *ghoti* is pronounced *fish*.

Although Shaw's bequest was disposed of in 1959—divided equally among four contestants—*The Oxford English Dictionary* remains intact today. For despite all the idiosyncrasies of English spelling and the continual complaints against it, those who use the language cherish it.[1] Defenders of traditional spelling point out, quite correctly, that the written form of any English word reveals its etymology; it may afford no clue as to pronunciation, but its ancestry is clearly disclosed. In the diversified letter combinations of English words, one may read the long tumultuous history of the British Isles. So far as American spelling is concerned, about all that has been effected since the days of Noah Webster (who advocated phonetic reforms) are one or two minuscule changes: the *u* has been dropped from *honour* and *colour*, and occasionally one encounters

[1] An experimental alphabet designed to accelerate the teaching of reading was introduced in a number of British schools in 1961 and has since been acclaimed as a remarkable success on both sides of the Atlantic. Created by Sir James Pitman, grandson of Sir Isaac Pitman, inventor of shorthand, it is known as the Augmented Roman alphabet. It consists of forty-three characters, of which twenty-four are conventional letters of the alphabet, and nineteen are diphthongs or diagraphs which indicate sounds phonetically and unvaryingly. Children who are taught to read with the Augmented Roman alphabet have been known to leap ahead of contemporaries using the regular alphabet by as much as a year. Around the third grade they are switched to traditional modes of spelling and are weaned, apparently, without difficulty.

such words as *tonite*, *thruway*, and *altho*. It would seem that the English-speaking people of the United States, like those of the United Kingdom, are reluctant to surrender their antiquated, irrational, exasperating, obsolete, indefensible, crazy, mixed-up system of spelling. The American attitude was perhaps epitomized by Mark Twain, when he remarked: "Simplified spelling is all right; but, like chastity, you can carry it too far."

No language is perfect, and for all its flaws English currently enjoys top rating, in the opinion of both critics and public, among the languages of the world today. Quite apart from its dominance in the rarefied realms of international diplomacy and commerce, quite apart from schools and colleges and all the other mainstreams of dissemination, English is infiltrating the countries of the world in a subtler, less obvious way. It is insinuating itself into other languages drop by drop, as it were—or rather word by word. Many English and American words are now completely international, not merely understood, but spoken and published around the world. Among the most familiar of these, universally employed on every continent, are: *baby-sitter*, *bar*, *bridge* (the game), *boyfriend*, *best seller*, *bikini*, *bulldozer*, *bus*, *beefsteak*, *cafeteria*, *cocktail*, *cover girl*, *cowboy*, *flirt*, *gangster*, *goddam*, *hamburger*, *holdup*, *hot dog*, *ice cream*, *jazz*, *juice*, *jeep*, *king-size*, *knockout*, *night-club*, *party*, *pipeline*, *pinup*, *radio*, *racket*, *sandwich*, *scooter*, *shorts*, *sex appeal*, *striptease*, *steak*, *taxi*, *whisky*, and *weekend*. It goes without saying that for years *okay* has been a universal expression of assent. Here and there certain American trade names have achieved international status as generic terms: e.g. public opinion polls are now generally known throughout Europe as *gallups;* stockings are *nylons;* and any paper tissue is a *kleenex*.

The interweaving of English words with indigenous idioms occasionally produces some curious bilingual effects. Thus Paris newspapers may print an item on their society pages reporting that a certain host "*a donné une surprise party dans son bungalow ce dernier weekend.*" In West Germany a pilot coming in for a landing may tell the control tower: "*Aber no sweat, boy. Ich habe normal letdown procedure gemacht.*" Many American words have become German verbs: *parken*, *twisten*, *hitchiken*. Many others have been Germanized, or translated in part or in whole: *Bei-product*, *brandneu*, *Herz-attacke* (heart attack), *Eierkopf* (egghead), *kalter Krieg* (cold war). In Japan the process of phonetic mutation has produced such haunting hybrids as *garu-furendo* (girl friend), *hittu parado* (hit parade), *doresu rihaasaru* (dress rehearsal), *kamera tesuto* (camera test), *kakuteiru* (cocktail), *sekkuso sutori* (sex stories), *hassaru* (hustle), and *purodakuchibichi* (productivity).

In Nigeria, according to a Princeton economist, Professor Frederick H. Harbison, who has made many trips there in recent years, a boy who finishes elementary school is known as a *megotbuk*, a boy who graduates from college is a *bigbigbuk*, and the exceptional young man who has studied at Oxford and returns home trailing clouds of culture is a *binto-jaguarfridgful*—a contraction for "He has been to England and come home with a Jaguar and enough money to keep a refrigerator full of frozen foods".

To those assisting in the spread of English the hope recurs that as linguistic barriers dissolve, national and political barriers may lose some of their traditional rigidity. If man's hope for an intellectual community depends on the free interchange of ideas, then the proliferation of English is abetting this purpose. For in many countries still uncommitted to East or West, people of all nationalities and every station of life—Buddhist monks, Yemenite sheikhs, Greek businessmen, Latin labour leaders—are participating in a learning process that brings them new insights as well as linguistic skill. By studying English they are discovering an identity of interest and understanding with other people in the world, such as they could obtain in no other way. The lessons themselves are opening intellectual windows. Many of those now studying the English language are learning for the first time the meaning of such words as liberty, justice, and independence. It is not without significance that these words entered the English lexicon as a result of historical processes which formulated the concepts they describe.

In a memorable address before an international conference of the English-Speaking Union in San Francisco in 1962, Prem Bhatia, editor of the *Times of India*, Delhi, said: "The English Language is mighty and strong in itself, but I think what is even more important is what the English language has brought with it. In my mind the real importance of the English language is not only that it is a means of communication, but also the scale of values it carries with it. The English language, wherever it has gone, has carried with it the idea of freedom—and there can be no more striking example than the fact that we in India got rid of the British through the English language. We got rid of the British through the effective use of the English language by quoting Macaulay, by quoting Edmund Burke, sometimes by quoting Shakespeare. But we not only got our freedom—we have kept a friendship through that language which I hope will be everlasting."

3

THE NATURE AND ORIGIN OF HUMAN LANGUAGE

And out of the ground the Lord God formed every beast of the field, and every fowl of the air; and brought them unto Adam to see what he would call them: and whatsoever Adam called every living creature, that was the name thereof.

GENESIS 2:19

In man's endless effort to understand himself, he is frustrated continually by his dual vision. On the one hand he sees himself as an observer, on the other as the object of his inquiry. The question that has troubled him from the dawn of history is: what sets him apart from the multifarious orders of the animal kingdom with which he shares the natural world and to which he is so unmistakably kin? To Aristotle and the ancient Greek philosophers it seemed evident that man's uniqueness lay in his power to reason. Theologians from the medieval scholastics down to the present have emphasized man's claim to a separable and immortal soul. Modern anthropologists note that *Homo sapiens* is endowed with a priceless constellation of physical assets—upright posture, stereoscopic vision, free and versatile hands, and an enlarged cerebral cortex. These special legacies are interrelated, and it was through their aggregate that man mastered his environment and evolved the ability to transmit culture—the accumulated experience of his entire past—from generation to generation.

Although all mammals instruct their offspring for varying intervals of time in the behaviour patterns, movements, sounds, and skills common to their species, man alone can reach back into the depths of time and evoke the collective knowledge of all his forbears—the sum total of their wisdom and folly, aspirations and achievements, triumphs, failures, and dreams since the morning of human life on earth. The talisman with which he effects this miracle of transcending time and death is language. It is this bequest, peculiar to the human family, that has placed man at the apex of the evolutionary ladder. Only man has language. It is possessed universally by man and it is unique to man. "Without language," says Weston LaBarre, anthropologist of Duke University, North Carolina, "it is safe to say man would never have become fully human."

What is language? How did man acquire it? The questions are inseparable, and neither admits of an easy answer. A classic definition of language that seemed adequate at the turn of the century stated simply: "Language is the expression of human thought by means of words." The ramifications of modern science have since revealed the lacunae in this description. Psychologists asked: what is thought? Linguists asked: what is a word? Zoologists observed that many animals and birds, and even insects, have systems of communication that may be regarded in a crude sense as languages. Physiologists pointed out that human language depends on an interplay between the highly complex vocal apparatus of a speaker and the equally intricate and remarkable auditory organs of a listener. And in its manifold aspects the study of language has involved physics, phonetics, acoustics, neurology, sociology, logic, information theory, semantics, statistics, and the branch of philosophy known as symbolism or theory of signs. To complicate matters still further the very word "language" presents problems by reason of its various meanings in the English lexicon, within which it must do double duty, connoting both language in the abstract, as the common possession of mankind, and language in the specific sense of *one* language—English, Arabic, Urdu, or any of the four thousand discrete tongues employed by communities of men around the polyglot world. The French vocabulary is more explicit. It provides the term *langage* to denote the totality of the four thousand *langues* that fragment mankind; and, in addition, the word *parole* to specify the vocal form of a particular *langue*, as opposed to a system of writing.

Since only about five per cent of the languages spoken on earth today have an ancillary written form, modern linguistic scientists—or Structural Linguists, as they are known academically—concern themselves essentially with language as a system of vocal communication. Writing is, of course, a relatively recent invention of man, dating only from the first flowering of Sumerian and Egyptian culture some five thousand years ago. There is no mystery about its origin. When Neolithic man discovered agriculture and abandoned nomadic life for life in a settled community, he developed a sense of property. With property came trade and with trade the necessity of keeping accounts. The earliest specimens of writing exhumed from the ruins of Sumer and neighbouring cities on the Tigris-Euphrates plain, from the valley of the Nile and the mountains of Crete are, therefore, business records. The idea of poetry—of language transcribed as a mode of art or as a medium of drama, narrative, or philosophical dialectic—came a little later. Writing is our carrier link with the past, and its advent marked the beginning of civilization and the start of history. Yet man had been a resident of this planet for more than half a million years prior to his discovery that information could be transmitted through time and space by visual symbols impressed in clay or inscribed on papyrus scrolls.

There is no doubt that from his initial emergence above the lower brackets of the hominid family, *Homo sapiens* had speech and the potential of evolving a complex system of language. His skeletal remains indicate that anatomically he was capable of producing the entire spectrum of vocal effects available to modern man. The testimony of his camp-sites and burying grounds suggests further that man has always been a social animal—and every pattern of social order in the animal kingdom is shaped and defined by the ability of its members to communicate. Human society could not exist without language. But the relationship is symbiotic; if society is a product of language, so language is a product of man's social nature.

To wonder at the phenomenon of human language, it is not necessary to contemplate it as the instrument of Homer, Shakespeare, or Lao-tse, but merely to contrast any of the thousands of tongues spoken by man with the communication systems that have evolved among other animal orders of the biosphere. Even the most primitive tribesmen in the rain forests of the Amazon or the gibber plains of Australia have complex and luxuriant languages, each the product of incomputable millennia of linguistic evolution, each endowed with its own intricate conventions of sound, sense, and structure (i.e. phonetics, vocabulary, and grammar) peculiar to itself and different from all others. "We know of no people," declared Edward Sapir, the great linguist and anthropologist of Yale University, "that is not possessed of a fully developed language. The lowliest South African Bushman speaks in the forms of a rich symbolic system that is in essence perfectly comparable to the speech of a cultivated Frenchman."

No less astonishing than the universality of language is its diversity. English, for example, is but one of 132 languages comprising the Indo-European linguistic family. But other linguistic families (of which there are seventeen to twenty-six, depending on systems of classification) claim many more members. Despite its small and steadily diminishing number of speakers, the North American Indian group embraces 351 separate languages, while the Sudano-Guinean family, ranging across central Africa, from the Indian Ocean to the Atlantic, has 435. The enormous diversification of human language points to a significant corollary: that language is a heritage of vast antiquity. Modern methods of linguistic analysis have shown that it takes approximately twenty thousand years for two sister languages to diverge beyond all semblance of relationship. But in the immense perspectives of prehistory, such an interval is but a moment. For, twenty thousand years ago, *Homo sapiens* had already evolved into the tall strong-chinned Cro-Magnon race of Western Europe whose finely wrought tools and enlarging social order foreshadowed the end of the Old Stone Age and the dawn of the New. Yet for more than half a million years before the ascendancy of Cro-Magnon man, various species of the genus *Homo* ranged the forests and grasslands of the Old World. And anthropologists agree that it must have been at least one quarter of a million years ago that *Homo sapiens*—prototype of modern, full-brained man—made his appearance on the planet Earth. Did he possess language? "It is doubtful if any other cultural asset of man," Sapir observed, "be it the art of drilling for fire or of chipping stone, may lay claim to a greater age. I am inclined to believe that it antedated even the lowliest developments of material culture, that these developments, in fact, were not strictly possible until language, the tool of significant expression, had itself taken shape."

Fragments of bone and flaked stone tools, painstakingly excised from ancient lake beds and the walls of timeless gorges, have enabled anthropologists to piece together the physical evolution of man and the sequence of his adaptations to the natural world. But until the revolutionary invention of writing—only yesterday in the stupendous span of human existence—he left no record of his language. The relics of his emotions—fears, hopes, intimations of immortality—are preserved in countless graves of the Paleolithic dead, interred in the floors of limestone caverns with ceremony and provision for the contingencies of an unknowable world. His sensibilities—his awareness and artistic delight in the varied aspects of his environment—are revealed in the exquisitely skilful murals limned by the artists of the Magdalenian culture on the walls of the famous Lascaux Cave in the Dordogne and more than a hundred other caves in France, Spain, and Italy some twelve thousand years ago. But the speech of those men who buried their dead with tender solicitude and decorated their shrines with consummate artistry vanished with the oscillations of the air on which their thoughts were borne, in the instant of transient utterance. How then can one reconstruct the steps by which early man, risen from small-brained forbears with beetling brows and receding chins and foreheads, evolved his complex systems of vocal sounds—arbitrary, symbolic, but conventionalized and recognized through common usage—by which all men communicate today?

Until quite recently the whole question of the origin of human language was considered so hopelessly insoluble that most serious anthropologists and students of language declined even to discuss it. The Linguistic Society of Paris went so far as to enact a standing rule, some fifty years ago, excluding from its proceedings any papers on the subject as inherently unscientific and probably crackpot. The justification for the ruling was that no actual evidence existed on which to base a theory. And one reason for the lack of evidence was that all philologists and linguists who tackled the problem were looking for something that could not be found—namely the vestiges of a primordial, universal tongue—common ancestor of all languages, living and dead, that ever cemented the societies of man. Their quest was inspired in part by Genesis 11: *And the whole earth was of one language and of one speech*—until, at Babel, *the Lord did there confound the language of all the earth.* It was stimulated also by the discovery by Sir William Jones in 1786 that most of the languages of Europe, India, and Persia—including ancient Greek, Latin, and Sanskrit—were members of a single great linguistic family that must have ramified in prehistoric times from a common ancestral tongue. From this discovery of the Indo-European family of languages, it was an easy leap to the conjecture that all of the world's linguistic families must have diverged in still more distant abysses of time from one single archaic *langue*, as the varied races of contemporary man evolved from a common progenitor.

On such assumptions, language scholars headed down two avenues of investigation. Since many areas of the planet had not yet been explored and hundreds of unwritten languages had not yet been studied or codified, one school of inquiry pursued the hope that in some part of the world there might exist a remote and isolated tribe of "living fossils" speaking a "fossil" tongue. Another group of scholars devoted a vast amount of effort to analysing contemporary languages in exhaustive detail, looking for common elements that might be interpreted as variants from a single primeval source. Both methods of attack proved futile, for at the time of their application, anthropology and linguistics were still in their infancy and had only begun to develop their respective disciplines. And geologists were only beginning to discern the immense antiquity of man. It was not, indeed, so long ago that many educated Europeans and Americans accepted the conclusion of Archbishop Ussher of Ireland, based on interpretation of the Scriptures, that man made his appearance on earth in the year 4004 B.C., on the morning of October 4, at nine A.M.[1]

[1] The notion that at one time all men spoke a single language is by no means unique with Genesis. It found expression in ancient Egypt, in early Hindu and Buddhist writings, and was seriously explored by several European philosophers during the sixteenth century. An interesting variation of the theme was set forth by the seventeenth-century Swedish scholar, Andreas Kemke, who contended that in the Garden of Eden the Lord spoke Swedish, Adam spoke Danish, and the serpent spoke French.

Today in the light of contemporary knowledge, linguistic scholars have abandoned the belief that they can ever exhume vestiges of an *Ursprache*, or universal, ancestral tongue. For nowhere on earth have they encountered a language that can be described as "primitive," in the sense of undeveloped—i.e. barren of complexities of grammar, vocabulary, or phonetic shadings. Moreover, the whole process of linguistic evolution, observable through seven thousand years of recorded history, has tended to reduce rather than multiply the languages of man. In every age and on every continent, local tongues have become extinct as dominant cultures imposed their speech on subject or colonial people. The process is plainly evident today throughout Africa where French, English and Arabic have supplanted hundreds of regional dialects. Across all of Asia from the Near East to the China Sea, English is spreading with astonishing speed. And around the shores of the Arctic Ocean, from Baffin Island to Mount Katmai, Eskimos and Aleuts are quickly forgetting their own rich and complex tongues as successive generations attend Canadian and American schools and listen nightly to radio broadcasts in English beamed not only from the south, but from Russia and China across the Pole. The tendency of dominant languages to overrun and obliterate regional tongues led Dr. Franz Boas, the great anthropologist of Columbia University, to a significant conclusion: "At a very early time the diversity of languages among people of the same physical type was much greater than it is now . . . It is reasonable to suppose that the number of languages that have disappeared is very large." More recently, Dr. Carleton S. Coon of the University of Pennsylvania declared: "We do not know what languages the hunters of the Late Pleistocene spoke, but we may be sure they were numerous."

In the total absence of any clue as to the speech patterns of prehistoric man, scholars could only speculate; and it was their fanciful speculations that irritated the Linguistic Society of Paris and provoked its ban on any discussion of the genesis of language. Today linguists allude to those nineteenth-century theories somewhat derisively by names which suggest both the essence of each theory and the attitude of its later critics. Most notable among such efforts to penetrate the mists of the early Pleistocene were:

• The Bow-Wow Theory, so-named by the Anglo-German philologist Max Müller, which proposed that language grew out of man's attempts to imitate natural sounds, as an infant learning to talk calls a locomotive a *choo-choo* or a cow a *moo*. According to this theory, man's first words must have been onomatopoeic or echo words—e.g. *thunder*, *bump*, *sneeze*, *splash*, *sizzle*, *slosh*, *cuckoo*, *moan*, *mumble*, *grumble*, etc.

• The Pooh-Pooh Theory held that speech originated from the spontaneous exclamations and interjections of the human animal; cries of fear, surprise, anger, pain, disgust, despair, or joy.

• The Yo-He-Ho Theory suggested that language evolved from reflex vocal utterances—grunts, gasps, glottal contractions—evoked by strenuous physical exertion, such as hacking up a carcass or dragging a heavy log through underbrush.

• The Ta-Ta Theory, to which Darwin lent some support, maintained that speech developed as a kind of obbligato, or vocal accompaniment, to the system of gestures or sign language by which man first communicated. In his treatise on *The Expression of Emotions*, Darwin observed that "persons cutting anything with a pair of scissors may be seen to move their jaws simultaneously with the blades of the scissors. Children learning to write often twist about their tongue as their fingers move, in a ridiculous fashion." Citing Darwin, Sir Richard Paget, chief exponent of the Ta-Ta Theory, wrote: "Originally man expressed his ideas by gesture, but as he gesticulated with his hands, his tongue, lips and jaws unconsciously followed in a ridiculous fashion 'understudying' the action of the hands. The consequence was that when, owing to pressure of other business, the principal actors (the hands) retired from the stage . . . their understudies, the tongue, lips and jaw, were already proficient in the pantomime art. Then the great discovery was made that if, while making a gesture with the tongue and lips, air was blown through the oral or nasal cavities, the gesture became audible. . . ."

• The Ding-Dong Theory postulated a kind of mystical or *a priori* correspondence between sound and sense. Enunciated about a century ago by Max Müller, the theory reiterated ideas first advanced by Pythagoras (*c.* 500 B.C.), and later sustained by Heraclitus and Plato, who held that language must have arisen by necessity from laws of nature and specifically an inevitable law of harmony which ordained that "everything which is struck rings; everything has its particular ring". Thus when prehistoric man first met prehistoric dog, he said "Dog" and that is how the dog got its name.

• The Sing-Song Theory contended that human speech arose out of primitive, rhythmic chants. Darwin also laid the basis for this theory in his *Descent of Man*, when he wrote: "Primeval man, or rather some progenitor of man, probably first used his voice in producing true musical cadences, that is in singing, as do some of the gibbon apes at the present day; and we may conclude from a widespread analogy, that this power would have been especially exerted during the courtship of the sexes—would have expressed various emotions, such as love, jealousy, triumph—and would have served as a challenge to rivals." The Sing-Song Theory found another formidable exponent in the distinguished Danish linguist, Otto Jespersen, who wrote in 1922: "Language was born in the courting days of mankind; the first utterances of speech I fancy to myself like something between the nightly love-lyrics of puss upon the tiles and melodious love-songs of the nightingale."

• The Goo-Goo Theory incorporated elements of all the others in a single eclectic package by stating (in the words of Harvard's great English professor George Lyman Kittredge): "All that is requisite for the beginning of language proper, is that any sound should come to be purposely uttered, however vaguely, and actually understood, and we have the promise and potentiality of the most cultivated human speech." The same concept had been expressed more graphically by Darwin, whose infinitely conscientious and non-partisan intellect led him always to examine every possible consideration: "May not some unusually wise ape-like animal have imitated the growl of a beast of prey, and thus told his fellow-monkeys the nature of the expected danger? This would have been a first step in the formation of a language."

Standing alone, each of these theories reveals flaws which are implicit in the baby-talk names by which they are contemptuously known. Each has been thoroughly criticized, rebutted, tarred-and-feathered, and ridden out of the pale of modern linguistic science. The Bow-Wow Theory, which was among the first and certainly the most familiar of these hypotheses, rests on the Biblical assumption that language was born when man started to invent descriptive or imitative names for the things he saw around him. There exists considerable doubt, however, that language began with nouns; and a great mass of evidence indicates that onomatopoeic or echo words represent but a small element in the vocabulary of any language. Many apparently onomatopoeic words evolved in relatively recent times from roots originally devoid of sound symbolism. Thus the English word *sneeze* derives from the Old English *fnēosan*, which stemmed in turn from the Greek *pnein* (to breathe), which exhibits no symptoms of hay fever at all. Even avowedly echoic words vary from language to language. Thus an English rooster greets the dawn with *cock-a-doodle-doo*, whereas his foreign cousins cry *cocorico* in France, *quiquiriquí* in Spain, *chicchericchi* in Italy, *kikeriki* in Germany, *kykeliky* in Denmark, and *kokke-kokko* in Japan.

Much more formidable objections impugn the Ding-Dong Theory which presupposes a natural, built-in fitness of words to designate their meaning. To accept such a metaphysical premise would raise the question of why, when prehistoric man first met prehistoric dog, he exclaimed *Dog!* rather than *Canis! Chien! Perro!* or *Hund!* Aristotle, father of grammar in the Western world,[1] perceived the fallacies in the Pythagorean-Platonic theory, and advanced the opposing view that language is altogether arbitrary and functions in any society by convention and the common consent of its speakers. No linguist disputes Aristotle's thesis today.

The chance that prehistoric man may have employed sign language before he talked, as proposed by Paget and other exponents of the Ta-Ta Theory, has received support from the branch of linguistic science known as *kinesics*. Studies in this

[1] Aristotle was the first Occidental scholar to analyse language, define parts of speech, and distinguish case and gender. The first great grammarian in history, however, was the Indian scholar, Pānini who, a century before Aristotle, wrote a consummately detailed analysis of the Sanskrit language that has remained authoritative for all time. Pānini's grammar described every inflection, derivation and syntactic usage of Sanskrit with a clarity and precision never surpassed by any later work. Modern philologists suspect it was because of Pānini's codification that Sanskrit later became the official and literary language of Brahmin India.

field have shown that the lexicon of human gestures includes more than 700,000 distinct and expressive movements of the hands, arms, fingers, and face by which information can be transferred without speech. The most highly developed gestural systems are those used by deaf-mutes—i.e. lip-reading and finger-talk. Others include the formal sign language of the North American Indian; the highly stylized hand imagery of the Hawaiian hula and the dances of Cambodia, Bali, and other Asian and Polynesian lands; the Japanese flirt language of the fan; the coded arm motions of football and hockey referees, baseball umpires, and other sports officials; the signalling patterns of semaphores, heliographs, and naval flags; and the varied and largely impromptu gestures used by traders in market-places the world over since travel and commerce began.

It is obvious that the more sophisticated systems of pantomime, such as the discourse of deaf-mutes, depend on a prior knowledge of language; and they were indeed devised as a substitute for speech. But it is equally evident, from studies of animal behaviour, that many species communicate successfully among themselves by a variety of non-vocal methods. Baboons, for example, rebuke their young and often reduce them to howls of terror simply by fixing them with an unwavering glare. Dogs and wolves also communicate expressively with their eyes —as well as with their tails. Certain species of birds and fish perform elaborate dances and other attention-getting rituals of display in the process of courtship. Monkeys and apes—and most notably chimpanzees—exhibit resources of facial and gestural expression far richer than those utilized by many deadpan pretenders to the human race.

The prevalence throughout the animal kingdom of visual, gestural, non-vocal communication suggests therefore that it must have antedated speech in the development of human society. But the gulf between sign language and the language of modern, articulate man is a profound one, and the route by which *Homo sapiens* crossed that gulf is by no means adequately defined by the Ta-Ta Theory. Similar shortcomings discount or depreciate each of the early hypotheses of linguistic origin, for each one is narrow in scope, vague in substance, and founded on flimsy knowledge of the physical and social evolution of early man. Yet scattered here and there among them lie fragmentary but sometimes suggestive clues.

To have reservations about the first valiant efforts to trace the stream of human language back to its sources in the dark oubliette of unrecorded time is not to say that those wellsprings are forever undiscoverable, nor that a reasonably valid theory of linguistic evolution cannot be formulated today. Current developments in many domains of science—especially paleontology, zoology, and both physical and cultural anthropology—have cast new light upon processes of communication in all orders of the animal world. An understanding of some of those processes is necessary to an understanding of the nature and uniqueness of human language.

Although animal communication is limited in range, the variety of methods by which it takes place is enormous at all levels of the evolutionary ladder. Insects, the largest class of living creatures both in number of individuals and number of species, transfer information by means of many highly specialized organs and codes. Some involve the auditory sense. Crickets, locusts, and cicadas, for example, "talk" by stridulation—the production of sound by friction between rough, file-like surfaces or plates on legs, wings, abdomen, and thorax. In Australia, incubator of many eccentric fauna, there is a "barking spider" whose utterance can be heard up to ten feet away. But much of the insect world is silent. Fireflies, glow-worms, and various luminous beetles identify their kind, summon mates, and discourage predators by the emission of cold light. Many moths and butterflies possess a delicacy of olfactory sense that enables them to interpret and respond to scent stimuli at distances of more than a mile. The social insects have still more specialized systems of information transfer. Termites, blind and deaf, secrete fatty substances from their skin surfaces which enable them to recognize the various castes of their hierarchical society in the eternal darkness of their woody labyrinths. Other ant species communicate in various ways—by the tactile sense of their antennae, by mouth-to-mouth exchanges of food, and by scent. The disciplined marches and manoeuvres of the army ants of Central and South America, Africa, and the Philippines are directed by chemical trails laid down by the advance echelons and followed undeviatingly by the rank and file.

The most extraordinary of all insect languages is the semantic dance of the honey bee, a phenomenon described in the classic studies of the German entomologist Karl von Frisch over several decades beginning in 1920. The remarkable feature of the dance is the quantity and accuracy of the information it conveys. When an individual bee has discovered a source of food, it returns to the hive, dusted with pollen, perfumed with nectar, and performs a dance on the vertical wall of the comb to attract the attention of its fellow workers and to announce its discovery. The configurations of the dance codify two kinds of information: the distance of the new-found food supply from the hive and the compass bearing in which it lies. If the food is nearby—less than 85 feet from the hive—the finder bee executes a series of swift circular figures. If it is farther away, the bee promenades in a straight line, broken at intervals by 360-degree pirouettes to right and left, wagging its abdomen in a rhythmic tempo directly proportional to the distance. The flight vector is indicated by the plotting of the dance figures on the wall of the hive: both the diameter of the fast circle and the direction of the slow straight promenade define by their deviation from the vertical the location of the food source with respect to the position of the sun *at that hour of the day*. The dance of the honey bee is an archetype of what linguists term a referential language. For though it is non-vocal, it has grammar—in the sense of structure—and it transmits information which evokes a responsive action from members of the society who understand its conventions.

Of all classes of animals, birds are the most continuously vocal and, save for man, the most versatile in their vocalizing. As in the human community, some birds sing and some are tone-deaf. Contrary to romantic tradition, songbirds pour forth their profuse strains neither out of unpremeditated joy nor leaden-eyed despair, but simply to proclaim their ownership of a particular bit of land and to repel intruders. The silent birds are, not surprisingly, the larger, often nocturnal, and generally solitary carnivores—hawks, owls, and condors. But between the predators and the songsters there exist many families of birds that communicate constantly by a multiplicity of calls, chirps, twitters, whistles, scolding sounds, and other vocal signals. Barnyard fowl, in addition to squawks of anger or alarm, keep up an almost incessant obbligato of what has been termed "conversational clucking", serving presumably to reassure the flock of its collective existence and well-being.[1]

Jackdaws, crows, and certain other species of highly gregarious and intelligent birds employ a variable range of vocal signals which are understood and uttered by their young apparently from the moment of hatching. The Swiss naturalist Konrad Lorenz made an extensive study of jackdaws and noted that their vocabulary consists of two flight calls—a departure call which he transcribed as *Kia* and a homing call, *Kiaw*—a nesting call, *Zick*, *Zick*, *Zick*; a language of love (jackdaws are monogamous and remain so for life) composed of soft, low notes suggestive of the sounds made by infant birds; and a harsh rattle of anger which, when uttered, convenes all jackdaws within hearing to collective attack or defence. From years of close observation Lorenz concluded that the code calls of European jackdaws are innate. On the other hand, studies of American crows conducted by Hubert and Mabel Frings of Pennsylvania State University convinced them that crow talk may be partially acquired—or at least subject to regional variation. They made a tape recording of crow calls in Maine and sent it abroad where it was played to crows in France. Unexpectedly, the French crows reacted to the assembly (attack) call of the Maine crows but listened to their alarm (dispersal) call without evident interest or response. When recordings of French crow calls were mailed back to America, the Maine crows ignored all of them. Later, however, the Frings found that recordings of the distress call of the French crows produced great agitation among crows in Pennsylvania. They deduced that the difference in response derived from differences in habit: crows that breed in Maine tend to be rather exclusive like many staid New England families, seldom mingling with other crows. Pennsylvania crows, however,

[1] Sociologists have noted that a human analogue of conversational clucking characterizes most large cocktail parties. In *The Meaning of Meaning*, C. K. Ogden and I. A. Richards observe: "Throughout the western world it is agreed that people must meet frequently, and that it is not only agreeable to talk, but that it is a matter of common courtesy to say something even when there is hardly anything to say."

winter in Florida and points south, where they encounter a varied and cosmopolitan community of birds and thus acquire greater sophistication than their stodgy Down East cousins.

The supreme vocalizers among birds, however, are the mimics—mockingbirds, catbirds, magpies, parakeets, parrots, and Indian and Chinese myna birds. One ornithologist has reported hearing an American mockingbird imitate the songs of fifty-five other bird species within the space of an hour. Parrots, which sometimes reproduce human speech with ludicrous accuracy, have been known to acquire vocabularies totalling as many as a hundred words which they may occasionally employ in correct association with people, objects, or events. But, for the most part, the dialogue of parrots and of myna birds (which mimic human speech, especially vowel sounds, even more precisely than parrots, though their vocabularies tend to be smaller) represents little more than conversational clucking, despite occasional purity of articulation. The vocal apparatus of birds is in general extremely complex and not yet fully understood: some species are capable of singing several notes simultaneously and thus producing a spectrum of harmonic chords. It is evident, however, that vocal organs, no matter how versatile, are not sufficient in themselves to engender true language. Other endowments are required—the most essential, of course, being intelligence.

The question is: what degree of intelligence? And what aspect of it? Mammals as a class comprise the most intelligent subdivision of the animal kingdom. The literature of every land abounds with tales of precocious animals—horses, dogs, lions, foxes, mice—that talk, and often out-talk and outwit man. But in actuality none has ever developed speech, although some species learn, with training, to respond correctly to human words. (Tests have shown that some elephants are capable of distinguishing up to twenty-four spoken commands.) In his youth some years before he invented the telephone, Alexander Graham Bell, who had studied the physiology of speech and had developed a method of teaching deaf-mutes to talk, trained his Skye terrier to growl steadily while he manipulated its lips and throat. Thus assisted, the dog eventually managed to produce a sequence of sounds that approximated *Ow ah oo gwah mah*. That was the closest it could come to "How are you grandma?" The close and immemorial relationship between man and his canine friend has established beyond doubt the truth of Bertrand Russell's dictum that "no matter how eloquently a dog may bark, he cannot tell you that his parents were poor but honest".

For true language neither the mimetic talents of a talking bird nor the sincerest efforts of a faithful dog are adequate endowments. Birds lack the brain power, and even such notably cerebral mammals as the elephant lack the requisite vocal equipment. Directly below man in the evolutionary scale, however, stand the anthropoid (Greek *anthrōpos*, man, plus *eidēs*, like) apes whose brains are relatively large with respect to their total body weight.[1] It is not surprising that zoologists and animal psychologists have been curious about these collateral cousins of man and have made rather intensive studies of their behaviour and modes of communication, not only in zoos and laboratories, but in their natural forest habitats—and in the human home.

All primates communicate by vocal sounds, but within the primate order, as within the species of man, some use their voices more than others; and the degree of loquacity, as is also the case with man, does not always reflect the degree of intelligence. Probably the most talkative of the primates are the Japanese monkeys (*Macaca fuscata*), whose vocabulary of more than thirty distinct calls or cries is the largest known to any animal other than man. Yet their intelligence ranks considerably below that of the least intelligent of the four anthropoid apes: the gibbon of South China and Malaysia. Smallest of the apes, it is also the most prolific, the most gregarious, the most spectacular aerialist, and the noisiest—both in volume of sound and redundancy. Endowed with a laryngeal sac and an enlarged hyoid throat-bone, it makes the jungle aisles quake with proclamations of its presence and state of being. Studies of the white-cheeked gibbon have shown that its vocabulary contains a total of fourteen distinguishable expressions, some indicating interior states of fear, sickness, satisfaction, or excitement,

[1] In gross brain weight, man ranks third in the animal kingdom. His 1,400 grammes of brain are exceeded by the elephant's 5,000 grammes and the whale's 2,050 grammes. The ratio between brain weight and body weight in man, however, is 1 : 40, as opposed to 1 : 40,000 in the whale, 1 : 150 in the gorilla, and 1 : 28 in the mouse.

some connoting, among other things, hunger ("Let's go find some fruit") or jealousy ("Keep your dirty hands off my wife!"). The gibbon's only ape relative in Asia is the orangutan (Malay, "man of the woods"), which dwells moodily in the low swampy forests of Sumatra and Borneo. Much larger and considerably more intelligent than the gibbon, the orangutan is dour, lethargic, and solitary—least gregarious of the apes and the least vocal. Some observers have reported that the adult male orangutan lives alone, save during the mating season, which would account for its taciturn nature.

The other two anthropoid apes—the gorilla and chimpanzee—live in Africa. The gorilla (*gorilla* is a supposed African word which first appeared in a Greek account of the voyage of Hanno, the Carthaginian navigator, in the fourth century B.C.) is the largest and most formidable of the great apes—six feet tall when standing erect, weighing up to six hundred pounds. It is also the most terrestrial and physically the most like man. Its impressive "forehead" rises high above beetling eyebrow ridges. But where man's vertical brow forms the outer façade of his overgrown frontal lobe, the gorilla's supraorbital structure is solid bone—a buttress mechanically necessary to sustain the muscles of its massive jaws. Although some zoologists believe that gorillas are the most intelligent of the anthropoids, the contention is difficult to prove owing to their shyness in the wild and their surliness and occasional ferocity in captivity. Moderately gregarious in their native habitat, gorillas tend to live in bands, comprising perhaps five associated families. They are, next to orangutans, the least articulate of the apes. Their vocalization consists for the most part of *Hu-Hu-Hu*, ranging from soft, low hoots to awesome, ear-splitting roars. They give voice most dramatically in the course of "displays"—recurring rituals, characterized by a crescendo of sound, combined with the breaking, tearing, and hurling of vegetation, leg kicking, "symbolic feeding", tree slapping, ground stamping, and winding up with a grand finale of chest beating—the reverberations of which may be heard a mile away. According to Dr. George B. Schaller, who observed gorillas in the wild as a member of the African Primate Expedition of 1959–60, displays are sometimes triggered by an unexpected disturbance, such as the approach of strangers—humans or another gorilla band. On other occasions, without any external stimulus, an individual gorilla may initiate a display, motivated apparently by some vague malaise—an accumulation of tension, general dissatisfaction with the simian world, or perhaps a sudden histrionic compulsion to show off. Whatever its inception, the force underlying any display is pent-up excitement, collective or individual, and the purpose of the display is to release it.

All of the anthropoid apes, from the silent orangutan to the garrulous gibbon, have their own special varieties of display —and so indeed has man. "Sporting events," Dr. Schaller observes, "are ideal locations for watching the behaviour of man when he is generally excited and emotionally off guard. A spectator at a sporting event perceives actions that excite him. Yet he cannot participate in them directly, nor does he want to cease observing them. The tension thus produced finds release in chanting, clapping of hands, stamping of feet, jumping up and down, and the throwing of objects."[1]

Of all the anthropoid apes, the chimpanzee (whose name entered the English lexicon in 1738 from a West African dialect: *chi-penzi*) is the best known and best liked. In contrast to the great, glum, glowering gorilla, the chimpanzee is animated, comical, imitative, sociable, sexy, talkative, and tractable—temperamentally far more like man (on one of man's good days) and far less dangerous to human observers. Adult males range from one hundred to one hundred and fifty pounds in weight. Some experts rank the chimpanzee above the gorilla in intelligence, though the question remains open. In vocalization it runs the gibbon a close race; it almost always has something to say, and its repertory of calls and cries exhibits both variety and volume. The most recent and remarkable investigation of chimpanzees in the wild was made in 1960–62 by Miss Jane Goodall, a young English zoologist who spent more than eighteen months in the forest of Tanganyika living in close proximity to the objects of her study. By exercising enormous patience, perseverance and courage, Miss Goodall, after weeks and months of discouragement, eventually established a rapport with a family band of chimpanzees solid enough to permit her thereafter to move among them without ado.

Commenting on the vocalization and communication of

[1] In *Natural History*, August–September 1963, p. 16.

chimpanzees, Miss Goodall reported: "If you judged from sound alone, you would imagine that wild chimpanzees were always fighting and quarrelling. When two groups meet there is sometimes a fantastic ceremony as the males call loudly, drum on tree trunks, and shake branches, while the females and youngsters scream and rush out of the way. But this is merely excitement and pleasure; with his highly emotional extrovert temperament, the chimpanzee likes to express his feelings in action.

"I am often asked, 'Do chimpanzees have a language?' They do not, of course, have a language that can be compared with our own, but they do have a tremendous variety of calls each one induced by a different emotion. The calls range from the rather low-pitched 'hoo' of greeting, and a series of low grunts that is heard when a chimpanzee begins to feed on some desirable food, to the loud, excited calls and screams which occur when two groups meet. One call, given in defiance of a possible predator, or when a chimpanzee, for some reason, is angry at the approach of another can be described as a loud 'wraaaah!' This is a single syllable, several times repeated, and is one of the most savage and spine-chilling sounds of the African forest. Another characteristic call is a series of hoots, the breath drawn in audibly after each hoot and ending with three or four roars. This is the cry of a male chimpanzee as he crosses a ridge. It seems to be an announcement to any other chimpanzees that may be in the valley below: 'Here I come.' These calls, while they are not a language in our sense of the word, are understood by other chimpanzees and certainly form a means of communication.

"In addition, chimpanzees communicate by touch or gesture. A mother touches her young one when she is about to move away, or taps on the trunk when she wants it to come down from a tree. When a chimpanzee is anxious for a share of some delicacy, he begs, holding out his hand, palm up, exactly as we do. He may pat the branch beside him if he wants a companion to join him there. When two animals are grooming each other and one feels that it is his turn to be groomed, he often reaches out and gives his companion a poke. Once, when three males were all grooming one another, I saw a female going around poking at each of them in turn. But she was completely ignored—and so sat down sadly and groomed herself! There are also many gestures of greeting and friendship. Sometimes when two friends meet after a separation, they fling their arms around each other in a delighted embrace. Despite this fairly well-developed system of communication, a chimpanzee suddenly confronted with danger gives no alarm to warn his companions, but simply runs off silently."[1]

Miss Goodall's observations in Tanganyika confirmed earlier studies of chimpanzees in captivity with respect to several points: (1) the vocal mechanism of the chimpanzee is potentially capable of articulating a large variety of sounds similar to those of human speech—including all the vowels (especially *o* and *u*), the labial consonants, *b* and *p*, the velar plosives, *g* and *k*, the aspirate *h*, and the nasals, *m* and *n*; (2) despite this potential, chimpanzees consistently use a vocabulary of only about two dozen "words" or utterances; (3) although much of the chimpanzee's vocalization is "phatic",[2] proclaiming only immediate emotional states—fear, joy, alarm—it can be semantic when it refers to external stimuli such as physical objects, food, other animals, friends, man. The consensus of all observers is that the chimpanzee lacks true speech, but not for phonetic reasons. What then is the barrier? Would environment make a difference? Can a chimpanzee be taught to speak? Several attempts have been made to do so.

In the summer of 1931, a female chimpanzee named Gua, seven and one-half months old, was taken from her mother at Orange Park Anthropoid Station, Florida, and moved to the nearby home of Professor and Mrs. W. M. Kellogg. There she was reared, for the better part of the ensuing year, as the younger sister of the Kelloggs's nine-and-a-half month old son Donald. Gua was diapered, bathed, powdered, brushed-and-combed, scented, enthroned on a high chair, fed with a spoon, and treated in every way like a human baby. During all her waking hours she was exposed to human speech, including Donald's infant babblings. From the beginning Gua showed her comprehension of English, responding differentially to various utterances, and surpassing Donald for the first five months in

[1] *National Geographic*, August 1963, pp. 289–90.
[2] This word was invented by the anthropologist B. K. Malinovski, rather as "conditioned reflexes" was invented by Pavlov.

the number of words and phrases she appeared to understand. But her own vocalizations were limited to the characteristic calls and cries of her species. Two of her commonest expressions —a "food bark" and a pathetic "oo-oo" cry of trouble or fear—took on extended meanings, becoming roughly assent and dissent, approval and disapproval, "yes" and "no". In the beginning for example, Gua would give her food bark at the sight of an orange; later she responded with her food bark when asked "Do you want an orange?" or "Do you want to go bye-bye?" But Gua never learned to utter a single human word, nor did she ever attempt to imitate new sounds, while Donald slowly but surely ascended from aimless prattle to semantic speech. More significantly, although Donald imitated Gua's barks and cries, Gua never tried to mimic Donald's babblings—nor did she ever babble herself. Every sound she uttered was evoked by either an internal or an external stimulus—there were no cooings, no lallation, no random noise for its own sake.

Observers of the experiment later suggested three possible reasons for Gua's muteness: (1) she had spent the first seven months of her life in chimpanzee society and might already have passed a point of no return; (2) the Kelloggs had given Gua every opportunity to learn to talk as children learn, but had made no extra effort to teach her; and (3) the experiment was terminated after nine months—perhaps too brief a time to produce significant results. Henry in 1947, with these considerations in mind, Keith and Cathy Hayes adopted another female chimpanzee, Viki, from Orange Park. They began visiting her at the station immediately after her birth, and took her home when she was six weeks old. Treating her like a somewhat retarded child, they worked assiduously to teach Viki to talk. From the beginning she uttered the same food bark and "oo-oo" cries as Gua. After three years of long and patient tutelage, Viki finally learned to say three words—*papa*, *mama*, and *cup*—none of them very well. At the same age a human child commands a vocabulary of at least two hundred words.

The Gua and Viki experiments, and others, have convinced psychologists and zoologists that the inability of apes to speak good English stems from more than faulty diction or an unhappy childhood. The evidence is not all in, however, on one mammal —the bottle-nosed dolphin or porpoise. Endowed with a brain one-third larger than man's and equally complex, the dolphin manifests its high intelligence in many ways: capacity for learning, speed of learning, social responsibility towards individual members of its species, and—most surprising—an extraordinary sensitivity, even kindliness, in its relations with man. The dolphin's communication system is extremely intricate. The sounds it makes are engendered in several ways, and range from tones as low as a bass viol's to a supersonic pitch of 200,000 cycles, far above the limits of human hearing. Its complex voice box can produce thousands of different effects that have been described as creakings, raspings, mewings, whistles, barks, squawks, and quacks. From the repiratory blowhole atop its head, it emits another variety of whistles and 'raspberries'. It also produces percussion effects by clacking its eighty-eight needle-point teeth. Dr. John C. Lilly of the Communications Research Institute of Miami, Florida, who has studied dolphins intensively for a decade, has discovered that they possess astonishing mimetic skill. Their utterances are hard to unscramble, however, as they are emitted with incredible rapidity. By playing tape recordings of dolphin talk at a tempo four times slower than the original recording speed, Dr. Lilly found himself able to distinguish, amid their incessant chatter, dolphin imitations of human laughter, of a baby crying, of a banjo, and of automobile traffic on a neighbouring highway. To his amazement he heard several words and phrases, which he himself had spoken a few minutes before the recording, now mimicked by a dolphin in "a very high-pitched, Donald Duckish" voice. "I believe," says Dr. Lilly, "that with proper care and preparation we can teach them to understand something of human speech and perhaps after some years of work actually to talk in a primitive way."

Like man, dolphins appear to possess both vocal versatility and superior intelligence—two of the preconditions of language. Yet there are other requirements as suggested by the fact that no animal, however clever in comprehension, however assiduously trained and tutored to talk, has ever engaged in a dialogue with man. Between the food bark of the hungry chimpanzee and the "What's for dinner?" of the hungry human lies a whole day of Creation—or a million years of evolution. The breakthrough from animal cries to the use of phonetic symbols opened the gates to all of man's subsequent triumphs. It gave him the power to abstract, to generalize, to synthesize—in short, to *think*. It signalled the most crucial single step in man's evolutionary ascent. It is clear that other elements besides the vocal and auditory mechanisms he shares with the apes have enabled man to develop his gift of language. Those elements lie embedded in the very nature of human language. And it is precisely those that are lacking in animal systems of communications.

To say that the vocalizing of apes is phatic—that it consists simply of noisy and redundant broadcasts of apish appetites and tensions—while human language is semantic—that *it* conveys meaningful information through the use of vocal symbols—is to oversimplify the case. The calls and cries of primates, monkeys as well as apes, often have semantic value, as when they alert the band to danger, convene them to repel invasion, or stimulate them to some useful common action. The fact that a gibbon emits a danger cry without specifying whether the dangers inheres in an approaching leopard or a waiting python does not flaw the semanticity of the warning. Conversely, much of human vocalization is essentially phatic—e.g. political oratory, television commercials, cocktail party chit-chat, the language of lovers, teen-age talk. There are, however, several aspects or "design-features" of human language which differentiate it totally from the communications systems of the apes and all other creatures on earth.[1]

• The fundamental feature of human language is that it has to be learned. Animal sounds are inborn and remain uniform within species, with only slight variations, wherever its members exist around the world. The fact that human language is acquired rather than innate is apparent in the multiplicity of man's tongues. If language did not have to be learned, there would be only one language and all men would speak alike. But each linguistic community has its own separate vocal code within which the relationship between the sound and the meaning of every word is a matter of local convention. That is why human children have to learn to talk: learning to talk is a

[1] The design features cited here were analysed and described by Dr. Charles F. Hockett, professor of linguistics and anthropology at Cornell University, in *Scientific American*, September 1960, pp. 80–96.

matter of learning the meanings their parents attach to the vocal sounds they make. Language is learned slowly and often with great effort, especially if the effort is made after infancy. Scattered cases of feral or isolated children—some thirty in all from Wild Peter of Hanover in 1724 down to Kamala and Amala, the wolf-girls of India in 1920—have shown conclusively that a child who is reared by animals, abandoned to live on its own in the wilds, or is otherwise cut off from human society, fails to develop speech. Isolation past the age of seven may render him permanently mute, despite the best efforts of teachers to repair the crippling effect of solitude. On the other hand, every normal child is born with the *capacity* to speak and a strong impulse to do so. The capacity and the impulse are both revealed in the moist and happy lallation of the infant babbler. It is significant that only the human baby takes pleasure in the aimless exercise of his larynx, lungs, lips, and tongue. The infant ape never tries, or learns, to babble.

• A second feature unique to human language is its ability to leap barriers of space and time, to describe past events and forecast future happenings, to speak of distant places and actions far removed. Animal communication deals only with the here and now, with the possible exception of the semantic dance of the honey bee which refers to something at a distance. Yet here too a distinction appears. The dancing bee is not like a returned diplomat reporting the results of his recent mission; it is going through what animal ethologists call "intention movements"—an attention-getting mechanism designed to incite its fellow workers to communal action. If the other bees do not respond at once, there is nothing the courier bee can do, save repeat the same dance over and over again. Its method of communication is instinctive, inflexible, and invariable; and the bee can refer to just one subject—food and where to find it. In contrast, human language is infinitely flexible. Man can talk about *anything*. He is, therefore, the only animal capable of lying.

• Human language also combines an incredibly rich variety of phonetic resources with consummate economy in their use. No language on earth uses more than a small fraction of the distinguishable sound which man's vocal apparatus is capable of producing. English, for example, employs only about forty separate speech sounds, or phonemes; yet from them more than half a million words have been made. (And many millions more *could* be synthesized from the same forty sounds.) An example of phonetic economy lies in the arrangement of sounds in *act*, *cat*, and *tack*. Only three sounds /*a*/, /*k*/, and /*t*/, are used, but they combine in different ways to form three distinct words. Animals have to rely on big sweeps of tone and volume to differentiate among signals. Man transfers meaning with minimal phonetic effort but absolute semantic effect.

• Perhaps the supreme attribute of human language is its limitless creativity. Alone of all creatures on earth, man can say things that have never been said before—and still be understood. Animals can only repeat the same limited utterances over and over again, as their countless forbears have done for seventy-five million years, since the dawn of the Cenozoic Era. But man has the capacity to create every time he speaks. It is within his power to coin new words, invent new phrases, evolve new modes of expression, invoke new ideas and concepts, seek new responses, by the process of arranging and rearranging familiar elements in accordance with the rules accepted by all speakers of his tongue. Language is thus, in one sense, a wondrously flexible system within which man spins tapestries of thought. It is also a living organism that changes constantly and will never cease to change as long as men have tongues.

The wonder of human language is transcended only by the enigma of its origin. We find no prototype of speech in the highest primates. No anthropoid ape has ever enlarged its lexicon of sounds or given a denotative name to anything. No talking bird has ever improvised a novel combination of the words it knows. No human child has ever developed speech instinctively when reared in isolation. Animals cannot be taught to talk, and children *must* be taught. It is clear that language is acquired only by human beings born into a linguistic community. Every community of man on earth today, no matter how primitive its way of life, has a fully evolved language system. Was ever a human child born into a human community that had no language?

The answer depends, obviously, on how one contemplates the words "human" and "language". As Carleton S. Coon has observed, "The threshold of becoming human which our ancestors once crossed was largely the barrier between communication by grunts, screams, facial grimaces, postures, nudges, and bites on one side of the line, and articulate speech on the other".[1] In other words, to become human is to acquire language—or vice versa. The statement involves no semantic sophistry. For the evolution of man and the evolution of language are one and the same story. The capacity for speech was latent in the primate family tree for seventy million years or more, but of its manifold branches only the line that led to the genus *Homo* and thence to man was able to exploit it.

From his primate forbears, prehistoric man inherited, among other assets: keen eyesight, prehensile hands, vertical posture, omnivorous taste in food, sociability, and a big voice. All of these evolved during millions of years of arboreal life. The hands were refined by brachiation—climbing and swinging from branch to branch. Stereoscopic vision to judge distance and depth was an obvious necessity for a wingless creature that lived in the trees. And so was vocalization. Terrestrial and solitary animals must exercise stealth in order to survive. For the gregarious primates, vocal communication was a means of keeping the family band together while gliding through the many-storeyed canopy of the dense primeval forest. In the long perspective of evolution it was a survival mechanism.

The ancestor of man might still be phatically soliloquizing in his leafy chambers; but with the advent of the Miocene Epoch, some thirty million years ago, there occurred one of the great climatic revolutions that cyclically alter the face of the planet. As a consequence perhaps of the uplifting of the Alps and Himalayas during the Oligocene, the air now grew cooler, rainfall dwindled, the forests shrank, and grasses spread across vast areas of the earth. The advent of grass profoundly affected the faunas of the Miocene. Many lines became extinct, many new forms evolved. Early in the Miocene—perhaps because of the climatic change, perhaps because of innate curiosity or restiveness—a number of primate groups descended from the vanishing sanctuary of the forest and took up life upon the ground. Among them was the ancestor of man. His new environment was hazardous, for the grasses grew high and hid the

[1] *The Origin of Races* by Carleton S. Coon (London: Jonathan Cape; 1963), p. 86.

slinking forms of many predators. While foraging for food upon the ground, the first terrestrial primates had only their keen eyesight and quick reflexes for defence. To see above the grasses it was necessary for them to stand erect. So by selection, those who stood tallest and perceived their environment most clearly survived. One of these was *Proconsul africanus*—a creature neither man nor ape who, many scientists believe, sired the common stock that led to both modern man and the modern apes before he became extinct ten million years ago.

New geological epochs wheeled by, the climate changed again, and many primate lines returned to the trees, where they abide today. But some members of the dynasty of Hominidae (the group of mammals that include living man, living apes, and a variety of extinct apelike creatures) remained on the ground. By now the progenitor of man walked fully erect. Although his face was still apish, with heavy jaws and projecting canine teeth, his lower limbs had become long and straight. He walked easily on arched feet unlike those of any other creature—engineered for flexibility of manoeuvre and firmness of support. And his hands were free, no longer shackled to the mechanics of locomotion, as were those of his simian cousins—and as they are still today. Alone in the animal kingdom he was truly bipedal, truly free-handed. Soon he began to use his hands in new and imaginative ways: he became *Homo faber*—maker of tools.

In time his upright posture and use of tools wrought changes in his brutish face, for he no longer needed massive jaws and fighting teeth, nor the powerful muscles that snapped the jaws, nor the bony eyebrow ridges designed to prevent the jaw muscles from crushing the eyesockets by their violent action. His teeth became even, and he developed a vertical chin and a deeper oral cavity, which allowed new freedom and flexibility in the movements of his tongue. Another important change occurred inside his throat. This was the opening of the valve of the pharynx which directs the flow of air and the passage of food at the intersection of the trachea and the esophagus. In quadrupeds the air tube runs in an almost straight line from lungs to nose, and the valve is habitually closed except when the animal, with conscious effort, expels breath through its mouth to vocalize. In man, as a consequence of his shift to an upright posture, the pharyngeal section of the throat is bent at a forty-five degree angle, the valve is habitually open, and air is free to pass from lungs to larynx to lips whenever he opens his mouth. He can thus vocalize without effort—a fact that helps to explain the phenomena of infant babbling and soapbox orators.

An even more momentous change occurred above the face. Relieved of its burden of jaw muscles, man's skull was able to expand upward and permit an enlargement of the brain, especially of the association centres of the cortex which underlie his heightened brow. Concurrently with the growth of man's brain came refinements in his nervous system affording him more delicate and precise control, by the motor nerves, over the muscles of his tongue and larynx, and a more exact correlation of their movements with his auditory sense. When these improvements had been effected, perhaps one quarter of a million years ago, *Homo sapiens* was fully fashioned, and equipped physiologically and mentally to talk—if he had not already done so.

When one has traced the evolution of man's physical capacity for speech, one has reached the limits of contemporary knowledge of linguistic genesis. Precisely when man uttered his first fateful denotative word, no one can say. Some theorists believe that even *Homo erectus*—Java Man or Peking Man—might have had some limited form of semantic speech. Their argument rests on the assumption that such collaborative activities as hunting and toolmaking must have required conversation. Others point out, in rebuttal, that successful hunting requires not speech but silence and stealth—the suppression of noise—and that the skills involved in toolmaking can be imparted by example, observation, and imitation. Hence Dr. Raymond A. Dart, anthropologist and first discoverer of the Australopithecines of South Africa, declares: "Articulate speech came only about 25,000 years ago and was preceded by about a million years of gesture and babble."

In opposition to the idea that language grew out of man's need to denote or give names to the things he saw about him, an English lawyer and sociologist, Dr. A. S. Diamond, published in 1959 a detailed and well-reasoned theory, supported by much philological evidence, that human speech began not with names, not with nouns, but with imperative verbs—commands.[1] At first, said Diamond, these commands were nothing more than exclamations, grunts, or gasps uttered in the course of violent or strenuous action. Then as man's social patterns became more stable, certain imperatives—calls for assistance or common action—acquired fixed, familiar, conventional phonetic forms and thus became authentic words. The first words, in Diamond's opinion, must have been monosyllables meaning "Strike!", "Cut!", "Break!", or "Kill!"

Given words—whether names or commands—how did man then expand and refine his first crude code into a structured system of language? How did he enlarge his lexicon, and learn to talk about abstractions, objects removed in space, events remote in time? A possible mechanism may be found in the process known as metathesis or blending—the transposition of letters or sounds in a word or sentence, resulting in a "slip of the tongue". Unintentional slips occur in conversation continually, often with comic effect as in the famous utterances of the Rev. William A. Spooner, Warden of New College, Oxford, at the turn of the century, whose original "spoonerisms" include: "The Lord is a shoving leopard", "Kinkering kongs their titles take", "You are occupewing my pie", and "half-warmed fish" (for half-formed wish). Apart from providing fun, such transpositions represent one way in which new words are formed. An analogous process might have abetted the growth of language in prehistoric times. Suppose, for example, that some man-ape or ape-man spied food and caught sight of a predator at the same time. Receiving the two optical stimuli a fraction of a second apart, he might start to utter the first sounds of a food cry and switch suddenly to a danger cry, thus producing a new phonetic pattern—and one, moreover, with a definite survival value. From such accidental blendings, recurring over thousands and tens of thousands of years, one can imagine the lexicon of proto-man slowly acquiring depth and shading. Blending also governs the learning process of a child just beginning to talk. Everything a young child says is either an exact repetition of something he has learned or a blended compound of familiar

[1] A. S. Diamond: *The History and Origin of Language* (London: Methuen & Co.; 1959).

utterances. He takes his first giant step toward language when he finally says something he has never heard before. For the rest of his life, every time he speaks or writes a sentence he is blending common elements, words, into new patterns, some trite and routine, some perhaps fresh and provocative.

The story of linguistic genesis, however, involves more than man's impulse to communicate. It is inextricably entwined with the whole history of the evolution of human behaviour. None of the hypothetical or actual processes described above could possibly have spurred the development of language were it not for man's biological inheritance—his identity as a mammal, bound to his mother by strong oral ties, and as a primate, destined to undergo years of infantile dependency. This protracted interlude of helplessness, unique to primates, affords a longer period of plasticity for learning, and, in the case of man, a crucially necessary time for the slow growth of the large, convoluted human brain and for fixing in the storage cells of its memory the rules and components of the particular language to which it has been exposed. From the biological evidence one suspects that language may have originated not with hunters, not with men demanding assistance or giving orders, but with mothers endeavouring to solace or reprimand their helpless, howling, impossible young.

One cannot ignore either, in any quest for the origins of language, the most baffling aspect of man's character—the *x*-factor that for want of a better term is called his spiritual nature. At once the most creative and destructive animal on earth, man is also a mystic, and has looked for a deeper reality behind the surface of things since the Neanderthals first laid their dead reverently to rest with relics designed to sustain them in another world. As a mystic, man is a maker of symbols, and through the ages he has found symbols in nature and used symbols to avert catastrophe and appease the gods. Tribal dances, rites, and incantations are symbols; monuments, flags, icons and tombs are symbols. And words are symbols. Contemplating the relationship between symbolism and language, Edward Sapir, perhaps the greatest of American linguists, wrote three decades ago: "Many attempts have been made to unravel the origin of language, but most of these are hardly more than exercises of the speculative imagination. Linguists as a whole have lost interest in the problem. . . . It is probable that the origin of language is not a problem that can be solved out of the resources of linguistics alone but that it is essentially a peculiar case of a much wider problem of the genesis of symbolic behaviour and of the specialization of such behaviour in the laryngeal region which may be presumed to have had only an expressive function to begin with."[1]

When he wrote these lines, Sapir may not have known of the "displays" of the mountain gorilla, and of chimpanzees and other apes. The truly brilliant insight in Sapir's statement lies in the phrase "the specialization of such behaviour in the laryngeal region". For although many of the subhuman primates are highly imitative and given to symbolic behaviour, their mimicry is essentially mute and their symbolic acts are in pantomime. It appears that only man has the capacity and the tendency to make symbols with his voice. With this unique endowment which he began to exercise at some undiscoverable moment in prehistoric time, he created the incredibly diversified and complex systems of vocal symbols that make up the seventeen great linguistic families and four thousand languages spoken in the world today. When history began, our own linguistic family—the Indo-European—was already fully evolved.

[1] From the article "Language" in *Encyclopaedia of the Social Sciences*, edited by Edwin R. A. Seligman and Alvin Johnson (London: Macmillan & Company; 1933), Vol. IX, p. 159.

4

THE GREAT RIVER OF ENGLISH

. . . Ther is so gret diversite
In English, and in wryting of oure tonge,
So prey I God that non myswrite thee . . .

GEOFFREY CHAUCER (1340–1400)

1.

These words, archaic as they seem today, represent the product of more than 4,000 years of linguistic evolution. The process began during Neolithic times when an unknown ancestral tongue which engendered the various languages known collectively as the Indo-European family group splintered into eleven main branches: Albanian, Armenian, Balto-Slavic, Celtic, Hellenic, Hittite, Indic, Iranic, Italic, Teutonic, and Tocharian. Two of these are now extinct: Hittite and Tocharian, a little-known tongue of Chinese Turkestan. The other nine flourish today around the world.

It was only recently that scholars began to discern the genealogy of this linguistic family by noting relationships between words in different languages: e.g. the English *father*, the German *Vater*, the Dutch *vader*. Upon the discovery of Sanskrit, a language of ancient India with texts dating back to 1500 B.C. and a formal grammar composed around 350–250 B.C., it became apparent that the varied languages of Europe and western Asia must at one time have been identical. Many basic words were obviously similar—so strikingly as to suggest a common origin. For example:

Sanskrit	*Greek*	*Latin*	*Italian*	*French*	*German*	*English*	*Russian*
mata	meter	mater	madre	mère	Mutter	mother	mat’
dvau	duo	duo	due	deux	zwei	two	dva
trayah	treis	tres	tre	trois	drei	three	tri
asti	esti	est	è	est	ist	is	est’

Variations in the phonetics of similar words in the different Indo-European languages were explained by the great German philologist Jacob Grimm in 1822. He noted, for example, that the *p* sound of the ancient Indo-Europeans, as preserved in ancient Greek and Latin, becomes an *f* in the modern Germanic languages. Thus the Latin *pisces*, *pes*, and *pater* become *Fisch*, *Fuss*, and *Vater* in German and *fish*, *foot*, and *father* in English. A number of other correspondences among consonants in the various Indo-European languages were studied and formulated by Grimm into a set of rules known collectively today as Grimm's Law. His evidence points overwhelmingly to the evolutionary descent of the Indo-European languages from an aboriginal ancestral tongue.

Another family trait that sets the Indo-European group apart from the languages outside it lies in the matter of sentence structure. The characteristic sentence in English and in other Indo-European languages is the so-called lineal or simple declarative sentence with a subject, a verb, and an object. Take for example this succinct description of action:

Man bites dog.

In many non-Indo-European languages, sentence patterns are static or situational, rather than active. The event might be described thus:

Time present: there is a man and a biting and a dog.

Even when the subject is not a person or even an animal but an idea or concept, the Indo-European sentence is still phrased in terms of action:

Manhattan stands on an island.

Many non-Indo-European languages would simply say:

Island place, Manhattan.

The geographical cradle of the ancestral Indo-European tongue cannot be fixed with certainty, but its probable location has been determined by ingenious linguistic deduction. Since all of the Indo-European languages have corresponding words for *winter*, for *snow*, and for *cold*, it is reasonable to assume that the original home of the family was situated in a northern climate. This is borne out by the fact that there are no ancient Indo-European words for *lion*, *tiger*, *monkey*, *elephant*, *rice*, *bamboo*, *palm*, *parrot*, and other tropical forms of life; however, the Indo-European languages include many well-distributed related words for *aspen*, *oak*, *beech*, *birch*, *willow*, *bear*, *wolf*, *otter*, *beaver*, *salmon*, *turtle*, *sheep*, *eagle*, *hawk*, *owl*, and *bee*.

In this list, the two most revealing words are *beech* and *bee*, not by reason of their phonemes, but by reason of what they represent. For the beech tree is virtually confined to Central Europe; it is not found east of Poland or the Ukraine. The bee is also indigenous to Europe. Moreover, words for *sea* do not appear in all Indo-European languages. Hence it has been inferred that the ancestral Indo-Europeans were originally an inland people, some of whom eventually migrated to coastal areas where they then invented a word for the great watery expanse on which they gazed for the first time with wonder and with awe.

Another clue to the location of the Indo-European home lies in the word for *hundred*. The family is divided into two well-defined halves known as the *centum* and *satem* groups from their pronunciation of the word for *hundred*—the former with a hard *c*, the latter with a sibilant. The *centum* division includes the Celtic, Hellenic, Italic, and Teutonic branches. The *satem* division consists of the Albanian, Armenian, Balto-Slavic, Indian, and Iranian branches. The line of cleavage between the two runs roughly from Scandinavia to Greece, suggesting that, from this central area with a common primeval tongue, one group of Indo-Europeans might have migrated westward, another eastward. It is significant that this region embraces Lithuania, seat of the oldest, most unchanged and unchanging language of the Indo-European family. Linguists believe therefore that the birthplace of the ancestral tongue of all branches of the family must lie in Central Europe, somewhere between Lithuania and the steppes of Southern Russia.

What sort of people were the progenitors of the Indo-European tongue? Their physical appearance is unknown, and indeed defies conjecture. Their descendants today include both the fair-haired, blue-eyed people of the Celtic, Teutonic, and Balto-Slavic divisions and the dark-skinned, dark-haired speakers of the Indian and Iranian tongues. Of their culture a few details have been ascertained by linguistic deduction and archaeological research. Their way of life was Neolithic, which means that they had discovered the arts of agriculture and animal husbandry and were no longer dependent on the random hunting and food-gathering economy of the Old Stone Age. They planted and reaped grain, raised cattle, and had begun to master the metallurgy of copper. They had evolved a social order, based on ethical ideas, and a religion, founded on a polytheistic pantheon of gods and a belief in the existence of the immortal soul and an afterlife transcending the visible world.

At some point between 3500 and 2000 B.C. the ancient Indo-European linguistic community disintegrated and dispersed in a series of great migrations that led them to both the east and the west. Throughout this epoch Britain was still inhabited by Palaeolithic (Old Stone Age) man—short and squat of stature, low-browed, under-chinned—who had dwelt there since mankind first ascended from the lower branches of the humanoid tree perhaps a quarter of a million years before. How did he first reach the British Isles across the stormy water-wall of the English Channel? For countless millennia of prehistory there was no English Channel; a low river plain creased by the estuaries of the Rhine and the Thames connected England with the continent of Europe. Then, not more than 9,000 years ago, following one of the deep interior convulsions to which the earth's crust is periodically subject, the plain slowly subsided and a channel opened between the Atlantic and the North Sea. And with the passing centuries, the channel widened as rushing tides ate away the chalk cliffs on either side. The life of prehistoric man in Britain is described by Sir Winston Churchill in his *History of the English-Speaking Peoples* in a single sentence: "Evidently, for prolonged, almost motionless periods, men and women, naked or wrapped in the skins of animals, prowled about the primeval forests and plashed through wide marshes, hunting each other and other wild beasts, cheered by the songs of innumerable birds." Of their language, nothing is known.

Nor is anything known of the language of the first invaders—

the first of many successive waves of strangers from overseas that would disembark on the English shore repeatedly as the mists of prehistory dissolved and gave way to the light of history, and for century after century thereafter. These first intruders were the Iberians, a people of Neolithic culture who came up from the Mediterranean area some time after 5000 B.C. and settled in the British Isles, swiftly obliterating and supplanting the Palaeolithic population. Unlike their nomadic predecessors, the Iberians lived in stilt-houses driven into the soft margins of lake shores and in marshes and fens. They knew how to weave and make pottery, and they buried their dead beneath mounds or barrows. They were a dark people, and it is thought that traces of their line may be seen today among strikingly dark-haired individuals in the populations of Ireland and Wales. Some scholars believe too that a remnant of their language still lingers on in Basque, a tongue unrelated to any other known on earth, and spoken now only in a tiny linguistic enclave in the Spanish Pyrenees.

2.

The long process of creating the historic seedbed of the English language actually began with the arrival of the first Indo-European elements from the continent. These were imported by the first invaders of historic times, the first whose language is still known today: the Celts. From the European continent they invaded the British Isles, beginning around 500 B.C. The Goidelic Celts (or Gaels) settled in Ireland and thence colonized Scotland and the Isle of Man. Their language survives today in Irish (Erse), Scottish Gaelic, and Manx. The Cymric or Brythonic Celts settled in southern and eastern England and remained for the better part of a millennium before the later Anglo-Saxon invaders drove them into the mountains of Wales and the peninsular refuges of Cornwall and Brittany. Here their original speech survives in Welsh, Breton, and vestigially in the Cornish dialect. The last of the three invading Celtic waves rolled in with the Belgae in the first century B.C. Closely akin to the inhabitants of Gaul, they were the most active and enlightened of the Celtic invaders. Horsemen and charioteers, they spread swiftly over the southern and eastern parts of the island. They had fought Caesar in Gaul, and Caesar found them waiting for him when he first landed on a British beach in 55 B.C.

Considering the length of time the Celts were either in sole possession of Britain or sharing it peacefully during the 400 years of the Roman occupation, it is surprising how few Celtic words remain in the English language proper. For the most part they survive in place names: especially those of rivers. The Thames was named by the Celts. The Cam perpetuates the Celtic word for "crooked". The Dee means "holy", and Aberdeen means "Mouth of the Dee". The Avon, the Esk, the Exe, and the Stour are various Celtic words meaning just "water". Other English rivers that have retained their original Celtic names include the Aire, the Derwent, the Ouse, the Severn, the Tees, the Trent, and the Wye.

In addition to rivers, other features of the landscape still bear Celtic names. The Celtic word *cumb* meaning "deep valley" lives on in such names as Duncombe, Winchcombe, Holcombe, Cumberland, Coombe, and the like; and the word *torr*, a "high rock" or "peak", survives in the towns of Torcross, Torquay, and Torrington. The name Bryn Mawr survives unaltered on both sides of the Atlantic—*bryn* means "hill", *mawr* "great". Many of England's leading cities bear names of Celtic derivation, among them London, though its origins are obscure; Exeter, from the Celtic *exe* meaning "water"; Dover from the Celtic *dove* meaning "black"; and York.

The evolution of the name York presents an example of English linguistic history in miniature. Its original Celtic name was *Eburācon*, meaning "the place of the yew trees". During the Roman occupation the name was altered slightly into the Latin *Eboracum* (New York is hence *Novus Eboracum* on the official seals of both city and state, on the diplomas of their various universities and graduate schools, and on other ceremonial documents in Latin). The Anglo-Saxons who poured into England after the Roman withdrawal translated *Eboracum* (which meant nothing to them) into *Eofor-wíc*, meaning "boar town". To the Viking invaders who followed them this sounded like *Iórvík*. With the passing of time *Iórvík* was shortened to *Iórk*, which finally was transliterated into the contemporary *York*.

Apart from place names, only a microscopic sample of Celtic

words lingered on in the evolving English tongue as it underwent successive permutations during the first millennium of its history. Among the few Celtic words of ancient origin still uttered today by English-speaking people are *bin*, *crag*, *curse*, *dun* (the colour), and possibly *ass*, which is believed to be a Celtic contraction of the Latin *asinus*. Such familiar and transparently Celtic words as *whisky*, *clan*, *shillelagh*, *brogue*, *bog*, and *bard* are recent importations, borrowed from the Irish and Scots in modern times.

The reason that so few old Celtic words were absorbed into the body of the English language is that the Celts were the first people to be dispossessed in the turbulent millennium of invasions and successions between the Roman and the Norman conquests. Almost invariably a dominant culture imparts its language to the inferior population it has mastered. To the Romans the Celts were definitely inferior, and throughout the Roman occupation (A.D. 43–410), Latin was the language of law, commerce, and government. It also became a second language for the upper-class Celts, much as French became the language of the aristocracy in Germany and Russia during the seventeenth and eighteenth centuries. When Christians began to convert Britain during the third century A.D., Latin was, of course, the language of the Church.

Although it is not surprising that the Romans borrowed little, if anything, from the Celts, it is extraordinary that they themselves left so little imprint on the speech of Britain at the time. For in Gaul and in Spain the influence of Latin had been profound, altering their languages forever. In a material way, moreover, the Romans had transformed the entire land of England north to Hadrian's Wall, between the Solway and the Tyne. The ruins of their fortifications, temples, villas, baths, and, most of all, their magnificent roads attest the extent of their enterprise and the benefits the Pax Romana brought to a hitherto barbaric people.

During the centuries of the Roman occupation, according to Churchill: "Britain enjoyed in many respects the happiest, most comfortable, and most enlightened times its inhabitants have ever had . . . In this period, almost equal to that which separates us from the reign of Queen Elizabeth I, well-to-do persons in Britain lived better than they ever did until late Victorian times.

From the year 400 until the year 1900 no one had central heating and very few had hot baths. A wealthy British-Roman citizen building a country house regarded the hypocaust (a system of radiant heating) as indispensable. For fifteen hundred years his descendants lived in the cold of unheated dwellings, mitigated by occasional roastings at gigantic wasteful fires. Even now a smaller proportion of the whole population dwells in centrally heated houses than in those of ancient days. As for baths, they were completely lost till the middle of the nineteenth century. In all this long, bleak intervening gap, cold and dirt clung to the most fortunate and highest in the land."

So thoroughly did the Romans mould and civilize the English Celts that for many years after the withdrawal of the Roman legions the inhabitants still proudly called themselves *Romani* and referred to Latin as "our language". Yet linguistic scholars can find only the barest sprinkling of Latin words, other than the elements of place names, that entered the English lexicon as a direct result of the Roman occupation. Quite a few Latin words were subsequently brought to England by the invading Anglo-Saxon tribes, who had learned them through their contacts with Roman legionaries and merchants on the European continent. Most of these pertain to trade life: e.g. *vinum* (wine), *cuppa* (cup), *caseus* (cheese), *discus* (dish), *mentha* (mint), *catillus* (kettle), *unio* (onion). Among the few English words whose lineage can be traced directly and uninterruptedly back to the Roman occupation are *port* and *portal* from the Latin *portus* and *porta* (meaning "harbour" or "gate"); and *mountain* from the Latin *mons*. The Latin word *castra* (camp), became *ceaster*, meaning a town or enclosed community, and now forms a familiar element in such place-names as Winchester, Manchester, Lancaster, Gloucester, Worcester. But the many thousands of Latin words that today compose half of the English vocabulary made their way into our language centuries later during the Renaissance.

For a full century before the departure of the Roman legions, there were premonitions of descending night. The golden afternoon of the Roman occupation, when the countryside lay at peace, dotted with opulent villas surrounded by fertile fields and park-like pastures, had begun to darken. Since A.D. 127

Hadrian's Wall, a stone rampart seventy-three miles long, studded with seventeen forts and 150 signal towers, protected in front by a thirty-foot ditch, and manned for its entire length by nearly 20,000 soldiers, had successfully shielded the lands of southern England from the barbarians in the north. But around A.D. 300 the pressures behind the wall increased. The wild Picts of Scotland periodically ruptured its defences, demolishing whole sections of the barrier and annihilating local garrisons. Along with these incursions the Irish recurrently emerged out of the sea mists to raid the western shores.

But most ominous of all, the first of the Teutonic tribes that ultimately would conquer Britain—the Saxons—crossed the North Sea in their long boats and began to harry and devastate the eastern coast from the Tyne to the Straits of Dover. A new front was thus added to the military burden of the Roman legions and their British auxiliaries, whose eyes had been alerted to danger only from the north and whose commander was known as the Duke of the Northern Marches. To meet the new danger, a line of fortesses was built along the eastern and southern coasts, and a new military command, the Count of the Saxon Shore, was created to organize and direct the coastal defence. For a time these fortresses, serving as bases for a combined British-Roman fleet, held the Saxons at bay. But as the decades passed, the power and frequency of the raiding thrusts increased. In the year 367, an alliance of Picts, Irish, and Saxons attacked simultaneously, breached the defences on every front, and looted and laid waste the countryside. Both the Duke of the Northern Marches and the Count of the Saxon Shore were slain in the savage fighting.

Again and again the imperial government in Rome sent reinforcements and new generals to defend its remote province across the misty strait. But the Empire as a whole had already begun to crumble from within. Its political and financial foundations were tottering: urban trade and industry were in a state of chaos; its famous highroads were infested with bandits and were unsafe for traffic and communications. And on every frontier hordes of barbarians beat at the gates of the Roman world. Erupting across the Rhine and the Danube, the Goths, Suevi, Burgundians, and Vandals overran all northern and central Europe down to the very heart of the Empire, the Italian peninsula itself.

To stem the threat to Rome, Britain was denuded of its defences, and in the course of this process the ranks of the remaining legions were eroded by defections, revolts, and mutinies. By the year 410 the last of the Roman legionaries, as well as all trained British auxiliaries, had been withdrawn from the island. The great northern Wall was unmanned, save by local volunteers. Britain lay bare before the invader's eye. In this hour of crisis, the Britons dispatched a final desperate appeal to Rome. The Emperor Honorius, beleaguered at his own threshold, sent his reply, the last official message Britannia was to receive from the Imperial Government: "The cantons should take steps to defend themselves." Thus ended Roman rule in Britain.

The events that followed can be only dimly discerned through the obscurity of an epoch without contemporary chroniclers. Yet the dark fifth century was historically an interlude of crucial importance, for it was then that the foundations of an English nation took form. According to the traditional accounts (Bede's *Ecclesiastical History of the English People*, completed in 731, and the *Anglo-Saxon Chronicle* of the ninth century), the Teutonic tribes that streamed across the North Sea in the wake of the Roman retreat and proceeded to conquer and occupy the seductive land came from western Germany and the Jutland (Danish) peninsula. There were four tribes whose descendants were later to become the English people: the Saxons who had dwelt in the river valleys and lowlands between the Rhine and the Elbe; the Frisians, seafarers from a narrow strip along the coast; the Jutes, from the northern part of Jutland; and the Angles, from southern Jutland and the area later known as Schleswig-Holstein.

For the first half of the fifth century the forays from across the sea continued on a small and sporadic scale—two or three shiploads at a time. Meanwhile the Irish and the Picts continued their depredations from the north and west. But there was a difference in the nature of the assaults. For the Teutonic invaders were not interested in booty alone; their aim was colonization; they had come to stay. The incursions of the Saxons, Frisians, Angles, and Jutes from the middle of the fifth century on constituted much more than a predatory, or even a military operation; they were the first phase of a great mass migration. As early as 441, a Celtic observer from Gaul reported: "The Britons in these days by all kinds of calamities and disasters are falling into the power of the Saxons."

The floodgates opened wide in 449. In that year a British chieftain named Vortigern, hard-pressed by the marauding Irish and Picts, decided to adopt the hazardous Roman tactic of importing mercenaries. According to legend, he made an agreement with two chieftains of the Jutes—Hengist and Horsa—offering land and pay in return for aid against his northern enemies. The Jutes kept their bargain; they were more than a match for the Irish and Picts. But they liked their new dominion so well that they stayed on, expanding it forcibly, dispossessing the resident British population, and establishing, in the south-eastern quarter of England, what became known as the Kingdom of Kent (from the original Celtic place-name *Cantion*).

Their success proved a stimulus to their neighbours, and before long new fleet-loads of Teutonic immigrants began to disembark on the beaches and on the banks of the wide, inviting estuaries of the eastern coast. For England, as Churchill has remarked, is an island "so tilted that its mountains lie all to the west and north, while south and east is a gently undulating landscape of wooded valleys, open downs and slow rivers. It is very accessible to the invader." The Saxons came next, landing on the south coast in 477 and consolidating themselves in Sussex, and, in 495, father to the west in Wessex. The migrations continued into the middle of the sixth century. Last to arrive were the Angles, who in 547 descended on the east coast and took over the downs and hill country north of the Humber.

The fate of the incumbent Celtic population during this period can only be deduced. From recurring patterns of history it would appear that the rich, the powerful, and the educated were exterminated. There is reason to believe that in Sussex the fierce Saxons, most ruthless of the Teutonic tribes, effected a total annihilation. Elsewhere resistant Celts took to the hills of Wales and the remote sanctuary of Cornwall, or else crossed the Channel into Brittany. It is only in these places that the language of the Brythonic Celts, with its vestigial echoes of Latin, is preserved in Welsh, Breton, and the nearly extinct Cornish dialect today. The Teutonic invaders called the evicted people *Wealas*, meaning "foreigners", from which the modern word *Welsh* derives.

During the eighth century seven shadowy kingdoms emerged from the chaos of the embattled island. Known as the Anglo-Saxon Heptarchy, they were: Northumbria, Mercia, and East Anglia—settled by the Angles; Kent settled by the Jutes; and Essex, Sussex, and Wessex—settled by the Saxons. Although each of the Teutonic tribes had its own dialect, whose traces persist today in variations of northern, midland, and southern idiom and inflexion, the settlers as a whole were relatively homogeneous in culture and in speech. In the beginning their Celtic victims referred to them collectively as Saxons, and Latin writers of the period called them *Saxones* and their expropriated domain as Saxonia. But owing, perhaps, to the political and cultural supremacy of the Northumbrian and Mercian settlements in the seventh century, the terms *Angli* and *Anglia* acquired dominance—referring not solely to the Angles in the north, but to all the immigrant Teutons on the island. In 601—a few years after the arrival of St. Augustine and his forty monks at the Kentish court of King Æthelberht in the first historic mission from Rome—Pope Gregory referred to Æthelberht as *Rex Anglorum*. By 700 the language of the entire land was known as *Englisc*; the people were called *Angelcynn* (kin of the Angles). It was not until about the year 1000, however, that the country as a whole became known as *Englaland* (land of the Angles). The shift of the initial *a* in *Angle* to the *e* in *England* is known to linguists as a "front mutation," and is related to the similar shift of *Frankish* to *French*, and the evolution of the singular *man* to the plural *men*.

The language which the Teutonic invaders brought to their adopted home completely supplanted Latin (save in the Church) and drove the Celtic tongue forever to the north and west. Its evolution from its advent in England down to the present time has been a continuous process, a march in the direction of ever-increasing simplicity and flexibility, unbroken for 1,500 years. Contemporary scholars distinguish three main chapters in its growth: 1. Old English, from about 450 to 1150 when the impact of the Norman Conquest began to alter the speech of all levels of society; 2. Middle English, from 1150 to 1500; and 3. Modern English, from 1500 on. Old English—or Anglo-Saxon as it is sometimes called—more nearly resembled Dutch than the English we speak today. Its word order was Germanic, and it imposed all the grammatical complications—elaborate declensions, conjugations, inflections of adjectives, articles, and pronouns—with which other modern European languages are still burdened, and from which modern English has, in the course of its long development, happily been freed. Like modern Dutch or German it had three genders—masculine, feminine, and neuter—distributed in a completely arbitrary and illogical way without regard for sex or meaning, capriciously attributing masculinity or femininity to sexless objects and the wrong sex, or no sex, to living beings. Thus, words like *mægden* (maiden) or *wīf* (wife) were neuter, while *wīfmann* (woman) was masculine.

The number of irregular verbs that cluttered Old English has been reduced to a mere 68 today (e.g. *sing*, *sang*, *sung*), and the number of mutated plurals to a mere seven: *feet*, *geese*, *teeth*, *men*, *women*, *lice*, and *mice*. Old English also included many so-called "weak" plurals, formed by adding an *n* or *an* (e.g. *naman* for names, *earan* for ears, *eagan* for eyes). Later, during the Middle English period, weak plurals included *treen* for trees, *worden* for words, *honden* for hands, *housen* for houses, *lambren* for lambs, *peasan* for peas, and *sistren* for sisters. Today we are familiar only with *children*, *brethren*, *oxen*, and in poetry *kine* for cows.

So far as pronunciation is concerned Old English remained emphatically a Teutonic language. Although many modern English words are pronounced much as they were a millennium and a half ago, their spelling has undergone major revisions. In Old English our *sh* sound was represented by *sc*, as in *scip* (ship), *scēap* (sheep), and *scēotan* (shoot); the *k* sound by *c* as in *cynn* (kin), *nacod* (naked), and *folc* (folk); the soft *g* sound by *cg* as in *bricg* (bridge); the short *a* sound by the diphthong *æ* as in *bæc* (back) and *græs* (grass); and the *th* sounds by two now extinct runic characters, *þ* (thorn) and *ð* (edh), as in *wiþ* (with), *þorn* (thorn), *þæt* (that; *bæð* (bath), *ðū* (thou), *ðē* (thee).

It has been estimated that of the original Old English vocabulary of about 30,000 words (of predominantly Teutonic origin and coloured by few of the thousands of words of Latin and French origin which today compose more than half of our modern English lexicon), only about 15 per cent survived the contingencies of time and change and remain unaltered in common use today. Yet the survivors make up the basic building-blocks of our language, the little words that hold a sentence together—the prepositions, pronouns, and conjunctions—the small but strong and sinewy auxiliary verbs, and a number of all-important words, both nouns and verbs, describing the quintessential things of life and human existence: *man*, *wife*, *child*, *house*, *meat*, *eat*, *sleep*, *drink*, *live*, *fight*.

Despite the paucity of Latin words, Old English was a remarkably flexible language. It continually extended its resources by making new words out of old ones—by combining two words together, by expanding the meaning of existing words, and by attaching affixes to native stems or foreign words recurrently imported from abroad. Thus, as in modern English we put two or more small, familiar words together to form new, self-explaining compounds—*bedroom*, *railway*, *steamboat*, *airline*, *one-way street*, *afternoon*—so the progenitors of Old English freely improvised to form such compounds as *ēarhring* (earring), *ealohūs* (alehouse), *medu-heall* (mead hall), *dægred* (dayred, hence dawn), *handcræft* (handicraft), *gimm wyrhta* (gem worker, hence jeweller), *fōtādl* (foot-ail, or gout), *fielleseōcnes* (falling sickness, or epilepsy), *læcecræft* (leech-craft, or medicine), and, obvious vestiges of the Roman occupation, *fiscdēag* (fish dye, or purple) and *eorþ-cræft* (earth-craft or geometry).

The versatility of Old English in word coinage is best revealed by its inventive use of prefixes and suffixes to modify or stretch the meaning of a root word. Among the prefixes most often used in this way—all of them still familiar in modern English today—are *ā*, *be*, *for*, *fore*, *mis*, *of*, *ofer*, *on*, *tō*, *un*, *under*, and *wiþ* (with). By attaching any of these to a simple root verb like *settan* (to set), Old English produced such variants as *āsettan* (to place), *besettan* (to appoint), *forsettan* (to obstruct), *foresettan* (to place before), *ofsettan* (to afflict), *onsettan* (to oppress), *unsettan* (to put down), and *wiþsettan* (to resist). In the same fashion, many Old English nouns and adjectives were formed by the addition of certain familiar suffixes that have passed on into modern English with only slight and recognizable variations: *dōm* as in *cyningdōm* (kingdom) and *eōrldom* (earldom); *sum* as in *wynsum* (winsome); *hād* as in *cildhād* (childhood); *scipe* as in *frēondscipe* (friendship); *wīs* as in *rihtwīs* (righteous); and *ig* as in *mihtig* (mighty), which eventually evolved into the *y* suffix common to thousands of adjectives in use today (misty, silly, speedy).

One of the most striking examples of how a single root word could be made to yield an abundant store of derivatives appears in the little noun *mōd* from which our "mood" derives. In Old English *mōd* was employed loosely to signify "mind," "spirit", and sometimes "courage" or "pride". Through combinations of *mōd* with affixes and other words, an astonishing variety of shaded and intensified meanings was obtained. Among these were such nouns as: *glædmōdnes* (kindness), *mōdhete* (hate), *mōdignes* (magnanimity), *mōdcaru* (care, sorrow), *mōdlufu* (love, affection), *mōdcræft* (intelligence), *mōdgemyd* (the mind), *mōdhord* (mind-treasure, i.e. understanding), *mōdlēast* (lack of courage), *mādmōd* (madness, folly), *mōdgeþoht* (thought), *unmōd* (despondency), and *ofermōd* (arrogance). Some adjectives formed with *mōd* were: *mōdfull* (haughty), *mōdlēas* (spiritless), *mōdlēof* (beloved), *hēahmōd* (highminded, noble), *stíþmōd* (stiff, obstinate), *micelmōd* (broadminded, magnanimous), *gemōded* (minded, disposed), *mōdig* (proud), *mōdcræftig* (intelligent), and *mōdsnot* (prudent, wise).

The capacity of Old English to embrace new concepts and give them expression within the confines of its own limited but elastic vocabulary was put to a crucial test when England was reconverted to Christianity in the seventh century. The abstractions of monotheism and Christian grace lay imbedded in Latin, and the conquering Angles and Saxons had not troubled to learn litanies any more readily than they had lent their ears to the common speech of their vanquished Celtic foes. All that remained of the Christian influence and Christian thought that had illumined the land through the latter tranquil decades of the Roman occupation had been swept northward and westward in the tempest of the Teutonic invasion. Vestiges of the once well-established British church still clung to outposts and hidden sanctuaries in the wilds of Wales; and the candles of faith were kept alight in Ireland by the disciples of St. Patrick and in Scotland by St. Columba from his rocky refuge on the isle of Iona off the stormy western coast. But the gulf between the warlike heathen Saxons and the warlike Christian Celts was too profound to be bridged until the advent of St. Augustine in Kent in 597.

King Æthelberht of Kent was a pagan, worshipper of the German pantheon of Wotan and Thor. His wife Bertha, however, was a Frankish princess and a Christian, and she had done much to prepare an auspicious climate for Augustine's mission. Within three months of his arrival, Augustine converted the king and in the ensuing seven years the whole kingdom of Kent. The little chapel which Æthelberht had indulgently built for Bertha near his palace at Kent-warabyrig (Canterbury) would soon become a cathedral and the seat of the Christian faith in England.

In the years that followed, other missionaries penetrated the unenlightened marches of northern England. Another half-century elapsed, however, before the unco-ordinated—and often conflicting—efforts of envoys from Rome and of Celtic monks from the Christian fringes of the island succeeded in converting the heathen kingdoms of East Anglia, Mercia, and Northumbria. Despite vicissitudes and periodic local reversions to paganism, the faith slowly but continually spread. In 664 the historic Synod of Whitby organized the Christian clergy of England into a national church under the aegis of Rome. Five years later a remarkable ecclesiastical statesman, Theodore of Tarsus, journeyed from Asia Minor to England to assume office as the first Archbishop of Canterbury. Under his skilful administration the number of English bishoprics increased from seven to fourteen, and before his death in 690 the island was completely and permanently Christianized from sea to sea.

The spreading of the faith had a profound effect on the language of the land. Latin words began to emerge from the cloisters and enter the everyday speech of man. Only a few were assimilated without change. Most underwent adaptations to suit them to the Anglo-Saxon ear and tongue. A sampling of words borrowed from the Latin at this early period which survive in only slightly altered form today follows:

MODERN ENGLISH	OLD ENGLISH	LATIN
abbot	*abbod*	*abba*
angel	*engel*	*angelus*
apostle	*apostle*	*apostolus*
candle	*candel*	*candela*
cleric	*clerc, cleric*	*clericus*
cowl	*cūgele*	*cuculla*
deacon	*diacon*	*diaconus*
devil	*dēofol*	*diabolus*
disciple	*discipul*	*discipulus*
hymn	*ymen*	*hymnus*
martyr	*martyr*	*martyr*
mass	*mæsse*	*missa*
minister, monastery	*mynster*	*monasterium*
monk	*munuc*	*monachus*
nun	*nunne*	*nonna*
offer	*offrian*	*offerre*
pall	*pæll*	*pallium*
pope	*papa*	*papa*
priest	*prēost*	*presbyter*
shrine	*scrīn*	*scrinium*

Even more interesting than the words which the Anglo-Saxons borrowed from Latin are those which they did not, preferring instead to utilize the treasure of their tongue whenever a concept could be faithfully represented within the confines of their own vocabulary. They saw no need, for example, to appropriate the Latin *deus* because they already had the word *god*—both in Old Saxon and Old Frisian—and retained it in its original form. They also had intimations of immortality and envisaged two possible destinations for man's immortal soul in the afterlife—*heofon*, which became our heaven, and *hell*, which has smouldered down through the centuries unchanged. Long before their conversion to Christianity they were well aware of churches and held them in high esteem—not as sanctuaries or shrines but as repositories of gold and silver ornaments and hence as pleasant places to be pillaged and plundered for profit; they clung therefore to their own word *cyrice* which later evolved into the Middle English *chirche*, thence into our modern *church*, ignoring the Latin *ecclesia* from which the French *église* derives.

Bending their own words constantly to encompass new ideas,

they translated the Latin *evangelium* (glad tidings) into *god-spell* (God's tidings or good tidings), which gave rise eventually to the modern word Gospel. In similar fashion they converted the Latin *spiritus sanctus* into *Hālig Gāst* (Holy Ghost). The word *gāst* means literally "guest" or "stranger", and is related to the Sanskrit *ghostis*, which is also the antecedent of the Latin *hostis*, meaning "stranger" or "enemy". Since a stranger may be either a guest or an enemy, modern English today preserves from the same ancestral root such apparently antipathetic words as hostile, hotel, host, hostess, hostage, hospital. The word Easter derives from the Saxon *ēastrun*, a vernal festival coinciding in the calendar year with the Feast of the Resurrection but celebrating the pagan goddess of spring *Eastre*.

Exercising their talent for making little words into big ones, the early English responded to the stimulus of Christian concepts by producing such syntheses as *prēosthād* (priesthood), *godferht* (God-fearing), *godsunu* (godson), *crīstendōm* (Christendom), and *ealdorman* (now alderman but used by the Anglo-Saxons to denote an administrative official and, specifically in Bible history, a high priest of Jerusalem). Not all of their inventions survived. Later generations reverted, in many instances, to words of Latin origin, rejecting the ingenious compounds of their early English forbears. Today we prefer *Trinity* to the Anglo-Saxon *þrynnes* (Three-ness); we have adopted *divinity* rather than *godcundnes* (God-kindness), *patriarch* rather than *hēahfæder* (high-father), *acolyte* rather than *taporberend* (taper-bearer), *chaplain* rather than *hīrendprēost* (hired, hence family, priest), *impious* rather than *godscyldig* (God-sinning), *episcopate* rather than *biscophād* (bishophood), and *diocese* rather than *biscopscīr* (bishopshire).

To the quick and casual modern eye, Old English presents a strange and foreign aspect, bearing little familiar foliage to identify it as the main stem of our linguistic family tree. Yet closer inspection reveals many similarities underlying the outer disguises of its lexicon. Here, by way of example, is the Anglo-Saxon version of the Lord's Prayer, with the modern English translation subjoined:

Fæder ūre,
Father of ours,

þū þe eart on heofonum,
Thou that art in Heaven,
sī þīn nama gehālgod.
Let thine name be hallowed.
Tōbecume þīn rīce.
Let come thine kingdom.
Gewurþe ðin willa on eorðan swā swā on heofonum.
Let be worth thine will on earth so so in Heaven.
Urne gedæghwāmlīcan hlāf syle ūs tō dæg.
Our daily-wanted loaf give us today.
And forgyf ūs ūre gyltas, swā swā wē forgyfað
ūrum gyltendum.
And forgive us our guilts so so we forgiveth
our guilt-doers.
And ne gelæd þū ūs on costnunge,
And do not lead thou us into temptation.
ac ālys ūs of yfele. Sōþlice.
But allay us of evil. In sooth.

If one bears in mind that the characters þ and ð are pronounced like *th*, the relationships between most of the Old English words in the prayer and their modern English counterparts become apparent. Only a few seem completely outside our lexicon. The word *rīce*, meaning "kingdom" is clearly a first cousin of the German *Reich*; and though it no longer exists as an independent noun, its traces linger on in the modern English words *rich* and *riches* and in the final syllable of *bishopric*. The word *syle* is a form of the verb *sellan* meaning "to give" or "to sell"; today only the latter meaning survives. (Our modern word *give* derives from the Old English *gifan* which meant specifically "to give in marriage"; the noun *gift* meant "the price of a wife".) Finally, the word *costnunge*, meaning "temptation", remained in use—along with its related verb *costian*, "to tempt"—until the thirteenth century, when they gave way to derivatives of the Old French *tempter* and vanished from the language. (Our modern word *cost*, incidentally, is no kin to *costian* but derives from the Old French *coust*, which became in time the modern French *coût*.)

Old English, therefore, was capable of expressing virtually every idea or concept that the human mind could engender—including the abstractions of Christian theology and metaphysics.

Philologists sometimes wonder how Old English might have evolved in isolation, without the subsequent importations of words and speech forms from across the Channel. One clue is provided by the richness and colour of Old English poetry, which began to flower with the gradual stabilization of the Anglo-Saxon community in the eighth century, and continued through the tenth.

The literature of the period reveals a confluence of pagan folklore and Christian thought. More than half of Old English poetry concerned itself with religion—with translations and paraphrases of the Bible, the lives of saints, and devotional and moralistic verses. Virtually all of the authors are unknown. But one whose name has come down to us through the centuries is Cædmon, lay brother at the famous monastery of Whitby, who wrote sometime between 657 and 680. A gentle and self-effacing cowherd, Cædmon was so shy that he invariably fled in dismay when it came his turn to sing after the evening meal in the great hall. But one night he became miraculously endowed with the gift of song. An angel appeared to him in a dream as he lay in the straw near his cattle, and told Cædmon that his mission on earth was to tell the story of the Scriptures and to hymn the glory of God. His first song—called simply *Cædmon's Hymn*—is the first English poem whose authorship is known, and Cædmon is thus the founder and forbear of the long illustrious line of English poets. According to Bede, who lived half a century later, Cædmon also turned several books of the Bible into the Northumbrian vernacular. Although these have been lost, they undoubtedly inspired the works of the second known English poet, Cynewulf, who wrote several poems on Biblical subjects and also enlarged the scope of vernacular verse by blending religious themes with the fables and imagery of classical Greece and Rome.

The volume of Anglo-Saxon poetry is small—perhaps some 30,000 lines in all. Of this total about one tenth is represented by the greatest single masterpiece of the period, the secular folk epic *Beowulf*, a poem of 3,182 lines first put down in writing some time during the eighth century, but subsequently revised and preserved in its present form in a manuscript dated by scholars around the year 1000. It recounts the heroic exploits of the young warrior Beowulf who fought and slew an amphibious monster named Grendel in a stupendous hand-to-hand battle, then descended deep into a fen to dispose of Grendel's vengeful mother, and finally lost his life to another foe in the form of a fire-breathing dragon. There is a good deal of evidence to indicate that as early as the ninth century *Beowulf* was already a classic which profoundly influenced or epitomized the poetic literature of the time.

In addition to *Beowulf*, Old English poetry encompasses a number of shorter poems in the form of war songs, gnomic verses, legal verses and riddles, and, especially, poems about wandering minstrels who tell of their travels and sufferings, of combat, exile, and the sea. The most famous of these are *Widsith*, *Deor*, the *Wanderer*, the *Ruin*, and the *Seafarer*—all imbued with vivid imagery and the melancholy of things remembered and pleasures past. Two great war poems, the *Battle of Brunanburh* and the *Battle of Maldon*, resound with the clash of arms and armies joined in conflict whose dubious causes are lost in the mists of time.

A cardinal characteristic of Old English poetry is its profusion of metaphors. In *Beowulf* there are 36 different ways of saying "hero", 12 terms for "battle", and 17 for the "sea". The king is variously the "leader of hosts", "giver of rings", "protector of earls", "victory-lord", and the "hero's treasure keeper". A warrior is a "shield bearer", wielding his "battle-brand" or "war-shaft" against the foe on distant shores to which he has sailed over the "sea-surge" or "whale-road", aboard his "wave-courser" or "sea-wood" or "broad-bosomed curved-stem". Unlike later English poets, the Anglo-Saxon bards did not concern themselves with rhyme. Instead they obtained their poetic effects through alliteration—the repetition of the same (usually initial) letter or sound in several words or syllables within each line. Thus a characteristic section of *Beowulf* reads:

Stræt wæs stān-fah, stig wisode
The street was stone-paved, the way well shown
gumum ætgædere. Gūð-byrne scān
to the band together. The war-byrnies (mail) shone
heard, hond-locen, hring-īren scīr,
hard-locked by hand, the ring-iron sheer,
song in searwum þā hie tō sele furðum

sang in their armour, as they to the first hall,
in hyra gryre-geatwum, gangan cwōmon . . .
in their grim war-gear, swung along . . .

The love of alliteration has continued down through all the generations of English poets, but after the fifteenth century it became secondary to the ending rhyme. It was Chaucer, for example, who, some five hundred years after *Beowulf*, wrote: "For aye as busy as bees been they." And two centuries after Chaucer, Shakespeare first used "care killed a cat", and "love's labour's lost". Thackeray disported himself alliteratively by referring to contemporary society chitchat as "faint fashionable fiddle-faddle and feeble-court slip-slop". And Tennyson once observed, "When I spout my lines first they come out so alliteratively that I have sometimes no end of trouble to get rid of the alliteration".

In the history of every language the development of poetry precedes that of prose. For poetry is the idiom of ritual and incantation, the tongue of passion and emotion that springs swiftly to the lips of the lover and the mystic and the minstrel, that is easily memorized and remembered, repeated, echoed, and preserved. But prose is the hard substance of exposition, the cold bone and marrow of thought and reason; it is the channel in which the stream of logic flows, ideally straight and limpid. To keep the channel clear of detritus demands a discipline not easily endured by man, in whose nature, since Stone Age times, emotion precedes reason. In the words of the famous Danish philologist Otto Jespersen, "The work of whole generations of good authors is needed to bring about the easy flow of written prose." It is a remarkable fact, therefore, that native prose evolved in England as early as the ninth century, at a time when most of the common people of the Western world—unable to read or write the Latin of statesmen and scholars—had only begun to produce verse in the vernacular of their native lands. English was the first European language, after the fall of Rome, to engender polished literary prose.

The period during which English prose developed was a time of recurrent crisis. For several hundred years after their initial colonization, the Anglo-Saxons had dwelt with relative security in the land they had wrested from the Romans and the

Celts. Their principal alarms and excursions arose from dynastic feuds among themselves—among the seven kingdoms of the Anglo-Saxon Heptarchy—and from the everlasting border skirmishes with the ever-restless Irish and Picts. But by the end of the eighth century, England was approaching national unity under the leadership of the Kingdom of Mercia whose king, Offa, styled himself *Rex Totius Anglorum Patriae* ("King of the Whole Land of the English") and who held sway at the time of his death in 796 over most of the island from Northumbria to Kent.

Little by little with the spread of Christianity and the growth of order, England entered upon a golden age of learning and culture, pointing to the ultimate fulfilment of its national genius. At the dawn of the ninth century, England stood at the forefront of Western civilization and at a peak of intellectual life which it would not see again for many centuries to come. Its monastery schools at Canterbury, York, Jarrow, and Wearmouth were internationally renowned for a succession of eminent teachers and scholars attracted from all parts of the Western world. The most famous of these, universally honoured as the greatest scholar of his day, was the Venerable Bede, a monk at Jarrow and a man of enormous and far-ranging erudition who wrote copiously on many subjects—grammar, poetics, astronomy, Greek and Latin literature, arithmetic, and Biblical exegesis. His best-known and most important work is the *Ecclesiastical History of the English People*, written in Latin and completed in 731; it remains to this day our principal source of knowledge of Anglo-Saxon England in those dim and distant times. It was Bede, incidentally, who first proposed a calendar, adopted long after his death, that would reckon the years backward and forward from the birth of Christ. A contemporary of Bede's, the Abbot Aldhelm of Malmesbury, wrote in both English and Latin on religious and secular themes and was indisputably, upon the sheer quantitative basis of the number of his works in circulation, the most popular writer in Europe. A generation after Bede the world's most illustrious scholar was Alcuin of York, whose fame was so great that Charlemagne summoned him to his court to direct the palace school and to promote the emperor's renaissance in the dominions of the Franks.

3.

The flowering of Anglo-Saxon civilization and learning was dramatically interrupted at this time by the sudden incursion of waves of fierce invaders from across the North Sea. Through the mysterious alchemy of ethnic history, the Scandinavian peoples of the Baltic—the Norwegians, Swedes, and Danes—had for obscure and complex reasons built up internal pressures imbuing them with a spirit of unrest and an irresistible charge of agressive and predatory vitality. Just as the fanatic armies of Islam had erupted from the Arabian desert wastes two centuries earlier, so now the Vikings (the name is from the Old Norse *vīk*, a bay or inlet of the sea) burst forth from their bleak and misty fjords and spread to east and west, plundering neighbouring lands, harrying, ravaging, devastating with fire and sword. The raids continued for the next 250 years.

They began on an inconspicuous scale. The first premonition of what was to happen befell on a summer's day in 789 when raiders from three Danish ships landed at Dorchester, slew defenders and local officials, and looted the town. The English were taken by surprise, for their relations with their Danish neighbours had hitherto been peaceful. They regarded them indeed as kinfolk, not-too-distant cousins whose language, blood, and background were notably similar to their own. Yet it was not long before monastic writers, who either witnessed or received reports of the continuing cruel and relentless depredations of the sea rovers, began referring to them as "this furious, ferocious, ruthless, wrathful, pagan people". Four years after the raid at Dorchester, in 793, a considerably more formidable Viking fleet attacked the wealthy monastery of Lindisfarne off the Northumbrian coast, massacred many of the monks, and bore the others off into slavery along with the abbey's rich hoard of gold and silver vessels, jewelled shrines, costly robes, and sacred treasure of all kinds as well as food and wine. The following year they returned and pillaged Bede's monastery at Jarrow (Bede had died a half-century before). In the spring of successive years they descended again and again on the coasts of Ireland and Scotland; Iona was sacked three times, the monastery at Kildare fourteen times. For the Vikings soon learned that monastery coffers were swiftly replenished after each raid by wealthy men who hoped through such benefices to win absolution for their sins and to improve their hopes of heaven in the life hereafter.

It was not until the middle of the ninth century that the full force of the Vikings' conquering fury was unleashed. In the earlier phase of their operations they had attacked in relatively small bands, struck swiftly, and vanished as soon as they had filled their boats with booty. But in the summer of 835 their activities underwent a marked change in quality and scale; it became apparent that their purpose was no longer simply plunder but conquest.

In this second epoch of the Viking Age, great fleets of 300 to 400 ships sailed up the rivers of Europe and the British Isles, pillaged the greatest cities of northern Europe—Paris, Hamburg, London—and, invading the Mediterranean, attacked the strongholds of Islam in North Africa and Spain. The Swedish Vikings, pointing their bronze-beaked longboats eastward, penetrated deeply into Russia, sacked the river towns, occupied Kiev, where they established the foundations of a Russian state, and ultimately laid siege to Constantinople. The Norwegian Vikings, plying westward, invested the Shetland Islands, the Faeroes, Scotland, Ireland (where they founded the city of Dublin), and then pushed on through unknown waters to Iceland, Greenland, Labrador, and the St. Lawrence River. The Danes headed south and west; one invasion force wrested the Dukedom of Normandy from Charles the Simple of France —an event that would prove of crucial historic importance two centuries later; other fleets of seaborne Danish warriors concentrated on England where the same flat shores and wide, slow rivers that had attracted the forbears of the Anglo-Saxon defenders 400 years before now lured them into the heart of the lush English countryside.

In the initial chapter of the Viking saga the longboats had landed with the first auspicious winds of spring; their crews then spent the summer in marauding, and with advent of autumn departed for their home bases along the bleak Baltic coasts. But in the year 865 the mighty invasion force which the Anglo-Saxon chroniclers later referred to as The Great Army descended on England with the intention of staying. For the next decade its warriors, travelling on horseback but fighting on foot, rampaged the length and breadth of the land.

Though the English fought bravely in many a bloody battle the Danes established themselves firmly on the conquered soil and virtually destroyed the political organization of the island. The Kingdoms of Northumbria, Mercia, and East Anglia ceased to exist. Only Wessex, under the leadership of Alfred, rallied in stubborn resistance and initiated the long, slow struggle to reconquer England for the English.

The fact that the Danes did not conquer all of England and stamp out the still young and vulnerable roots of Christian society and culture was due in huge measure to the dauntless courage, skilled diplomacy, and wisdom of King Alfred, who, alone of English monarchs, has been invested by history with the appellation of The Great. Yet even Alfred was forced to yield more than half of England to the district called the Danelaw—the territory where Danish sovereignty and law held sway. Throughout his reign (871–99) he alternated coolly and resourcefully between stubborn military resistance and periodic payments of ransom (Danegeld) in order to preserve his rule and the independence of the English people within their limited domain.

The combination of Alfred's statesmanship and the solacing passage of time served in the end to produce a relatively peaceful and rather thorough mingling of the invaders and their unwilling hosts. The Danish settlements were, in the early years of the occupation, little more than armed camps. But gradually as conditions stabilized the Northmen began to transplant their families—as the Anglo-Saxon pirates had done four centuries earlier—and the historic sequence of conquest and colonization repeated itself again. The soldiers of one generation thus became the progenitors of the farmers and artisans of the next.

The differences between the invaders and the resident population were far less deep than those that had divided the Anglo-Saxons from the earlier Celts. For the English and the Northmen had much in common in their Teutonic heritage, social customs, and language. The Old Norse spoken by the Danes was quite intelligible to the English, as was Old English to the Danes. Indeed, according to the British historian J. R. Green, the Vikings "were in fact Englishmen bringing back to an England that had forgotten its origins the barbaric England of its pirate forefathers. Nowhere over Europe was the fight so fierce, because nowhere else were the combatants men of one blood and one speech. But just for this reason the fusion of the Northmen with their foes was nowhere so peaceful and so complete."

During the two centuries that elapsed between the advent of the Viking Great Army in 865 and the arrival of William the Conqueror in 1066, the Danes intermarried with the English and sank quietly into the society around them. New waves of invaders continued to storm ashore at intervals, and some of the bloodiest battles found second and third generation Anglo-Danish colonists fighting shoulder to shoulder with the native English defenders to repel the newcomers. But by their presence those who had come earlier and adopted Christianity tended to mitigate somewhat the violence of the Viking tradition. Imparting to later émigrés some awareness of the virtues of a tranquil existence and the benisons of peace, they helped to convert them in turn.

The impact of the Viking onslaught on literature and learning, however, was disastrous. By the time Alfred came to the throne, most of the great monasteries of Northumbria and Mercia lay in ruins, and with their destruction the intellectual fervour that had placed England in the forefront of European scholarship had swiftly decayed. Reflecting sadly on the decline of education and disciplines of the mind that had occurred in the stormy decades prior to his accession to the throne, Alfred lamented the golden days of Bede and Alcuin when "the sacred orders were zealous in teaching and learning". In a famous epistle to the Bishop of Worcester, the king observed: "It has come into my remembrance what wise men there formerly were among the English race, both of the sacred orders and the secular . . . and how foreigners came to this land for wisdom and instruction." Yet by 871, when he became king, "so clean was it fallen away in the English race that there were few on this side of the Humber who could understand their (Latin) mass-books . . . or translate a letter from Latin into English; and I ween that there were not many beyond the Humber. There were so few of them that I cannot remember a single one south of the Thames when I came to the kingship. . . . There was also a great multitude of God's servants, but they had very little knowledge of the books because they were not written in their language."

Despite constant crises and his preoccupation with military operations and affairs of state necessary to the preservation of his beleaguered kingdom, Alfred somehow found time to foster the revival of learning, law, and religion. He restored ruined monasteries and churches and established new ones, and in an effort to promote a desire for education among his people he undertook to provide them with books in the English vernacular. For it was Alfred's inspired notion that the cause of education could be served best by employing English rather than Latin as the basic medium of communication, both in schools and in books for adults. To this end, when approaching the age of forty, he set about learning Latin and proceeded to translate the most important books of his age into English, adding prefaces and interpolated comments. It is impossible today to determine precisely how many of the volumes attributed to Alfred he personally translated or how much of the work was completed by scholars in his court or his employ. But among the great books of the ninth century which he either translated or commissioned for translation from Latin into English were: Pope Gregory's *Cura Pastoralis*, as a manual and guide to the demoralized clergy; Bede's *Ecclesiastical History of the English People*, because he believed strongly that his people should know something of their past; Orosius's *Universal History*, an earlier work by a fifth-century Spanish priest, which traced the rise and fall of ancient civilizations to refute the notion that the Roman Empire had collapsed as a result of the abandonment of pagan gods, in favour of Christianity; Pope Gregory's *Homilies*; and Boethius's *Consolations of Philosophy*, a classic of the fifth century.

Alfred's greatest contribution to the development of a native English prose was his instigation in 891 of the *Anglo-Saxon Chronicle*, which recounted the history of England from the time of Caesar's invasion in 55 B.C. Assembling the earlier story from fragmentary sources down to the accession of Alfred, the anonymous authors of the *Chronicle* thereafter kept abreast of events with accuracy, and often with eloquence, for two and a half centuries after Alfred's death until its termination in 1154. The most intellectual of all English kings, Alfred was the founder of English prose, the father of English education, and for these achievements among others has been venerated for more than a thousand years as the greatest of all rulers of the sceptred isle.

Although Alfred laboured throughout his reign to revive the spirit of learning, his efforts did not achieve fruition in his lifetime. Nevertheless his vision kindled a spark in the land and his able successors nurtured and propagated his ideals. His son Edward, who succeeded to the throne in 899 and reigned until 925, his three grandsons—Æthelstan (925–40), Edmund (940–6), and Edred (946–55)—and his great-grandsons, Eadwig (955–9) and Edgar (959–75), maintained a social and political climate in which Anglo-Saxons and Danes were able to intermingle in a united Christian community and in which English literature, art, and scholarship once again began to flourish. By the end of the tenth century the splendid illuminated manuscripts, written in English and produced in English monasteries, were becoming famous throughout Europe. Among those who lent distinction to the new medium of English prose were the Abbot Ælfric and his contemporary, Bishop Wulfstan, both of whom lived on into the early eleventh century and died some forty years before the Norman conquest. In their works—consisting of homilies, sermons, the lives of saints, and commentaries on the Bible—the English vernacular was polished and refined into a versatile medium that put into words far more flexibly than the Old English of earlier times any idea or abstraction that Latin could express. Educated men now wrote in English, as well as Latin, and the development of English as a form of literary expression began. It was the first vernacular to attain this eminence in the Western world.

But the Viking storm had not spent itself. As rapidly as the Scandinavian sea rovers settled in their expropriated homesteads, new invaders arrived. And at the outset of the eleventh century the Viking hegemony reached its peak with the defeat and exile of Edgar's son, Æthelred the Unready, and with the accession to the English throne of the Danish King, Canute. For the next quarter-century England was ruled and dominated by the Danes. This was the high-water mark of the Viking conquest. For Canute also held sway over Norway and the entire Scandinavian world from Iceland to Russia.

• • •

As a consequence of three centuries of Viking aggressions, a great part of England absorbed lasting and indelible traces of Scandinavian culture. The Vikings left their imprint on the island in many ways—in government, legal procedures, language, and even arithmetic. They transmitted to the English with whom they dwelt, among other things, their duodecimal system. That is to say, they did their counting in twelves instead of tens, thus establishing to this day the marketing unit of a dozen, the measuring formula of 12 inches to a foot, the monetary equation of 12 pence to a shilling, and the legal entity of a jury of 12 good men and true.

The heritage of the Scandinavian conquest survives today in many words of the English language and most especially in place names. More than 1,400 villages and towns in England bear names of Scandinavian origin. Most of these are in the northern and eastern areas that once constituted the Danelaw. In certain centres of heaviest Viking settlement where the invaders outnumbered and supplanted the Anglo-Saxon population—in Yorkshire, Lincolnshire, Cumberland, Northumberland, Westmorland, and parts of Norfolk—up to 75 per cent of the place names are Danish or Norwegian.[1] The Scandinavian word *thorp* or *torp*, meaning "village", is affixed to some 300 communities in modern England—Woodthorp, Althorp, Linthorp, and the like. The word *thwaite*, meaning "an isolated piece of land", survives in almost as many village names—Applethwaite, Braithwaite, Cowperthwaite, Satterthwaite. The word *toft*, "a piece of ground" or "private property", appears in about 100 modern place names—Brimtoft, Langtoft, Mapletoft, Lowestoft, Nortoft. Other Scandinavian terms that live on today in English place names are *beck* (brook), as in Birkbeck and Troutbeck; *brack* and *breck* (slope) in Haverbrack and Norbreck; *fell* (hill) in Scafell and Whinfell; *garth* (yard) in Applegarth and Arkengarthdale; *gill* (ravine) in Gaisgill and

[1] Philologists find it difficult to distinguish Danish from Norwegian place names of the period, for Old Danish and Old Norse were even more similar to each other than they were to Old English. The Anglo-Saxon chroniclers tended to refer to all the Vikings as Danes, perhaps because Canute was a Dane, but more probably because the Danes were found everywhere in the Scandinavian settlements while the Norwegians were concentrated in certain definite districts.

Garrigill; *keld* (spring) in Hallikeld and Trinkeld; *mel* (sand-dune) in Cartmel and Rathmel; *rigg* (ridge) in Crossrigg and Lambrigg; *scough* (wood) in Ayscough and Myerscough; *slack* (shallow valley) in Nettleslack and Witherslack. But perhaps the most ubiquitous vestige of the Viking Age is the suffix *by* from the Scandinavian *bȳr* meaning "village", "farm", or "town". All in all more than 600 places in England—many of them famous like Derby, Rugby, and Whitby—still attest to the extent and permanence of the Viking occupation. There are no less than seven communities named Normanby, from *Norðmanna bȳr*, or "Village of the Northmen". Similarly the modern communities of Denby and Denaby, of which there are several in various parts of the island, come from *Dena bȳr* or "Village of the Danes"; and four communities named Irby derive from *Ira bȳr* or "Village of the Irish"—the Irish in this case being Vikings who settled first in Ireland and then migrated back to England.

Personal names also reveal the degree of intermingling—and intermarriage—between the sea rovers and the native population. Today all the multitudes of familiar English and American patronymics ending in *son*—like Jackson, Thompson, Stevenson, Johnson—clearly manifest their Scandinavian origin. The extent to which the Vikings adopted Christianity early in their occupation is evident from the numbers of monks and priests, as well as donors of land to abbeys and churches, whose obvious Scandinavian names are preserved in official records from the eleventh century on.

It is not only in the names of people and places that the Vikings left the traces of their tongue. The syllable *by* survives also in the expression *by-law*, meaning "town-law" or "local ordinance". The word *law* itself is Scandinavian—derived from the Danish *lög* (which later evolved into *logh*)—and means "that which is laid down". Its adoption and preservation—along with its many derivatives, such as *outlaw, in-law, lawyer*—is significant of the profound influence that the Scandinavian system of jurisprudence exerted upon the legal structure and legal terminology of England. In local government the words *husting* (from *husþing*, or "house assembly") and *riding* (originally *thriding* or "third part"—one of the three divisions of Yorkshire) survive beside the Anglo-Saxon *shire* and *hundreds*. The word *husband* was originally a legal term, stemming from the Scandinavian *hūsbōndi* or "householder"—one who runs or owns a house, quite apart from love and marriage. Similarly the word *fellow* derives from *fēlagi*, one who lays down a *fē* (fee), hence a partner or shareholder. Many Danish legal terms which displaced their Anglo-Saxon counterparts disappeared in turn when they were supplanted after 1066 by the imposition of Norman law.

The intermingling of Scandinavians and English was a continuing process sustained by the recurring debarkations of new immigrants or invaders and the lively flow of trade across the North Sea. In many districts people became bilingual, which was not too difficult an accomplishment since most of the commonest words in the two languages were nearly identical. Yet regional variations inevitably arose; here the Scandinavian idiom prevailed, there the English. (In parts of Scotland, Old Norse was still spoken as late as the seventeenth century.) It is only through the study of early Anglo-Saxon manuscripts, set down before the Viking conquests, that linguists can determine the genealogical history of certain words. One clue to the problem of Scandinavian versus English antecedents applies to words containing *sh* and *sk* sounds. At an early date in the development of our language such Old English words as *disc*, *fisc*, *scip*, and *biscop* became palatalized into *dish*, *fish*, *ship*, and *bishop*. And at the same time many Scandinavian words with the hard *sk* sound were absorbed into the English vernacular without change—e.g. *scrape*, *scrub*, *skill*, *skin*, *bask*, *whisk*, *tusk*. But the Scandinavian words *screde*, *skelle*, and *skere* gave way to the English *shred*, *shell*, and *sheer*, as the Scandinavian *bennk* succumbed to the English *bench*. Yet the Scandinavian *kettle* won out over the English *chetel*. In some instances hybrid forms evolved, like *shriek* and *screech*, preserving within themselves both the Scandinavian *sk* and the English *sh*. One of the neatest examples of this phonetic relationship lies in the coexistence in modern English of the words *shirt* and *skirt*—the first from the Old English *scyrte*, the second from the Scandinavian *skyrta*, both originally describing the same garment. The sartorial differentiation developed centuries after the verbal.

There are other indications that enable etymologists to trace the genealogy of Scandinavian and Old English words. In general the hard *g* as in *get*, *give*, *gild*, and *egg* reveals Scandinavian ancestry, as does the hard *k*. In districts where Scandinavian and English words were used interchangeably, sometimes the former survived, sometimes the latter. Thus the Scandinavian *syster* (sister) displaced the Old English *sweostor* and flourishes phonetically intact today. Today too we say *weak* instead of the Old English *wāc*, and we say *window* (from the Old Norse *vindauga* or "wind-eye") instead of *eye-hole* (from the Old English *eagþyrel* or *eye-thirl*). But this old final syllable does survive in *nostril*, a "nose-hole". In many instances Scandinavian words that did not eliminate their Old English counterparts relegated them instead to the role of secondary synonyms. The Scandinavian *angr* now dominates the Old English *irre*, and the Scandinavian *sky* has thrust the Old English *wolcen* into the obscurity of such archaic, poetic phrases as "make the welkin ring". Conversely the Old English *church* is dominant, and the Scandinavian *kirk* is heard only in Scottish dialect (and at Hollywood funerals in The Wee Kirk O' The Heather).

Sometimes the Old English form survived, but with a variant Scandinavian meaning attached. For example, the Old English word *drēam* originally meant "joy", but in the later evolution of the language it absorbed the meaning of the Danish *dröm*. Similarly the Old English *eorl* meant loosely a "brave warrior" or just plain "man", but later took on the connotations of the Scandinavian *jarl*, a powerful nobleman or governor of a division of the king's realm. The English word *plōh* meant "a measure of land" until it merged with the Scandinavian *plōgr* to signify the implement *plough*. In Old English the verb *steorfan* meant "to die" until the Scandinavian *deya* overtook it, reducing the native term to its present meaning of "to starve".[1] And the Old English *lēas* has been superseded by the Scandinavian *loose*, and it survives only in the adjectival suffix *-less*.

Other examples of Old English and Scandinavian words that have survived side by side in modern speech, with slight differences of spelling, meaning, or usage are:

[1] It is still common in certain English dialects, particularly in the North of England, to say that one is "starved with cold", i.e. dying of cold.

ENGLISH	SCANDINAVIAN
no	*nay*
from	*fro*
whole	*hale*
bathe	*bask*
rear	*raise*
shatter	*scatter*
carve	*cut*
ditch	*dike*
shift	*skip*
wish	*want*
craft	*skill*
hide	*skin*
rind	*bark*

One of the best-documented cases of verbal rivalry between Old English and Scandinavian usage is found in the long struggle between the two words for "egg": the Old English *ey* (with its plural *eyren*), and the Scandinavian *egg*. As late as the end of the fifteenth century, William Caxton, the first English printer, noted this confusion in a preface to his translation of a French version of Virgil's *Aeneid*. Writing in 1490, Caxton, who was also a linguist, remarked: "And certaynly our language now used varyeth ferre from that whiche was used and spoken when I was borne. . . . And that comyn englysshe that is spoken in one shyre varyeth from a nother. In so moche that in my dayes happened that certayn marchauntes were in a shippe in tamyse [The Thames], for to have sayled over the sea into zelande [Holland], and for lack of wynde, thei taryed atte forlond, and wente to lande for to refreshe them. And one of theym named Sheffelde, a mercer, cam in-to an hows and axed for mete; and specyally he axed after eggys. And the goode wyf answerde, that she coude speke no frenshe. And the marchaunt was angry, for he also coude speke no frenshe, but wolde have hadde egges, and she understode hym not. And thenne at laste a nother sayd that he wolde have eyren. Then the good wfy sayd that she understod hym wel. Loo, what sholde a man in thyse days now wryte, egges or eyren. Certaynly it is harde to playse every man by cause of dyversite & chaunge of langage."

Soon afterward the conflict between the *egg* and *ey* ended with the permanent victory of the Scandinavian form.

By far the most important influence which the Scandinavians exerted upon Old English was their inception of the long process of eroding grammatical complexities. Words may pass from one language to another, but inflexions are seldom transferred. Just as in modern pidgin English a Melanesian may say "Me got three-fella house", so in any language men have managed to communicate through the ages without bothering too much about inflexional endings, grammatical gender, adjectival agreement, and all the other impedimenta that clutter the highroads of human speech. It is precisely because England assimilated so many waves of invaders that the English language has been planed free of most of its inflexions, and it was the Vikings who began the levelling process.

In addition to hacking out complexities, the Northmen also reduced ambiguities. In Old English a good deal of confusion prevailed with respect to the third-person pronoun. It was difficult phonetically, to distinguish between *hē* (he) and *hī* (they); between *hire* (her) and *hira* (their); and between *him* (him) and *heom* (them). To clear up matters, the Scandinavians clung to their own plural pronouns, *þā* (they), *þāra* (their), and *þōem* (them), and since men generally prefer to be understood, it was not long before the Scandinavian plurals were adopted by the Northern English and became a basic element of our tongue.

During the two centuries between the advent of the Viking sea rovers and the landing of William the Conqueror, the English and Scandinavian languages thus intertwined as their users turned from enemies into neighbours, intermarried, and dwelt peaceably side by side. Philologists estimate that more than 900 words in modern English usage can claim a pure Scandinavian pedigree, but when this number is augmented by those of *probable* Danish or Norwegian origin, plus others locally employed in the regional dialects of northern England and Scotland, then the total soars into the thousands. Analysis of these so-called "loan words" reveals that they refer mostly to the objects and acts of ordinary, everyday existence. Even without historical records, the testimony of these homely, commonplace words would suggest that the relationship between the two peoples became a close and democratic one and that they met and conversed eventually as social coequals and not as conquerors and conquered or as aristocracy and proletariat. Today one cannot write in English about religious, intellectual, or philosophical subjects without employing our vast heritage of Latin and Greek words, nor can one discuss the arts, the social world, or the domains of high fashion and *haute cuisine* without drawing on our rich legacy from the French. But for the quintessential things of the human condition, we constantly require words which the Scandinavians introduced into the Anglo-Saxon vernacular more than a thousand years ago. In addition to the words mentioned previously (and omitting words that were identical in both languages), these ancient and highly useful imports, all made in Denmark and Norway, include:

NOUNS: *axle, band, bank, birth, boon, booth, brink, bull, calf, crook, dirt, down, dregs, freckle, gait, gap, gate, girth, guess, hap, haven, keel, kid, knife, leg, link, loan, mire, race, rift, root, scab, scales, score, scrap, seat, skull, slaughter, snare, stack, steak, thrift, tidings, trust, wing.*

ADJECTIVES: *awkward, flat, happy, ill, low, meek, muggy, odd, rotten, rugged, scant, seemly, sly, tattered, tight, ugly, wrong.*

VERBS: *bait, batten, call, cast, clasp, clip, crave, crawl, dangle, dazzle, droop, drown, flit, gape, gasp, glitter, guess, happen, hit, kindle, lift, lug, nag, rake, ransack, rid, scare, scowl, scream, skulk, snub, sprint, take, thrive, thrust.*

Even more important, perhaps, than words like the above, which evoke an image or define an action, are the little words, sometimes referred to by grammarians as "form words" or "empty words", which constitute the bare bones of every language, the unnoticed substructure that sustains the linguistic edifice. In this category the Scandinavians contributed such structural elements as: *at, both, less, lesser, rather, same, though, till, until, together, worse, hence, thence, whence,* and the verb form *are.* The ever-present phrase *they are* is pure Scandinavian.

4.

The era of Danish influence reached its zenith during the reign of King Canute from 1017 to 1035, but with the accession of Edward the Confessor seven years after Canute's death, the linguistic climate began to undergo a change, limited at first but ultimately of profound importance to the national speech. For Edward spoke French. His mother was a Norman, and he had been reared in Normandy, the maritime province which had been ceded by Charles the Simple of France in 912 to the

Viking chieftain Rolf the Ganger, thereafter known as Rollo, First Duke of Normandy. Although in the beginning Normandy (Nor-man-dy or "Northmen's Land") was simply another Danelaw imposed upon France, the Vikings who settled there adopted French customs and French speech so swiftly that two generations later Rollo's grandson had to be sent from Rouen, the Norman capital, to Bayeux for tutoring in Danish as that was the only place in the entire dukedom where the Scandinavian tongue was still spoken. In striking contrast with the linguistic evolution of England, no Scandinavian words survive in Normandy today—even in local dialect—save for a few place names ending in *bec*, *beuf*, *dalle*, *ham*, and *tot* (e.g. Bolbec, Quillebeuf, Dieppendalle, Ouistreham, and Yvetot).

The relations between England and Normandy were close for more than half a century before the Conquest. When Canute drove Æthelred the Unready into exile, the ousted English king took refuge in Rouen, for his wife Emma was a sister of Richard, fourth Duke of Normandy and grandfather of William the Conqueror. Their son Edward (later called the Confessor) was then only nine years old. When he was recalled to England in 1042 to assume the throne of his forbears, he was, at the age of 38, the finished product of French society and a French education. He proceeded to surround himself, to the considerable resentment of the Anglo-Danish nobility, with Norman advisors and Norman favourites, and he appointed Normans to important positions in the government and church hierarchy. In the course of Edward's reign of 24 years, French became the dominant speech of important elements of the ruling classes. In many ways he paved the way for the imminent—and permanent—Conquest which would change the political and social history of England and alter its language forever.

When the Confessor died childless in January 1066, he left the succession in doubt. He had at one time encouraged the aspirations of his cousin, William of Normandy, and perhaps had even assured him of accession to the throne. But for the last twelve years of his reign, Edward's principal advisor had been Harold Godwin, the able and dynamic Earl of Wessex who boasted some royal blood on his mother's side. On the day following the Confessor's death, the English Witan (Council), weary of French favourites, elected Harold king. Infuriated,

William assembled a fleet and an army—one-third of them Normans, the others land-hungry mercenaries from all over Europe—and landed in England on September 28, 1066. A fortnight later the bloody, all-day battle of Hastings resolved the issue. Harold fell in the late afternoon when a random arrow pierced his eye. On Christmas day, in Westminster Abbey, William the Conqueror was crowned King of England.

For all the decimation of England's finest warriors at Hastings, resistance to the Norman foe was by no means extinguished. During two decades after the invasion, the Normans dwelt uneasily and warily, barricaded behind earthen forts and wooden stockades, later in great stone castles, a hated and beleaguered army camped in a hostile land. William was an exponent of the psychology of terror, and through the years that followed his accession to the throne, he conducted relentless campaigns of subjugation, suppressing resistance mercilessly by fire and spoliation, by death and mutilation, by slow hanging and flaying alive, by cutting off hands and burning out eyes with hot irons, and by all the other methods of deterrence, repression, and retaliation that we now call "frightfulness". As the great estates of the English nobility were overrun and occupied, and their owners put to painful deaths, William paid off his debts to those who had abetted his conquest. In all parts of the realm, Normans were rewarded with lands, castles, and high positions in the church and government.

By 1072 only one of the twelve earls of England was an Englishman, and he was executed four years later. The two archbishops of England—Canterbury and York—were replaced by Normans; and of all the English bishops who held office when William became king, only two remained at the end of his reign, and their dioceses were in the remote west country where the Norman storm had not reached full fury. In the monasteries change occurred more gradually. A decade after Hastings, 13 of the 21 principal abbots of the realm were still English. But as vacancies arose through death or other causes, they too were replaced by Normans, and when William died in 1087, there were only three English abbots. New monasteries were established and staffed entirely with monks from France.

Unlike their Viking predecessors, the Normans did not assimilate with the local population and had nothing but scorn for local customs and language. They entered England as a ruling class and they brought with them not only Norman soldiers to garrison their castles, but Norman merchants and craftsmen to provide them with goods and services. Their interests were constantly focused across the Channel, where most of them had estates on French soil. The only real culture was French, and those members of the English gentry who had somehow managed to preserve or salvage part of their possessions sent their sons to France for their education. For two centuries after the Norman Conquest the language of the governing classes was French, and for more than three centuries all the kings of England spoke French. With the exception of Henry I (1100–35), no king married an English woman until the end of the fifteenth century. Indeed most of them spent the greater part of their time in France. William the Conqueror and his sons, William II and Henry I, lived in France for at least half of their successive reigns. Henry II, for all his great contributions to England, passed nearly two-thirds of his 35-year reign in France, administering his vast dominions in Normandy, Anjou, and Aquitaine. His son, Richard Cœur de Lion, despite the legend of "Good King Richard", was completely French, devoted most of his adult life to crusading in the Near East, and spent only a few months of his ten-year reign in England. It was not until Henry IV, who came to the throne in 1399 (one year before the death of Chaucer), that England had a king whose mother tongue was English.

Since the government, the military, the church—and therefore education—were all dominated by French-speaking Normans who regarded the English as boors and louts and their vernacular as a barbarian tongue, it is not surprising that the written language fell into a decline during the twelfth century. What literature was produced in England—poetry, history, romances, devotional works—was all set down in French. Only the monks at Peterborough continued to record the events of English history in the *Anglo-Saxon Chronicle* begun by King Alfred two and a half centuries earlier.

Yet inevitably the mere fact of proximity on a small island produced in time a fusion of the two peoples. Men who came into contact with both the ruling classes and the ruled—local officials such as stewards, and bailiffs, and parish priests—

eventually became bilingual. Meanwhile many of the more ambitious and intelligent English, eager for advancement in trade or military service began learning French. Through the ever-recurring agencies of commerce and intermarriage, and the stimulating associations of military service, Normans and English gradually forgot the bitterness of the past and converged toward common loyalties and a unified national culture. Save for the court itself and the upper strata of the nobility, the fusion of the population progressed so rapidly that by the end of the twelfth century an English jurist wrote: "Now that the English and the Normans have been dwelling together, marrying, and giving in marriage, the two nations have become so mixed that it is scarcely possible today, speaking of free men, to tell who is English, who of Norman race." Following the loss of Normandy by King John in 1204, even the ruling classes ceased to orient themselves toward France and turned inward upon the land they had won and held for a century and a half.

During this initial hundred and fifty years of the Norman occupation, the infiltration of French words into the English language progressed slowly. The two tongues existed side by side without mingling. The sparse examples of written English preserved from the twelfth century contain very few words of French origin. A treatise known as the *Ancrene Riwle* ("Rulle for Anchoresses") contains about 500 French words in a total of 200 pages. The *Ormulum*, a collection of Gospel paraphrases and saints' lives, employs only twenty French words in 20,000 lines. Layamon's *Brut*, a translation of a French romance, has only 150 French words in 56,000 lines. These works plus others reveal that prior to the thirteenth century, only about 1,000 French loan words entered the English language. Of these the largest number (and the first to be introduced) were of an ecclesiastical character. They included such words as: *preach*, *pray*, *prayer*, *relic*, *friar*, *clergy*, *parish*, *baptism*, *sacrifice*, *orison*, *homily*, *honour*, *glory*, *chaplain*, *procession*, *nativity*, *cell*, *miracle*, *charity*, *archangel*, *religion*, *service*, *trinity*, *saviour*, *virgin*, *sermon*, *virtue*, *vice*, *grace*, *evangelist*, *passion*, *paradise*, *sacrament*, *saint*, *chaste*, *covet*, *desire*, *pity*, *descipline*, and many more all bearing witness to the Norman devotion to the church, memorialized still today by the soaring cathedrals and cloistered abbeys with which the conquerors adorned the English countryside. Other major categories of loan words from this period include those pertaining to:

GOVERNMENT: *court*, *crown*, *council*, *counsel*, *empress*, *legate*, *govern*, *reign*, *realm*, *sovereign*, *country*, *power*, *minister*, *chancellor*, *authority*, *parliament*, *exchequer*, *people*, *nation*, *fief*, *feudal vassal*, *liege*, *peer*, *baron*, *viscount*, *marquis*, *duke*, and *prince* (but not *king*, *queen and knight*, English words which the Normans did not supplant).

LAW: *Just*, *justice*, *judge*, *jury*, *suit*, *sue*, *plaintiff*, *defendant*, *plea*, *plead*, *summon*, *cause*, *assize*, *session*, *attorney*, *accuse*, *crime*, *felony*, *traitor*, *damage*, *dower*, *heritage*, *property*, *real estate*, *tenure*, *penalty*, *injury*, *case*, *marry*, *marriage*, *oust*, *prove*, *false*, *heir*, *defend*, *prison*, *robber*, *rich*, *poor*, *poverty*, *money*, *interest*, *rent*.

ART AND ARCHITECTURE: *art*, *beauty*, *colour*, *image*, *design*, *figure*, *ornament*, *paint arch*, *tower*, *pillar*, *vault*, *porch*, *column*, *aisle*, *choir*, *transept*, *abbey*, *cloister*, *palace*, *castle*, *manor*, *mansion*.

PLEASURES: *pleasure*, *joy*, *delight*, *ease*, *comfort*, *flower*, *fruit*, *falcon*, *quarry*, *scent*, *chase*, *leisure*, *sport*, *cards*, *dice*, *ace*, *deuce*, *trey*, *partner*, *suit*, *trump*.

COOKING: *sauce*, *boil*, *fry*, *roast*, *pastry*, *soup*, *sausage*, *jelly*, *dainty*, *feast*, *viand*, *cuisine*. In this category it is interesting to observe that words connoting such items of meat as *beef*, *veal*, *mutton*, *pork*, *bacon*, and *venison* are all French words, while the living animals from which they are derived (*ox*, *cow*, *calf*, *sheep*, *pig*, *swine*, *boar*, *deer*) retain their English names. Equally provocative is the fact that *dinner* and *supper* are French words, while *breakfast* is English.

During the thirteenth century certain events of history combined to lift the English language from its humble estate as the vernacular of a conquered people and to impel it on its slow climb back to ascendancy as the national tongue. The loss of Normandy, coupled with the growing menace of King Philip II of France, compelled the Anglo-Norman nobles to choose between trying to cling to their precarious holdings across the Channel or devoting themselves single-mindedly to their English estates. In many instances families divided, with one son returning to France, the other remaining in England. By mid-century a large proportion of the nobility no longer thought of themselves as Normans but essentially—and politically—as English. Their new sense of nationality was further stimulated by the advent of hordes of foreigners who poured into England during the reign of Henry III. For, in 1236, Henry married a French princess from Provence and proceeded to surround himself with her numerous and needy friends and relatives. National resentment against the rapacity of these royal favourites, who monopolized the appointive offices, dipped greedily into the exchequer, and scandalously exploited the lands and holdings which the king had bequeathed to them, precipitated a revolt of the English baronage with the full support of the middle class. The watchword was "England for the English". And the outcome was a linguistic, as well as a political, victory for the English. For Henry was forced to agree to the appointment of a commission for reform of government whose proposals were embodied in the Provisions of Oxford in 1258. The king accepted the provisions in a historic proclamation issued in English, French, and Latin—the first official document to employ the English language since the Norman Conquest.

Devotion to England and its ancient vernacular now developed such strength that Henry's son, the great and energetic Edward I, was able to rally the support of Parliament in 1295 for war against France by declaring that it was Philip's "detestable purpose, which God forbid, to wipe out the English tongue". Although the nobility still conversed in French, deeming it a mark of culture (as did the ruling classes of every country in Europe), Englishmen of all lesser ranks were beginning to regard it with some hostility. And although French remained the language of diplomacy and international commerce, of the law courts and of Parliament, it was accepted as an official and mandatory system of communication, imposed by tradition and convention, rather than as a mother tongue inherited from anyone's ancestors. By the dawn of the fourteenth century there were indications that even among the upper classes—especially the bucolic aristocracy—there were some who no longer could speak French at all.

Year by year, generation by generation, English invaded the citadels of government and became a necessary implement of official intelligence. In 1327 when Edward II granted certain privileges to the City of London, the royal edict was first read in French to the assembled aldermen and other functionaries in the Guildhall and then explained to them in English by the city chamberlain. Ten years later when Edward III convened Parliament to consider his claim to the throne of France, the king's spokesman addressed the session in English "to the end that he might be better understood by all". A still more notable milestone was reared in 1362, when, for the first time in history, Parliament was opened by the king's chancellor with an address in English, and only in English. In that same year Parliament enacted the Statutes of Pleading, ruling that all lawsuits would henceforth be conducted in English, "for the French tongue is much unknown in this realm". In 1399 the articles of accusation that deposed Richard II were read to Parliament in both Latin and English; a few days later his successor, Henry IV, used English in his speech when accepting the throne. In 1404 during diplomatic exchanges between England and France, the English envoys objected to the use of the French language in negotiations, claiming that French was as unknown to them as Hebrew—an assertion which was probably less a statement of truth than a bit of linguistic gamesmanship.

There were other events of the fourteenth century which accelerated the spread of English through all levels and estates of the realm. One was the Hundred Years War, for, upon its outbreak in 1337, French at once became the language of England's enemy. Another was the Black Death whose terrible onslaught in 1348–50 cut the population of England almost in half, thus causing a crucial shortage of labour. As a consequence the importance of the working classes, of artisans and craftsmen, was greatly enhanced; wages soared, and the resultant ascendancy of the yeoman in the country and the bourgeois in the town—both of whom spoke only English—further abetted the use of the native tongue. Moreover hundreds of teachers and scholars perished during the seasons of the great plague. Faced with a dearth of instructors versed in French and Latin, many schools resorted to English as a common medium of instruction. By 1385 the practice became general, and even universities and monastic institutions began conducting their curricula in English.

This development awakened misgivings among some

educators. Commenting on the new trend, John of Trevisa wrote in 1385:

So that now, the yere of oure Lorde a thowsand thre hundred and foure score and fyve, and of the secounde Kyng Richard after the conquest nyne, in alle the gramere scoles of Engelond, children leveth Frensche and construeth and lerneth in Englische. . . . Here avauntage is, that they lerneth ther gramer in lasse tyme than children were i-woned [used] to doo; disavauntage is that now children of gramer scole conneth no more Frensche than can hir left heele, and that is harme for them and [if] they schulle passe the see and travaille in straunge landes and in many other places.

This emergency action induced by the Black Death engendered an educational reaction. Alarmed by the decline in the general knowledge of other languages, schoolmasters prepared and published manuals and handbooks of French grammar. Oxford and Cambridge enacted statutes requiring students to construe and compose in both English and French "lest the French language be entirely disused". Concerned with the new insularity of English education, Parliament decreed that all "lords, barons, knights, and honest men of good towns", should teach their children French. The historical significance of these developments lay in the fact that by the fifteenth century the ability to speak French had come to be regarded as an accomplishment. In schools and universities, French was taught, like Latin, as an ancillary language requisite to the cultural wardrobe of the properly educated man. Government officials who lacked this accessory had to retain on their staffs a "secretary in the French Language". The linguistic balance had shifted for ever. By the end of the fifteenth century William Caxton observed: "For the mooste quantyte of the people understonde not latyn ne frensshe here in this noble royame of englong."

5.

Of all the forces conducing to the supremacy and dispersion of English, none had greater effect than the increasing use of the vernacular as an instrument of artistic expression. All the great popular literature of England from the middle of the fourteenth century was composed in the native tongue. The five decades from 1350 to 1400 proved a period of extraordinary florescence.

Within this half-century, which still stands as the high noon of mediaeval literary creation in England, there emerged the following immortal works: *Piers Plowman*, a long allegorical poem by William Langland; John Wycliffe's English translation of the Bible; *Sir Gawain and the Green Knight*, finest of chivalric romances, by an unknown poet; and, above all, *The Canterbury Tales*, *Troilus and Cressida*, and the many other poems of Geoffrey Chaucer.

Chaucer, the first poet to write in English, stood on the threshold of the modern language. Behind him lay the transitional period of early Middle English with its vestiges of Anglo-Saxon inflexions and spelling and its incipient assimilation of French words. Before him shone the glories of modern English which reached full flower with the advent of Shakespeare two centuries later. The age in which Chaucer wrote marked a high tide in the flow of French words into English speech. For as the upper classes slipped away from conversational French and turned increasingly to the common tongue, they nevertheless continued to resort to French words when at a loss for an English phrase or synonym. As a consequence the French vocabulary, quite apart from syntax or grammar, was wafted constantly through the English air into the ears and consciousness of all levels of society. A notable example of the linguistic dichotomy of the time survives in a letter written in 1403 by the Dean of Windsor to King Henry IV, which begins in French, switches midstream into English, and concludes in a relaxed combination of both:

Jeo prie a la Benoit Trinite que vous ottroie bone vie ove tres sentier sauntee a tres longe durre, and sende yowe sone to ows in helth and prosperitee; for, in god fey, I hope to Al Mighty God that, if ye come youre owne persone, ye schulle have the victorie of alle youre enemyes. And for salvation of youre Schire and Marches al aboute, treste ye nought to no Leutenaunt. Escript a Hereford, en tres graunte haste, a trois de la clocke après noone, le tierce jour de Septembre.

In the period between 1250 and 1400, the year of Chaucer's death, an estimated 10,000 French words slid unobtrusively into English speech; of these 75 per cent are still in common use today. The trend is manifest in Chaucer's own works. Of his poetic vocabulary of approximately 8,000 words, slightly more than 4,000 are of Romance origin. (Like Shakespeare, Chaucer was neither a pedant nor a snob; he addressed himself to a wide and popular audience, but, also like Shakespeare, he was a writer of enormous erudition.) Chaucer foreshadowed in his writing the quantitative balance of Modern English which consists today, roughly, of one half Germanic (Anglo-Saxon and Scandinavian) words, and one half words of Romance (French and Latin) derivation. He was thus the first great writer to demonstrate the richest resource of the English language: the treasure trove of native and borrowed words that endows its skilled practitioners with a wealth of synonyms and near-synonyms which may be employed to achieve both subtle nuances of meaning and the varied rhythms of poetry and rhetoric.

In his description of the Prioress in the Prologue to *The Canterbury Tales* Chaucer revealed not only his recognition of the decline of Norman French as a national tongue, but his amused awareness of the difference between the authentic speech of continental France and the kind of French heard in England (and still, for that matter, spoken by Englishmen and Americans today):

> Ther was also a Nonne, a Prioresse,
> That of hir smyling was full simple and coy;
> Hir Gretteste ooth was but by sëynte Loy;
> And she was cleped madame Eglentyne.
> Ful wel she song the service divyne,
> Entuned in hir nose ful semely;
> And French she spak ful faire and fetisly,
> After the scole of Stratford atte Bowe,
> For Frensh of Paris was to hir unknowe.

There is no question that Chaucer, whose works were no less relished in his age than they are revered today, was a powerful agent in the process of crystallizing the English language. He could have written with equal facility in any one of three languages—French, Latin, or English. He chose to write in English. According to Theodore Morrison of Harvard, poet and Chaucerian scholar whose rendition of Chaucer's works in contemporary rhymed pentameter is widely known: "Chaucer threw his whole strength both as translator and poet into the use of English as it was spoken in his day." The prolific body of his work endures today as a turning-point in the evolution of the English language, for it signalized the blossoming of a hybrid vocabulary of Anglo-Saxon, Scandinavian, and French derivation, fused at last into a fluid and flexible instrument of both precise and poetic expression.

An incidental but no less significant by-product of Chaucer's work was the establishment of the East Midland dialect as standard English speech. Aware of the fragmentation of English in the many dialects of the north, south, and west, Chaucer wrote in an epilogue to *Troilus and Cressida:*

> Go, lytle booke,
> And for ther is so gret diversite
> In Englissh, and in writyng of oure tonge,
> So I pray I god that non myswrite thee,
> Ne thee mys-metre for defaute of tonge,
> And wherever thee may be rede,
> I pray god thee may be understoode.

The dominance of the East Midland dialect was fostered by several factors. England's two great universities, Oxford and Cambridge, lie in the East Midland region, as does London, the capital and most populous city of the realm. Moreover London was then, as now, the centre of the printing trade, and the role of the printer proved of enormous importance not only in transmitting knowledge but in stabilizing the national vernacular. While Chaucer may have been the literary progenitor of modern English, it was William Caxton and his successors who froze the mould, stabilized spelling, and disseminated uniform conventions of grammar and syntax among the reading public. (It has been estimated that half of the population of London in Shakespeare's time could read.) As a consequence of the printer's work, the language of the common people, English, began to receive recognition slowly in the field of learning—but very slowly, for Latin continued to be the language of scholarship.

Among the interior changes that occurred in English at this time was the final expunging of grammatical complexities—levelling of inflexions, elimination of artificial gender in nouns, adjectives, and such—in short, completion of the process of linguistic simplification that had begun with the Viking invasions and had accelerated after the Norman Conquest. Scores of irregular verbs (akin to our still extant *sing*, *sang*, *sung; drive*, *drove*, *driven; wear*, *wore*, *worn*) gave way to regular verbs (like *talk*, *talked*, *talked; love*, *loved*, *loved*). Nearly a third of the irregular verbs current in Old English usage died out during the Middle English period. Even in Chaucer's time the past tense of *ache* was *oke*, the past tense of *step* was *stope*, the past tense of *climb* was *clomb*, the past tense of *shave* was *shove*. The tendency to eliminate irregular conjugations and convert all verbs into regular verbs continues today whenever a child (or a foreigner or uneducated person) employs a construction such as "The wind blowed hard", "I seed him go home". It is thus that grammar evolves in the direction of simplicity.

During this same period several other developments of fundamental importance occurred in the long process of transforming Old English—a highly inflected language—into the analytical language that English is today In addition to abandoning case endings in nouns and elaborate conjugations of verbs, English also dropped for ever the idiocy of grammatical gender. Here again good sense prevailed. The common people, although they recognized the necessity of natural gender—the logic of distinguishing between the pronouns *he*, *she*, and *it*—gradually came to ignore the artificiality of the Old English convention which classified such a word as *wīf* (wife) as neuter and the word *wīf-mann* (woman) as masculine. Thus true sex prevailed over unnatural gender, and English was swept clean of all the tortuous mutations of adjectives, participles, and articles required (in all other European languages) by the law of agreement of modifiers. Today we have the single definite article *the* as opposed to the French *le* (masculine), *la* (feminine), *les* (plural); and the German *der* (masculine), *die* (feminine), *das* (neuter), and *die* (plural).

A further stride in the direction of simplicity came with the adoption of the letter *s* to indicate the plural form of all nouns. Early in the Middle English period the manifold plural endings of Old English were reduced to only two: *-s* and *-en*. As late as the thirteenth century the *-en* form was dominant in the south of England (*eyen*, *shoon*, *housen*, *peasen*). But the northern *-s* eventually prevailed and during the fourteenth century it became the standard plural throughout the land with very few exceptions such as *oxen*, *children*, *feet*, *mice*, and the like. Its victory may have been abetted by the fact that *-s* was and is still the standard plural in French.

These linguistic developments were doubtless inspired by the Normans—not directly but indirectly—by their making French the language of the educated classes and scorning English as the patois of the illiterate. For it is always the educated man who is the purist in speech and writing and it is the untutored fellow who disregards the lace frills and meringues glacées of language and heads for the simpler staples of communication. In this way the common people simplified English. At the same time they enriched it, by adding countless new words to its vocabulary. Since Anglo-Saxon days, the English had continually invented new terms by putting two or more small words together or by adding prefixes and suffixes to existing stems (see pp. 84–5). Now, during this formative period when hundreds of French words were circulating in common use, the English once again employed their special talent for creating compounds. As a result, a vast number of hybrid words combining elements of both languages came into being.

One of the earliest examples of the process is found in the French word *gentil*, which was adopted by the English and was widely used by 1225. Before many decades had passed, the English wordmakers had combined *gentil* with the Anglo-Saxon *man* and *woman* to form *gentleman* and *gentlewoman*; not long afterwards they added the suffixes *ly* and *ness* to create *gently* and *gentleness*. Such familiar Anglo-Saxon suffixes as *-ly*, *-ness*, *-less*, *-ship*, *-ful*, and *-dom* were attached to French words to produce countless bilingual compounds: e.g. *nobly*, *princely*, *courtly*, *faintly*, *easily*, *naïvely; richness*, *poorness*, *faintness*, *closeness*, *simpleness; faithless*, *artless*, *colourless*, *fruitless; courtship*, *companionship*, *scholarship*, *clerkship; artful*, *beautiful*, *dutiful*, *powerful; dukedom*, *martyrdom*. Conversely, but more rarely, the wordminters reversed the process and combined Anglo-Saxon stems with French endings. The French suffix *-age* gave rise to *acreage*, *leakage*, *breakage*, *cleavage*, *roughage*, *shortage*. From the French *-ess* (the feminine *-esse*), we have *goddess*, *shepherdess*, *seeress*; from *-ment*, we get *endearment*, *enlightenment*, *fulfilment*; and from *-ance* we derive *hindrance*, *forbearance*, *furtherance*. But incomparably the most versatile French suffix now wedded to Anglo-Saxon stems is the adjectival ending *-able*. It flourishes today in the modern English lexicon in thousands of hybrid words such as: *bearable*, *liveable likeable*, *kissable*, *readable*, *eatable*, *drinkable*, *suitable*, *answerable*, *unmistakable*, *understandable*, *unutterable*. Shakespeare coined the word *laughable*, and George Eliot, in a letter, invented the word *knock-upable*. And of course, throughout the English-speaking world today, such words as *washable*, *nonshrinkable* and *disposable* are among the most indispensable, ineluctable, not-to-be-got-along-without-able adjectives of modern living.

Another small building-block of French which has been fitted into the edifice of our language is the verbal participial ending *é* (as in *aimé*, *trouvé*, and the like). In English this has become the suffix *-ee*, attached to nouns defining a person on the receiving end of some transaction (*lessee* as opposed to *lessor*, *mortgagee* as opposed to *mortgagor*). Originally entering the language through legal terminology (as in *legatee*, *appellee*, *trustee*), its use has been extrapolated beyond the vocabulary of law, so that today we also have such words as *nominee*, *referee*, *presentee*. Some writers of the past played with this little suffix more than we do today. Laurence Sterne used the combination *jester* and *jestee*, and Richardson *lover* and *lovee*. Carlyle adduced the words *cursee* and *laughee*. Elsewhere one also finds *flirtee*, *flogee*, *beatee*, *bargainee*, *gazee*, *staree*, *callee*, and *wishee*. And in the word *trusteeship*, the French participle stands squarely in the middle of one of the most exuberantly international words in the English language, a trilingual construction composed of the Scandinavian stem *trust*, the French *ee*, and the Anglo-Saxon suffix *-ship*.

As new words entered the vernacular, many of the old Germanic and Danish expressions died out, victims of the laws of selection and of survival of the fittest, which operate in speech as in nature. The momentous and fundamental changes that so profoundly transformed the language during the Middle English period (1150–1500) were in some cases direct consequences of the Norman Conquest; others were the inevitable end-products of linguistic evolution. In any event, the 331 years between the reign of Henry II, first of the Plantagenets, and Henry VII, first of the Tudors, were crucial years of transition when the architecture of modern English with all its beauty and felicity, complexity and simplicity, symmetry and balance, was taking shape stone by stone, alternately embellished and scoured, emblazoned and hewn clean by generations of nameless artisans. By the end of the fifteenth century, English had ceased to be a foreign language, alien in structure and vocabulary, and was assuming the guise by which we recognize it today. Although for vast periods of time it had been despised as an inferior tongue, ridiculed by the ruling classes, disdained by scholars, and inundated again and again by waves of foreign words, it was now to ascend with incredible swiftness, in the next hundred years, to heights of literary splendour never attained by any language before or since.

6.

The year 1500 is often fixed as the point of transition from Middle to Modern English. Although the spoken word still varied from region to region, coloured by local dialects, the written language had begun to crystallize into a uniform, standard mould. This was the English of London. For inasmuch as the printing trade (which had grown rapidly since William Caxton set up England's first press in 1476) was centred in London, it tended to employ the conventions of London speech. And by reproducing these conventions in thousands of books and pamphlets and distributing them throughout the land,the printers of London established the local idiom as that of English literary composition henceforth.

London English was, of course, the English of Chaucer and of Wycliffe, whose translation of the Bible appeared almost concurrently with Chaucer's poems. But, no less importantly, it was the English of the royal court. During the reign of Henry VIII (1509–47), the criteria of spoken English, as well as written English, became fixed. For just as today the speech of the educated Englishman is regarded as the hallmark of cultivation and status, so in the sixteenth century, the dialect of the court was the élite form of English, the form to be studied and imitated by anyone with either literary or social aspirations. Henry VIII, as a matter of fact, was a poet of considerable talent, and the

English he wrote and spoke was in more ways than one The King's English.

No living language ever ceases to change, and during the sixteenth century—the first century of modern English—two new forces began to exercise a powerful influence on the national speech. One was the impact of the Renaissance, the revival of classical learning which had been kindled in Tuscany three centuries earlier and had radiated progressively northward and westward through France, Germany, the Low Countries, and finally to England. The other was the growth of national pride, which began to flower in mid-century with the Reformation, swiftly gathered momentum, and reached its culmination amid the triumphs and glories of the brilliant Elizabethan Age.

The extraordinary surge of interest in the classics opened the gates of the English language to a new verbal invasion—this time of Latin and, to a lesser extent, Greek words—as drastic as any that had ever occurred before. Although there never had been a time when Latin was not read and written in England since the legions of the Emperor Claudius invaded and subjugated the island in A.D. 43, the linguistic legacy of the Romans to the English vocabulary, despite 400 years of occupation, was surprisingly small (see p. 78). Following the conversion of England to Christianity by St. Augustine and his followers, a greater number of Latin words found their way into the common tongue. Yet virtually all of these pertained to religion and the physical symbols of the church. And even though Latin was employed constantly in religious rituals, academic activities, and state ceremonies, its individual components did not seep into the English vernacular. Now abruptly the new passion for the antique past, the zeal for reading the classic works of Homer and Virgil, of Horace, Catullus, and Marcus Aurelius in the original texts and, moreover, for employing the ancient languages in written and spoken disquisitions, precipitated a wholesale diffusion of Latin and Greek words and phrases which came into widespread use and soon found permanent niches in the English lexicon.

The phenomenon of this linguistic incursion remains something of a mystery to historians of language. Why did Latin suddenly penetrate the English language at this relatively late date when it had failed to do so earlier, despite four hundred years of Roman occupation and a thousand years of Christian worship conducted in the Latin tongue? One reason, of course, lies in the difference between the repetition of a set ritual and the excitement of encountering new ideas. Many of these new ideas were not susceptible to precise translation, and so scholars often simply retained the Latin terms for want of proper counterparts. One translator of the time apologized for the inadequacy of his work on the ground that "ther ys many wordes in Latyn that we have no propre Englysh accordynge therto". Many Latin and Greek terms, mostly of an abstract philosophical or scientific character, were taken over intact by scholars and entered the language through the medium of *writing*—not talk, as was the case with the Scandinavian and French borrowings. Many of these classical words, though originally of a narrow or specialized application, later acquired general connotations and eventually became familiar and commonplace elements of everyday speech.

Another factor may have served to facilitate the invasion of Latin words at this time. According to Otto Jespersen: "The reason seems to be that the natural power of resistance possessed by a Germanic tongue against these alien intruders had been already broken in the case of the English language by the wholesale importation of French words. They paved the way for the Latin words which resembled them in so many respects. . . . If French words were more *distingués* than English ones, Latin words were still more so, for did not the French themselves go to Latin to enrich their own vocabulary?"

As the sixteenth century wheeled into the seventeenth and the horizons of human knowledge receded outward in space and time, English writers dipped increasingly into the rich granaries of Greek and Latin to express new concepts in the realms of art, philosophy, literature, and, above all, science. To this day the terminology of such scientific disciplines as biology, botany, chemistry, physics, and medicine is overwhelmingly (and often, to the layman, incomprehensibly) Latin and Greek. It is not without significance that the words *arithmetic*, *grammar*, *logic*, *rhetoric*, *geometry*, *astronomy*, and *music* are all of Greek origin. So are most words connected with the theatre such as: *drama* (first recorded in 1515), *comedy*, *tragedy*, *prologue*, *dialogue*, *epilogue*, *episode*, *scene*, *climax*, *critic*, and the word *theatre* itself. And in every domain of knowledge, educated men relied more and more on Greek and Latin terms in preference to the resources of their own supposedly inelegant native tongue.

Upon entering the English language, many of these borrowed words underwent slight adaptations (such as the dropping of case and verb endings). But others were lifted straight from the Greek and Latin in their original form and still circulate today, unaltered in meaning or spelling from the days of ancient Greece and Rome. From the pure Latin, we have *arbitrator*, *executor*, *explicit*, *finis*, *gratis*, *index*, *item*, *major*, *minor*, *memento*, *memorandum*, *neuter*, *pauper*, *persecutor*, *prosecutor*, *proviso*, and *simile*. And from the Greek, virtually unchanged save in the transliteration of alphabets, we still use: *acme*, *anonymous*, *criterion*, *ephemeral*, *idiosyncrasy*, *lexicon*, *ostracize*, *polemic*, *tantalize*, *thermometer*, and *tonic*.

Language scholars have been able to fix the precise years at which certain words were exhumed from the classics and welcomed into the living vocabulary of England. Among these linguistic débuts the *Oxford English Dictionary* lists: *arbiter*, 1502; *genius*, 1513; *pollen*, 1523; *acumen*, 1531; *folio*, 1533; *area*, 1538; *circus*, 1546; *axis*, 1549; *vacuum*, 1550; *species*, 1551; *terminus*, 1555; *decorum*, 1568; *ignoramus*, 1577; *omen*, 1582; *radius*, 1597; *virus*, 1599; *premium*, 1601; *equilibrium*, 1608; *specimen*, 1610; *series*, 1611; *census*, 1613; *arena*, 1627; *apparatus*, 1628; *veto*, 1629; *curriculum*, 1633; *formula*, 1638; *impetus*, 1641; *focus*, 1644; *complex*, 1652; *pendulum*, 1660; *maximum* and *minimum*, 1663; *lens*, *status*, 1693; *momentum*, 1699; *nucleus*, 1704; *inertia*, 1713; *propaganda*, 1718; *auditorium*, 1727; *ultimatum*, 1731; *insomnia*, 1758; *prospectus*, 1777 . . . and so on.

In many instances, philologists have been able to specify not only the dates at which Greek and Latin words first appeared in the English language but also the authors who initially used them. John Wycliffe was the first and most prolific classical importer; it has been estimated that in his translation of the Bible and other works he introduced perhaps one thousand Latin words into the English lexicon. Sir Thomas More also drew heavily on the classics; among the many Greek and Latin words he uncovered and used for the first time, we find such now familiar specimens as: *absurdity*, *acceptance*, *anticipate*, *combustible*, *compatible*, *comprehensible*, *congratulatory*, *contradictory*, *denunciation*, *dissipate*, *endurable*, *exact*, *exaggerate*, *exasperate*, *ex-*

plain, *fact*, *frivolous*, *impenitent*, *implacable*, *indifference*, *insinuate*, *inveigh*, *inviolable*, *monopoly*, *monosyllable*, *necessitate*, *obstruction*, *paradox*, and *pretext*.

Shakespeare thrust his pen boldly and resourcefully into the fountainhead of Latin and Greek words, which by the end of the sixteenth century were flowing freely through all channels of literate expression. Many of the words that he appropriated were extremely new, appearing in English only a year or two before he found use for them. But he also produced some innovations of his own. Words which Shakespeare claimed from the classics and introduced into the English language through the medium of his plays include: *accommodation*, *apostrophe*, *dexterously*, *dislocate*, *frugal*, *indistinguishable*, *misanthrope*, *obscene*, *pedant*, *premeditated*, *reliance*, *submerged*—and many more.

In addition to simple borrowing—the use of a Greek or Latin word with its original meaning intact—English writers occasionally indulged in more complex forms of linguistic poaching. Sometimes, anxious to express a vague or general concept for which no English word came readily to mind, they would expropriate a word from the classics and edit or extend its meaning to suit their own purposes. Thus the statesman-scholar Sir Thomas Elyot, groping for a single word to express "all manner of lerning, which of some is called the world of science, of other the circle of doctrine" reached into the store-house of ancient Greek and came up with *encyclopaedia*. And again, seeking a word for "the manner of governaunce called in Latin *popularis potentia*, in Englisshe the rule of the comminaltie", Sir Thomas naturalized the Greek word *democratia* into *democracy*. It was Elyot also who first used the word *education* (from the Latin *educare*, meaning specifically "to rear a child") in its modern sense.

The passage of time also produced mutations in the meaning of many words that came into the language on the crest of the classical wave. Some integrated themselves so completely into common English usage that their original connotations have been for ever lost. Today, for example, only Greek scholars are aware that the word *athlete* means literally "a contestant for an *athlon* or prize"; that the word *atom* means something that is "uncut" or "indivisible" (and in modern Greek means simply an "individual person"); that an *acrobat* is a "point-walker", one who walks on his tiptoes; a *character* is an "engraving"; a *catastrophe* is a "down turn"; a *crisis* is a "selection" or "judgment"; and a *protagonist* is the "first actor" in a dramatic troupe. Sir Thomas Elyot's fine word *en-cyclo-paedia*, incidentally, is derived from the Greek words *en kyklos*, meaning "in a circle" and *paideia*, "teaching of children", which perhaps suggested to Elyot the broader connotation of some kind of universal classroom or round-table discussion, hence a compendium of knowledge.

Whenever the classical reservoir failed temporarily to slake their thirst for new expressions, inventive writers and scholars resorted to the old Anglo-Saxon trick of creating hybrid compounds as their forbears had done with French roots and affixes in an earlier century. Now they disported themselves with Greek and Latin suffixes such as *-ism*, *-ist*, and *-ize*, and prefixes such as *anti-*, *co-*, *de-*, *ex-*, *inter-*, *pre-*, and *pro-*, combining them with root words from every strain in England's linguistic past, and thus creating compounds in enormous profusion. The process has never ceased; it continues at the present time, and not least of all in the United States. Among the thousands of quasi-classical compounds that swell the English language today, a sampling of a few random specimens, old and new, might include:

With *-ism* (from the Greek *-ismos*, Latin *-ismus*, denoting a process or result of action): *behaviourism*, *classicism*, *colloquialism*, *Communism*, *Darwinism*, *expressionism*, *Fascism*, *futurism*, *hedonism*, *mannerism*, *modernism*, *nudism*, *realism*.

With *-ist* (from the Greek *-istes*, Latin *-ista*, denoting one who does or makes a practice of): *cellist*, *columnist*, *dentist*, *economist*, *florist*, *individualist*, *jurist*, *manicurist*, *oculist*, *psychiatrist*, *receptionist*, *scientist*, *sexologist*, *socialist*, *terrorist*, *tourist*, *ventriloquist*.

With *-ize* (from the Greek *-izein*, Latin *-izare*, meaning to subject to the action or process defined by the root): *demoralize*, *fraternize*, *hospitalize*, *itemize*, *jeopardize*, *lionize*, *mechanize*, *modernize*, *pressurize*, *socialize*, *solemnize*, *slenderize*, *winterize*.

Insofar as the prefixes are concerned, a quick glance at the dictionary will reveal the hosts of words of every extraction that can begin with any one of them. The Greek prefix *anti-* (meaning against) runs through the long annals of human conflict like a perpetual counterpoint, separating *papists* from *anti-*

papists, *Federalists*, from *anti-Federalists*, *vivisectionists* from *anti-vivisectionists*, *New Dealers* from *anti-New Dealers*, and *segregationists* from *anti-segregationists*. Arrayed opposite them, of course, have always been the *pro's*—the embattled legions who at various times have been *pro-slavery*, *pro-war*, *pro-suffrage*, *pro-German*, *pro-Roosevelt*, or *pro-Castro*. The prefix *ex-* has even wider application; the passing years bestow it on one and all, converting *kings* and *presidents* into *ex-kings* and *ex-presidents*, *wives* into *ex-wives*, *husbands* into *ex-husbands*, *champions* into *ex-champions*, and thus down through all the ranks of humankind. With respect to verbs, the prefixes *de-* and *re-* are equally versatile, for they enable one to reverse or repeat an action with just two letters: one can *nationalize* or *denationalize*, *mobilize* or *demobilize*, *humidify* or *dehumidify*, *compose* or *decompose*, similarly one can *act* and *react*, *write* and *rewrite*, *create* and *re-create*, *tell* and *retell*, *paint* and *repaint*, *negotiate* and *renegotiate*. In a class by itself, towering above all other creations of England's verbal genius, stands the greatest masterpiece of cumulative affixes ever assembled in one place, that splendid, historic cosmopolysyllabic construction: *antidisestablishmentarianism*.

In long-range effect, the great Graeco-Latin invasion involved more than the mere mathematical matter of adding thousands of new words to the English vocabulary. Far more significant was the fact that these new words introduced yet another linguistic element into the already highly variegated national tongue. Thus enriched, English came into full leaf as a medium of literary expression. Poets and playwrights, endowed with a wealth of synonyms found in no other language, were able henceforth to achieve subtle nuances of shading and sound, meaning and metre, that led to the creation of the greatest literature ever engendered by any nation on earth. From the vast lexicon at their disposal, English writers could now pick and choose within a wide range of analagous words of varied linguistic origins. In one context a writer might prefer the Latin *paternal* to the Anglo-Saxon *fatherly*; in another he might favour the native English *youthful* over the Latin *juvenile*. Or for different reasons he might select a word of French derivation as opposed to either the Anglo-Saxon or Latin forms.

The English language thus provides at least two and often

three or more synonyms for most of the general concepts—actions, objects, or qualities—that man has occasion to describe. The literary value of these "doublets" and "triplets" lies in the fact that they are seldom completely synonymous. They differ not only in sound, but usually too in some slight and tenuous variance of interior sense that the percipient eye or ear discerns. It is the challenge of this verbal chiaroscuro that renders the English language such a delicate and, at the same time, difficult medium of artistic expression. A few examples of doublets and triplets from our main linguistic lines reveal the typical range of semantic shading in English synonyms.

ANGLO-SAXON	FRENCH	LATIN
size	*calibre*	*magnitude*
faith	*fealty*	*fidelity*
wretched	*miserable*	
weighty		*ponderous*
blessing	*benison*	*benediction*
reckon	*count*	*compute*
readable		*legible*
kingly	*royal*	*regal*
share	*portion*	*part*
weak	*frail*	*fragile*
watery		*aquatic*
lawful	*loyal*	*legal*
daily	*quotidian*	*diurnal*
	purvey	*provide*
heavenly		*celestial*
same		*identical*
break	*sever*	*separate*
settled	*sure*	*secure*
womanly	*female*	*feminine*
manly	*male*	*masculine*

In the final category, it may be noted, there is also a fourth synonym, *virile* (from the Latin *vir*, man), created no doubt to affirm the adjectival superiority of the manly, masculine male.

During this period of vocabulary expansion, when the language was approaching its era of greatest glory, some of England's most eminent men wrote exclusively in Latin. Sir Thomas More composed his masterpiece *Utopia* (1516) in Latin, whence it was translated into French during his lifetime, but not into English until a generation later. In the next century Sir Francis

Bacon published all of his most important works in Latin. Sir William Harvey, the great surgeon who discovered the circulation of blood, employed Latin to report the final results of his research in 1628. And in 1687 Sir Isaac Newton released his *Principia*, the supreme scientific work of all time, in Latin—not necessarily for love of the language but, as he observed, to spare himself the nuisance of future correspondence with "little meddlers in mathematics".

The craze for the classics and love of Latin did not equally inspirit all constituents of the academic and literary worlds. For there were linguistic patriots then as there are today, defenders of the vernacular, who upheld the excellence of the English tongue and proclaimed its virtues in competition with Latin and Greek as an equally broad and gracious highway to the accumulated knowledge and experience of mankind. Foremost among these champions of English was Richard Mulcaster, Headmaster of the Merchant Taylors' School in London, who exclaimed: "But why not all in English? I do not think that anie language, be it whatsoever, is better able to utter all arguments, either with more pith, or greater planesse, than our English tung is . . . I love Rome, but London better, I favour Italie, but England more, I honour the Latin, but I worship the English." And the poet Sir Philip Sidney (1554–86) declared: "But for the uttering sweetly and properly the conceit of the minde, which is the end of speech, [English] hath it equally with any other tongue in the world."

In addition to such convictions, held by many scholars and writers, other forces contributed to the ultimate victory of English over Latin as the language of literature and learning. One was the increasing popular demand for English translations of the classics. The bright light of the Renaissance had illuminated the intellectual treasures of antiquity. But they were available at first only to those familiar with the ancient tongues. Now, caught up in the intellectual ferment of the times, men in every calling clamoured for access to the classics in English. Along with translations, original English commentaries appeared in profusion. By 1640, a century and a half after Caxton introduced the printing press, more than 20,000 individual works had been published in England in English.

It was with such considerations in mind that Mulcaster, over and above his eloquent eulogy to the English tongue, confessed frankly that he was also desirous of reaching the widest possible audience, for "he that understands Latin very well can understand English farre better". Roger Ascham (1515–68), Regius Professor of Greek at Cambridge and the greatest classical scholar of his day, prefaced one of his books with the remark that although it would have been "easier and fit for my trade in study" to have used either Greek or Latin, nevertheless out of concern for the "pleasure or profit of many . . . I have written this Englishe matter in the Englishe tongue, for Englishe men". There is also on record a letter of rejection from an Elizabethan printer to one Thomas Drant who had submitted a manuscript in Latin. "Though, sir, your book be wise and full of learning," the printer wrote, expressing a worry as prevalent in publishing circles today as in 1567, "peradventure it will not be so saleable."

Historians of our language have estimated that by the end of the great age of Elizabeth and Shakespeare, the English lexicon had been enriched by more than 10,000 new words. Of these by far the largest number (though not all) came from Latin and Greek, and most of them survive today in modern English usage. Those that flourished but briefly and died fell into two categories which purists of the time termed "aureate" and "inkhorn" words. The former referred to fancy, florid words put forth by poets, the latter to pompous, ponderous words produced by pedants. Some aureate words that blossomed briefly early in the classical age were *abusion*, *dispone*, *equipolent*, *palestral*, *sempiterne*. Inkhorn words that irritated contemporary language critics included *lubrical*, *magnificate*, *strenous*, *obstupefact*, *turgidous*, and *ventosity*. A few inkhorn words, though censured at the time, eventually won acceptance in English: *audacious*, *defunct*, *egregious*, *hermaphrodite*, *inflate*, *reciprocal*, *spurious*.

Commenting on such innovations, Ben Jonson wisely remarked: "A man coins not a new word without some peril and less fruit, for if it happens to be received, the praise is but moderate; if refused, the scorn is assured." The short-lived aureate and inkhorn words, however, represented only a small fraction of the total Graeco-Latin invasion. A quantitative study by the late Professor George Lyman Kittredge of Harvard disclosed that out of all the words listed in a standard Latin dictionary one out of every four or five had moved over into the English dictionary and there lives on as a permanent resident today.

In addition to Latin and Greek words, the Elizabethans borrowed freely from other sources. For the fifteenth and sixteenth centuries also witnessed the great age of exploration, world trade, and colonial expansion. As a consequence new and strange words and phrases were borne into England under sail from many far lands. Indeed the vocabulary of the late sixteenth century contains words derived from no less than fifty foreign languages.

Some of the earliest of these came from the Dutch, verbal products of the wool trade, like *pack*, *spool*, *stripe*, and *scour*; or of brewing, like *hops*, *tub*, and *scum*; or painting, like *easel*, *etch*, *sketch*, and *landscape*. But by far the most important group of Dutch loan words reflects the maritime supremacy of Holland up to the middle of the seventeenth century. A great number of the principal terms in our nautical vocabulary are of Dutch origin, among them: *ahoy!*, *avast!*, *belay*, *bowline*, *bowsprit*, *boom*, *buoy*, *commodore*, *cruise*, *deck*, *dock*, *freight*, *iceberg*, *keel*, *leak*, *lighter*, *marline*, *pump*, *schooner*, *skipper*, *sloop*, *yacht*, and *yawl*. Spanish and Italian words also crossed the seas with the growth of international commerce. From Spain at this time came *anchovy*, *armada*, *banana*, *barricade*, *bravado*, *cannibal*, *cargo*, *cocoa*, *desperado*, *embargo*, *escapade*, *hurricane*, *maize*, *mosquito*, *mulatto*, *Negro*, *potato*, *sombrero*, and *tobacco*. (These were only the first of thousands that later entered the language with the development of Latin America.) Meanwhile from Italy came: *balcony*, *cameo*, *cupola*, *design*, *granite*, *grotto*, *piazza*, *portico*, *stanza*, *stucco*, *trill*, *violin*, and *volcano*. And thanks to a steady increase in travel and tourism in France and a growing interest in French literature, the already large body of French words in the English language was augmented further by a number of new imports from Paris, among them *alloy*, *bigot*, *bizarre*, *bombast*, *comrade*, *detail*, *duel*, *entrance*, *equip*, *essay*, *explore*, *genteel*, *moustache*, *naturalize*, *probability*, *progress*, *retrenchment*, *surpass*, *ticket*, *vogue*, and *volunteer*.

The influx of foreign words irritated purists no less than the coining of inkhorn terms. Sir John Cheke, predecessor to Ascham in the Regius chair at Chambridge, wrote in a letter to a friend: "I am of this opinion that our own tung should be written cleane and pure, unmixt and unmangeled with borrowing of other tunges." But the dynamics of the English language defeated conservatives like Cheke who sought to put up barriers against the entry of immigrant words. Its whole tradition had been one of free verbal trade. And the Elizabethan Age was above all one of open intellectual windows, of enlargement, innovation, and adventure. The Elizabethan dramatists were intoxicated by words; they borrowed them, they invented them, they drew on every linguistic resource—and none more exuberantly than Shakespeare. For Shakespeare wielded the largest vocabulary of any writer in any age—20,000 to 25,000 words (depending on the numeration of compounds and inflected forms), as compared with 4,800 in the King James version of the New Testament, 5,642 in the Old Testament, and 8,000 in the works of Milton.

Although the advocates of unadulterated Anglo-Saxon have continued to inveigh against Latin derivatives right down to the present time, every great work of English poetry or prose refutes them with its own inner harmonies produced through the interweaving of Romance and Germanic linguistic tones. Perhaps the best defence of verbal integration or word-mixing was adduced by John Dryden in 1697 in a preface to his own translation of the *Aeneid*: "I will not excuse but justify myself for one pretended crime, with which I am liable to be charged by false critics: that I latinize too much. 'Tis true that when I find an English word, significant and sounding, I neither borrow from the Latin nor any other language. But when I want at home, I must seek abroad. If sounding words are not of our growth and manufacture, who shall hinder me to import them from a foreign country? I carry not out the treasure of the nation, which is never to return; but what I bring from Italy, I spend in England. Here it remains, and here it circulates; for if the coin be good, it will pass from one hand to another. I trade both with the living and the dead for the enrichment of our native language."

It was not simply the magnitude, nor even the variety, of its vocabulary that lifted Elizabethan English to a pinnacle of grandeur unattained before or since; no less important were the daring and virtuosity with which its practitioners put it to use.

Although the underlying skeletal structure of the language had hardened in the patterns set since Chaucer's day, the Elizabethans blithely disregarded many of the grammatical relationships which purists are careful to observe. They looked upon parts of speech as interchangeable—they used nouns for verbs, adjectives for adverbs, and scattered prepositions indiscriminately as their fancy chose. Shakespeare was foremost among these verbal alchemists. He transmuted a noun into a participle in the famous phrase "*stranger'd with an oath*". In *Antony and Cleopatra* he astonishingly used the noun *window* as a verb (in the sense of "placed in a window") when Antony asked: "*Wouldst thou be window'd in great Rome*?" And he fabricated an original verb out of an esoteric Latin adjective in Macbeth's protestation:

"No, this my hand will rather
The multitudinous seas incarnadine."

Similarly in *The Tempest* he employed the adverb *backward* as a noun in the haunting phrase, "*in the dark backward and abysm of time*". In other now-familiar expressions such as "*cudgelling one's brain*", "*breathing one's last*", "*beggaring all description*", "*backing a horse*", Shakespeare beguiled himself by converting the formal functions of words in a way possible only in English, and specifically in Modern English. For it was in the transition from Middle to Modern English that inflexional endings withered and died. In an inflected language like French, for example, one could not use *amour* as a verb or *aimer* as a noun. The reason our ears accept Shakespeare's functional conversions without any sense of strangeness or antiquarian surprise is that we perform the same trick every time we utter a phrase like "*on the make*", "*in the know*", "*dog his steps*", "*contact a client*", "*ape our betters*", "*lord it over others*", "*the haves and have-nots*", "*the might-have-beens*", "*a down-and-outer*", "*he was thoroughly cowed*".

The plasticity of Elizabethan English is seen too in the prevalence of other usages frowned upon today—for example, the double negative which in Shakespeare's time was regarded not as a grammatical crudity but rather as a special form of emphasis, a *strong, strong* negative. Shakespeare could write: "*Thou hast spoken no word all this while—nor understood none neither*", and "*Nor never none shall mistress be of it, save I alone*". The same principle applied to double comparatives and double superlatives such as "*more larger*", "*most boldest*", and Antony's famous "*This was the most unkindest cut of all*".

Apart from a few minor deviations of usage, the English language of the seventeenth century differed little in its fundamentals from twentieth-century English. In its basic structure, in the architecture of its sentences, word order, and word forms, Elizabethan English was Modern English. Among nouns, the old Anglo-Saxon *-n* and *-en* plurals had given way almost completely to the universal *-s*. Among pronouns, the singular *thou*, *thee*, *thy*, and *thine* were swiftly surrendering to the plural *you*, *your*, and *yours* as the common form for both. A few archaisms remained in verb constructions. Where Shakespeare wrote "*Goes the king hence today*?" we now say "*Is the king going away today*?" Instead of Polonius's question, "*What do you read*, *my Lord*?" we now use the progressive form, "*What are you reading*?" With the disappearance of *thou*, the inflexion *-est* in the second person singular also vanished, so instead of "*Whither thou goest*" we now say "*Wherever you go*". Similarly the third-person ending *-eth* was displaced by *-s* (he *tells* instead of *telleth*, *says* instead of *saith*, *does* instead of *doth*). In Chaucer's day the *-eth* inflexion was standard. The *-s* began to take over during the fifteenth century and became dominant in the spoken language by the end of the sixteenth, though the *-eth* ending survived in poetry and formal prose. Shakespeare used both as his iambics and the milieu of his plays dictated.

The principal differences between seventeenth- and twentieth-century English lie mostly in the realm of pronunciation and spelling. To this day, of course, pronunciation varies wildly from place to place within the global domain of the English language, and spelling remains a problem for even the most literate of those born to the tongue. During the Middle English period, spelling was more or less phonetic: that is to say the sounds coincided fairly well with the written symbols—both vowels and consonants—that represented them. The final *e* in words like *name*, *stone*, *dance* was sounded, and the final *ed* in participles like *pierced*, *laughed*, *seemed* was awarded full syllabic value. But in the two centuries between Chaucer and Shakespeare the final *e* in both instances lost its stress and became silent. Thousands of two-syllable words were thus reduced to one.

The other change that occurred in pronunciation between 1400 and 1600 is known as The Great Vowel Shift. In Chaucer's day, the letter *a* was pronounced like the *a* in *farm* or *barn*; the letter *e* was pronounced like the *e* in *they*; the *i* in *kine* sounded like the *ee* in *keen*; *mouse* rhymed with *moose*, and *moon* rhymed with *moan*. But The Great Vowel Shift flattened the Middle English *a* into the *a* of *cat*, and altered the phonetic values of other vowels into approximations of the way they are pronounced today. Meanwhile the spelling remained more or less constant. And it is for this reason that foreigners find themselves so bewildered by the discrepancies between spelling and sound in English. In the early years of the printing press, the confusion was often confounded further by printers who, to "justify" a line of type—line up the right-hand margin of the printed page—added or dropped letters in accordance with their notions of typographical aesthetics. Indeed the notion that spelling should be uniform is an idea of relatively recent inception. The Elizabethans could not have cared less, and Shakespeare spelled his own name in different ways at different times.

Of all the linguistic events of the sixteenth and seventeenth centuries, perhaps the most important was the inception of a blazing sense of pride among the English in the opulence of their native tongue. The virtuosity of the great playwrights, Marlowe, Jonson, and Shakespeare, as well as the poets, Donne, Herbert, Herrick, and others, impressed upon the word-loving English people the orchestral power and splendour of the language to which they were born. As a consequence of their national, linguistic pride, English became an object of study and analysis. Its users became self-conscious and introspective. Criticism was born, and with it the long slow drift toward rules of style, standardization of spelling, precepts of grammar and syntax, and all the other controls that the unfettered Elizabethans never knew.

The English language attained its final fullness of fruition at the start of the seventeenth century—in a decade within which Shakespeare produced his greatest plays, and the gifted translators and authors of the King James version of the Bible completed their collaborative masterpiece. Now at last, English speech which started as a trickle of dialects in the earliest dawn-light of history had become a swelling mainstream that would spread its influence around the world. The language would continue to evolve. But in its lifetime up to now it has never surpassed and rarely equalled this age of glory. In the words of the literary historian George Saintsbury: "The plays of Shakespeare and the English Bible are, and ever will be the twin monuments not merely of their own period, but of the perfection of English, the complete expression of the literary capacities of the language at a time when it had lost none of its pristine vigour, and had put on enough but not too much of the adornments and the limitations of what may be called literary civilization."

As a twentieth-century scholar, Saintsbury was able to look back and evaluate Elizabethan English with respect to what came afterward. More significant, perhaps, is the prophetic insight of the great educator Richard Mulcaster, whose long career coincided with the most brilliant years of Tudor history. Sensing somehow that the English language was in its era of greatest lustre, Mulcaster asserted: "I take this present period of our English tongue to be the very height thereof, because I find it so excellently well fined, both for the body of the tongue itself, and for the customary writing thereof. When the age of our people, which now use the tongue so well, is dead and departed there will another succeed, and with the people the tongue will alter and change. Which change in the full harvest thereof may prove comparable to this, but sure for this which we now use, it seemeth even now to be at the best for substance, and the bravest for circumstance, and whatsoever shall become of the English state, the English tongue cannot prove fairer than it is at this day."

Mulcaster died in 1611. Just four years earlier, in 1607, Captain John Smith and a small group of English settlers landed at Jamestown, in what is now Virginia, and founded the first English colony in America. The language they brought with them was the fair tongue which Mulcaster loved and advocated so well.

5

VARIATIONS ON THEMES BY SHAKESPEARE

England and America are two countries separated by the same language.

GEORGE BERNARD SHAW (1856–1950)

In the century that saw its full flowering in the poems and plays of the Elizabethan Age, the English language began its circumnavigation of the world. Its first syllables had reached the Western Hemisphere in 1497 when John Cabot, an Italian-born explorer in British employ, sailed from Bristol across the uncharted ocean and claimed Newfoundland in the name of King Henry VII. Although many ships of other nations soon spread nets upon the teeming waters of the Grand Banks, Cabot's claim held fast, and a contemporary chronicler, Anthony Parkhurst, wrote in 1578 that "the English are commonly lords of the harbours where they fish". Soon thereafter Queen Elizabeth granted letters to Sir Humphrey Gilbert, commanding him to establish a colony on Newfoundland's bleak shore. But the harsh climate and bitter trade rivalry frustrated English attempts to colonize Newfoundland on a durable basis for another half-century. Meanwhile, farther south, Captain John Smith planted the first permanent English settlement in North America at Jamestown in 1607. And in 1620 the *Mayflower* landed at Plymouth Rock.

The enormous wilderness of Canada, first pioneered by French *voyageurs* who called it New France, became British territory in the middle of the eighteenth century. The English-speaking community of Halifax was founded on the south-east coast of Nova Scotia in 1749. A decade later, in the decisive battle of the Plains of Abraham, a British army captured the French citadel of Quebec and thus opened the way for the march of English westward to the Great Lakes and beyond. And in 1776 the American Revolution, though a setback to England's colonial ambitions, created a vigorous new domain wherein English speech would flourish and diversify remarkably in years to come.

On the other side of the globe, the process of linguistic expansion was also gaining headway. It had begun in 1600 with the founding of the East India Company in response to the Dutch maritime challenge. Within the next few decades the first English-speaking settlements in Asia were established at Madras, Bombay, and Calcutta. Midway in the eighteenth century the English language reached the antipodes, when Captain Cook raised the English flag over New Zealand and Australia. In 1795 it came to Africa with the occupation of Cape Town, and thence spread gradually northward to the Nile.

Thus radiating to all points of the compass from London town across thousands of miles of perilous seas, the winds of trade and business enterprise conveyed the language of England in its literary heyday to the far places of both hemispheres. It was during this century and a half of empire-building that English, transcending its limited use as the local tongue of a small island in the North Sea, began to grow into an international language echoing around the world. Writing in 1754, Lord Chesterfield remarked on the "sensible pleasure" he experienced "in reflecting upon the rapid progress which our language has lately made, and still continues to make". In this progress the already cosmopolitan vocabulary of English continued to be enlarged and enriched by the addition of many thousands of words from strange and distant lexicons and by many new words invented to meet changing needs.

1.

Of all modulations of English spoken in the world today, American English is the oldest, as well as the most influential and farflung. For although England's trading colonies in India antedated those in the New World by a few years, British influence in the East remained inconsequential until the collapse of the Mogul Empire in the middle of the eighteenth century. But the growth of the English language in America has been continuous and uninterrupted from the start.

The first colonists arrived in America at a time when the plays of Shakespeare, Marlowe, and Ben Jonson were magnificently unfolding the splendours of their native tongue—the time of *Hamlet*, *Macbeth*, *Doctor Faustus*, and *Volpone*. The language that disembarked at Jamestown and Plymouth was Elizabethan English, rich and resourceful, fluid and flexible, ready to borrow and invent, quick to clip or compound words, or to interchange parts of speech. And so, since the colonial period when the Old World and the New were separated by vast spans of open sea and months of travel time, the American language has sailed down its own roadsteads on a course of its own devising.

Many features of standard American speech—so-called "Americanisms", words and idioms which purists on both sides of the Atlantic have noted and often deplored—were inventions contrived to meet the necessities of a new existence and made possible by the virtuosity of the English tongue. For how else were the pioneers to describe the features of a strange new land, mantled with strange trees and shrubs, haunted by strange animals, flecked with strange birds, and peopled by strange aborigines speaking a strange language and pursuing strange ways of life? Many Americanisms are borrowings from this strange language. Yet curiously, many others are in fact archaisms, relics of the pure Elizabethan speech imported by the original colonists and preserved in the United States, while the mother tongue of the homeland gradually digressed and diverged from the seventeenth-century forms and accents once shared in common.

The survival of these Elizabethan elements in American speech is, however, no unique linguistic phenomenon. All transplanted languages tend to preserve their conservative features. Today similar vestiges of the past live on in Canadian French, in Icelandic Norse, and in the Spanish of Latin America, though they have long since evaporated from the ancient fountains of speech whence once they sprang. The fact that many Americanisms are actually survivors from the golden age of English literature has been known to scholars for more than a century. It inspired James Russell Lowell's dry observation that the American colonists "unhappily could bring over no English better than Shakespeare's".

The areas of divergence between American and British

English exist mostly in vocabulary and pronunciation—the spoken word. Literary English remains more or less standard on all continents. Differences in grammar and syntax are inconsequential, and where they do appear it is often American English that has preserved the earlier form. A notable example is found in the past participle of the verb *to get*. Americans employ two forms—*got* and *gotten*. In the United States one may say "I've got five dollars"—connoting present possession. One also say "I've just gotten a new car"—indicating recent acquisition. An Englishman never uses *gotten*; he considers it incorrect, discordant, and an Americanism. But *gotten* was once the proper participial form. In Middle English the infinitive of the verb *to get* was *geten*; the past tense was *gat* (still very much with us in the Old Testament's list of "begats"); and the past participle was *getten*. In time *gat* became *got*, and *getten* became *gotten*. Toward the middle of the seventeenth century the final syllable of *gotten* withered and faded away in England, though it flourishes as lustily as ever in both written and spoken American usage today.

Another small grammatical distinction between British and American English lies in the treatment of collective nouns—like *government*, *crowd*, *company*, *team*. In England the tendency is to regard such words as plural and to follow them with plural verbs and pronouns: "The government have committed themselves to . . ." An analogous sentence in the United States would read: "The administration has committed itself to . . ." Similarly, in another domain, a British newspaper reporting a regatta won by the crew of Jesus College, Oxford, might headline its story: "JESUS ROW TO CLOSE VICTORY". But on the other side of the Atlantic every baseball fan can quote the immortal remark of the Brooklyn Dodgers' former manager, Charlie Dressen: "The Giants is dead".

In spelling as in grammar the differences between Old and New World English are few and relatively unimportant. Many derive from Noah Webster, compiler of America's first great dictionary and an advocate of spelling reform, who as early as 1789 urged the amputation of the *k* from *critick*, *frolick*, and *publick*. On this point he won victory on both sides of the Atlantic. But his campaign to change the vestigial French *-our* and *-re* endings of certain nouns to *-or* and *-er* succeeded only in his native land. So today Americans write *color*, *favor*, *honor*, *humor*, *odor*, while the British cling to *colour*, *favour*, *honour*, *humour*, *odour*; similarly Americans prefer *center*, *fiber*, *somber*, *theater* to the British *centre*, *fibre*, *sombre*, *theatre*. (America still adheres, however, to *acre*, *lucre*, *massacre*, and *ogre*.) Webster also proposed dropping one *l* from *traveller and travelled*. Hence in a great class of words like *canceled*, *chiseled*, *equaled*, *jeweled*, *labeled*, *rivaled*, *totaled*, et cetera, American form now elects the single *l* where British requires two.

Certain other vestiges of the long history of the language which survive in England have vanished from American orthography. Americans have cropped the Greek and Latin diphthongs *oe* and *ae* in such words as *amoeba*, *diarrhoea*, *encyclopaedia*, *hyaena*, *mediaeval*, and *palaeontology*, so in the United States they appear as *ameba*, *diarrhea*, *encyclopedia*, *medieval*, and *paleontology*. Similarly French forms like *catalogue*, *cheque*, *gramme*, *omelette*, and *programme*, have been curtailed and anglicized in American spelling to *catalog*, *check*, *gram*, *omelet*, and *program*. The general tendency among writers and editors in the United States has been to eliminate unnecessary letters. Over the years American spelling has reduced the British *aluminium* to *aluminum*, *aeroplane* to *airplane*, *axe* to *ax*, *draught* to *draft*, *hiccough* to *hiccup* (though we retain the *ough* elsewhere), *idyll* to *idyl*, *mould* to *mold*, *phial* to *vial*, *plough* to *plow*, *waggon* to *wagon*, and *woollen* to *woolen*. In a few instances, however, it is the British who have adopted contracted forms. Where Americans write *burned*, *learned*, *leaned*, *spelled*, *spilled*, and *spoiled*, the British generally prefer *burnt*, *learnt*, *leant*, *spilt*, and *spoilt*. And, as opposed to the American *connection*, *inflection*, and *reflection*, British style inclines towards *connexion*, *inflexion*, and *reflexion*.

It is not always possible, therefore, to generalize about the distinctions between British and American spelling. Only the most exhaustive etymological research can uncover the reasons for some mutations. Why, for example, does an American writer describe a colour as *gray* while an Englishman sees it as *grey*? Both forms of the word go back through Middle English *gray* and *grey* to Old English *græg* and *grēg*—both of which stemmed from the earlier old Frisian *grē*. Thus after some 1,500 years of peaceful coexistence *gray* has triumphed in the United States and *grey* in England. Equally complex histories underlie the

American's preference for a *brier* pipe to a *briar*, and explain why he likes *catsup* better than *ketchup*, takes *offense* rather than *offence*, stands on the *curb* instead of the *kerb*, prefers *pajamas* to *pyjamas*, and changes a *tire*, not a *tyre*.

Yet it is amid the rocky ranges of pronunciation that the deepest chasms of the English-speaking world lie gaping. "We and the Americans have much in common," Oscar Wilde once observed, "but there is always the language barrier." Pronunciation varies with time, as well as in space, and many of the accents and intonations of the United States today derive from those which the seventeenth-century settlers transplanted to American soil. A good number of those initial immigrants were educated citizens of the middle class, schooled at a time when standards of English were becoming stabilized around the idiom of the Tudor court and literary London, whence they radiated outward to the surrounding shires. The great majority of the pioneers who arrived in the first wave of immigration came from the southern and eastern counties nearest London, and their speech contained many intonations that still echo in the accents of New England and Virginia today. The nasal twang so often disparaged as a jarring American peculiarity in fact originated in East Anglia, chief stronghold of the Puritans, and was long associated with Puritans in England by various British writers, among them Shelley who, in a vignette of an unpleasantly pious Puritan, wrote:

His eyes turned up, his mouth turned down;
His accent caught a nasal twang.

In seventeenth-century England, no less than in England and America today, regional dialects varied widely. Sir Walter Raleigh, for example, spoke with a broad Devonshire accent. And even among the London literati, uncertainties of pronunciation were rife. Elizabethan poetry reveals that no hard and fast sound barrier lay between the long *e* of *meet* and the long *a* of *mate*. Shakespeare rhymed *please* alternatively with *knees* and *grace*; elsewhere he made puns indicating an identity or near-identity of the vowel sounds in *grace*, *grass*, and *grease*. He also rhymed *grapes* with *mishaps*, *serve* with *carve*, and *convert* with *art*. Queen Elizabeth wrote *defar* for *defer*, *parson* for *person*, *wark* for *work*, *hiar* for *hear*, and *hard* for *heard*. It is clear that the *ar* sound in such words was correct in Elizabethan English, and it remained so until the end of the eighteenth century. Today in England only a few traces of it remain—e.g. in the words *clerk* and *Derby*, which in British speech are still pronounced *clark* and *Darby*. In America it is embalmed in the writings of nineteenth-century comic dialecticians—in such phrases as "book-larnin' ".

Inasmuch as three centuries have elapsed since the advent of the colonists, it is not surprising that the accents and inflexions of England and America have grown apart. Many of the divergences derive from the preservation by descendants of the first settlers, and transmission from generation to generation, of archaic but once perfectly correct forms of pronunciation that have gradually become obsolete in England. One of the most striking instances of phonetic deviation—indeed a badge of nationality in the English-speaking world—is the contrasting treatment of the letter *a* in such sentence as: *The calf came down the path to take a bath.* Where most Americans, confronted with these words, use the flat *a* of *cat*, most Englishmen (save in the North) employ the long *a* of *father*, and the sentence emerges from his lips as: *The cahff came down the pahth to take a bahth.* Such a pronunciation was unknown in Elizabethan times, at least not in polite court circles where *calf*, *path*, and *bath* were pronounced as they are in America today. As late as 1791 an English pronouncing dictionary classified the broad *a* as vulgar and the flat *a* as "characteristic of the elegant and learned world". Precisely why the broad *a* began to gain a foothold is not known, but its origins were, ironically, Cockney. Not until the second quarter of the nineteenth century did it become a hallmark of the cultivated accent in British society. It is in American speech, therefore, that the older "elegant" pronunciation has been preserved, while the adoption of a once-vulgar form occurred in the linguistic homeland.

An equally notable divergence between English and American speech developed with changing articulations of the letter *r*—especially in such words as *bird*, *word*, *heard*, *infer*, *learn*, and *turn*. Before Shakespeare's time the individual vowels in these words had quite separate and distinct values: the *i* in *bird* was pronounced like the *i* in *bid*; the *o* in *word* was like the *o* in *worn*; the *ea* in *heard* was like the *ea* in *health*; the *e* in *infer* was like the *e* in *infect*; and the *u* in *turn* was equivalent to the *oo* in *took* (hence *toorn*). During the sixteenth century these separate combinations, having in common only the letter *r*, began to converge into a uniform pronunciation approximating the sound *err*. The merging process apparently originated in the lower- or lower-middle-class dialect of London as early as 1560, and then crept gradually upward through various shadings into educated and court circles. Today poets on both shores of the Atlantic can rhyme *learn* and *turn*, *firm* and *worm*, and *bird*, *inferred*, *heard*, *word*, and *curd*.

At this time, another evolutionary process had also come into play. Little by little the consonantal strength of the *r* slowly waned in southern England and by the end of the eighteenth century it had faded away entirely. In Walker's *Critical Pronouncing Dictionary*, published in 1791, it is noted that "in England, and particularly in London, the *r* in *bar*, *bard*, *card*, *regard*, etc. is pronounced so much in the throat as to be little more than the middle or Italian *a*, lengthened into *baa*, *baad*, *caad*, *regaad*". Transplanted to America by the settlers of New England, this mannerism has flourished and still flourishes in the vicinity of Boston. It provides the distinctive colour of the so-called "Haavaad accent". Elsewhere in America, notably in the West and Midwest, the strong consonantal *r* resounds vigorously, perpetuated by the descendants of later waves of immigrants from the northern English counties and Scotland.

Modulations of cadence and stress also differentiate the quality of British speech from that of the United States. In such words as *dictionary*, *necessary*, *oratory*, and *secretary*, the trailing syllables receive full value from Americans, while the British swallow them, so that the words emerge as *diction'ry* *necess'ry*, *orat'ry*, and *secret'ry*. Here again it is the American pronunciation which has descended from Elizabethan times and the British which represents a modern elision. For the existence of the secondary stress in Shakespeare's day is clearly revealed by the scansion of Hamlet's famous line, *Nor customary suits of solemn black*. Summing up the differences between America and British pronunciation, the famed English actor, George Arliss, once remarked: "The chief fault in speech in America is sloppiness and the outstanding defect in England is snippiness."

It is in the field of vocabulary, however, that American English can best lay claim to being, if not a separate language (as some linguistic chauvinists like to insist), at least the most important tributary in the great mainstream of our common tongue. In colonial America, as elsewhere in the expanding British empire, new words were invented, improvised, borrowed, and translated from native lexicons to describe new things, experiences, flora and fauna, occupations and activities for which no counterparts existed in England. New and special vocabularies came into being and, as they circulated, many words worked back into the central treasury of the English tongue.

The first borrowings to enter the language from America were Indian words. At the time of the colonial landings an estimated one million aboriginal tribesmen, sparsely distributed and fragmented by some 350 languages, ranged the enormous wilderness of the North American continent. Since most of the main linguistic families with which the settlers came in contact —Algonquian and Iroquoian in the east, Muskogean in the south, Siouan in the Great Plains region, and Uto-Aztecan in the south-west—contained sounds which do not occur in English, the pioneers could only approximate them in speech and spelling. Hence the word *raccoon*—one of the very first Indian words to enter the English language—made its début in Captain John Smith's *A True Relation*, published in 1608, with a thick Algonquian accent as *rahaugcum*, *raugroughcum*, and *raughroughcums*. Some years later, Smith honed down the spelling to *rarowcun*. But it was not until 1672 that the raccoon finally emerged in its present neat phonetic attire. Another animal described by Smith as having "an head like a swine, a taile like a rat, and is of the bigness of a cat", entered the arena in 1610 as an *apossoun*, in 1612 as an *opassom*, but not until 1763 as an *opossum*. Through similar mutations the Narragansett word *moosu* (meaning "he trims smooth", i.e. he strips branches and bark from trees when feeding) became *mus* by 1613, *mose* by 1637, and *moose* in 1672. Other early loan words lifted by the colonists from the Indians' lexicon of nature were: *hickory* (from *pawcohiccora*), *persimmon* (from *putchamin*), *muskrat* (from *musk-wessu*), *skunk* (from *seganku* or *segongu*, later *squunck*), and *wood-chuck* (from *otchock*).

Besides new animals and plants, the settlers were confronted also with new objects, artifacts, and concepts unique to Indian culture. Here too they simply appropriated the native terms: e.g. *hominy*, *moccasin*, *papoose*, *pemmican*, *powpow*, *squaw*, *tepee*, *terrapin*, and *wigwam*. In the naming process some words were taken over into English virtually intact, others were abbreviated or revised. The Narragansett *askútasquash* was shortened to *squash*, *misikquatash* was simplified to *succotash* and *wampampeag* was reduced to *wampum*. Sometimes the settlers, instead of borrowing an Indian expression outright, translated it into English. The term *firewater* is a literal translation of the Algonquian *scoutiouabou*; *paleface* is English for the Ojibway *wâbinêsi-win*. Other Anglo-Saxon renderings of Indian terms, real or imagined, produced such well-known compounds as *warpath*, *war paint*, *war club*, *peace pipe*, and *Great White Father*. Language scholars estimate that, all told, the American Indian enriched the English language by some 1,700 words—counting both straight loan words and derivatives—of which about half were in common use by the end of the seventeenth century.

Perhaps the greatest heritage bequeathed by the red man to the United States, however, may be seen on the map—in the profusion of Indian place names. At the dawn of the colonial period the homesick pioneers nostalgically transplanted English names to American soil—like Jamestown and Plymouth Rock. Hence there are in the United States today 28 Newports, 22 Londons and New Londons, 19 Bristols, 19 Bostons and New Bostons, 15 Princetons, and 12 Richmonds. But as they pushed deeper into the wilderness the settlers increasingly retained local Indian names for rivers, mountains, lakes, and other features of the landscape. Today more than half of the states in the Union bear names of Indian origin; so do four out of five of the Great Lakes, several mountain ranges, the nation's longest river, second city, and greatest waterfall, and more than a thousand assorted waterways, lakes, and ponds. The state of Maine especially is liberally splattered with such names as Allagash, Caucomgomac, Chemquassabamticook, Oquossoc, Passadumkeag, and Unsuntabunt. The first Indian place-name appropriated by the colonists was *Rarenawok*—which survives today in mutated form as Roanoke, Virginia.

The Indians provided only the initial freshet in the torrent of new words that soon would swell the reservoir of the American language. For increasingly as the years passed, the colonists coined, rather than borrowed, terms of their own to describe indigenous features of their adopted homeland. Among their earliest creations were *ground hog* (1656) and *bullfrog* (1698). Later they invented *black alder*, *catfish*, *canvasback*, *katydid*, *mockingbird*, *mud hen*, *potato bug*, *sweet potato*, and *whippoorwill*. The Lewis and Clark Expedition of 1803 gave names to no fewer than 412 previously unrecorded plants and animals which were observed on their historic trip to the Far West—among them *bull snake*, *catbird*, *copperhead*, *cottonwood*, *ground squirrel* and *tumblebug*. Features of the landscape unknown in England presented a challenge, and the pioneers met it by coining new terms—*bottomland*, *underbrush*, *water gap*—or else by endowing existing words with new meanings, as in the case of *bluff* and *creek*.

As their initial holdings enlarged, the English colonists increasingly came in contact with their competitors—the French, Spanish, and Dutch—who were also endeavouring to carve chunks of empire from the apparently unbounded wilderness. At many points of encounter along the broken and disputed frontier, the rival languages met and mingled, and words—of various kinds—were exchanged.

From the French *voyageurs* and *coureurs des bois*, the Anglo-American settlers picked up such useful words as *butte*, *charivari* (now often *shivaree*), *chowder* (from *chaudière*), *gopher* (from *gaufre* meaning honeycomb), *levee*, *prairie*, *rapids*, and (via French from Indian) *bayou*, *caribou*, and *toboggan*. With the Louisiana Purchase in 1803 they acquired *praline*, *picayune* (originally the French name for a Spanish coin), and *buccaneer* (applied first to early French settlers in the West Indies).

Like the French, the Dutch had previously exported a wealth of words—particularly involving painting, weaving, and navigation—to their English neighbours across the Channel prior to the seventeenth century. Now in America they handed over a few more to their English neighbours in New Amsterdam

—*boss*, *coleslaw*, *cookie*, *cranberry*, *dumb* (meaning stupid), *Santa Claus*, *sleigh*, *snoop*, *spook*, *stoop* (a small porch), *waffle*, and *Yankee* (a corruption of Jan Kees, meaning "John Cheese", a derisive nickname applied to Dutchmen by their rivals in the New World as early as 1683). Their most important gift to the American language was the almighty *dollar*[1]—from the Dutch *dalar*, from the German *thaler*. The so-called Pennsylvania Dutch, as opposed to the New York Dutch, were actually Germans from the Rhenish Palatinate who migrated to America in the seventeenth century. To eighteenth-century American menus they gave the *noodle*, the *pretzel*, and *sauerkraut*. Other German specialities followed later.

Of all the European languages which have augmented the American vocabulary, none has contributed more liberally than Spanish. With the opening of the West, following the Mexican War and the California gold rush of 1848, Spanish words of many categories became part of everyday speech in the western and south-western portions of the United States. Among these early loan words were: topographical terms like *canyon*, *mesa*, and *sierra*; mining terms like *bonanza*, *Eldorado*, *placer*; building terms like *adobe*, *patio*, *plaza*; articles of clothes like *chaps* (from *chapareras*), *poncho*, *sombrero*; legal terms like *calaboose* (from *calabozo*, dungeon or jail), *desperado*, *incommunicado*, *hoosegow* (from *juzgado*, court of justice); articles of food like the *tortilla*, and (via Spanish from Indian) *chile*, and *tequila;* ranching terms like *buckaroo* (from *vaquero*), *bronco*, *burro*, *cinch*, *corral*, *coyote* (via Spanish from Indian), *lariat*, *lasso*, *mustang*, *ranch*, *rodeo*, *stampede*, and *vamoose* (from *vamos*, "Let's go."). Two of the most interesting Spanish loan words are *cockroach* and *tornado*. The former (from *cucaracha*) is one of the very oldest borrowings, first mentioned by Captain John Smith in 1624; the latter, a pure Spanish word, is also pure American, for only in the United States do tornadoes occur. The state name *California* itself is a Catalan word signifying—though its Chamber of Commerce does not publicize the fact—"hot oven". Profuse as they were, these early borrowings represented only the vanguard of far greater hosts of Spanish words that would

[1] Established as the monetary unit of the United States by Congress, July 6, 1787.

invade the American language in the twentieth century with the gradual knitting of Western Hemisphere ties.

Keeping pace with the weedlike growth of the American vernacular as it spread across prairies, deserts, and mountains to the Pacific Ocean, thirstily absorbing foreign words and phrases on every frontier, was another more orderly process of growth—a growth of national pride in the language of America and an increasing sense that it had entered on a destiny of its own, distinct from that of the mother tongue in England. This feeling, this new lingustic awareness began with the winning of independence and the founding of the American republic.

On September 5, 1780, John Adams addressed a letter to Congress proposing an academy "for refining, correcting, improving and ascertaining the English language". Pointing out that England had failed to establish such an institution despite the precedents of Italy's Accademia della Crusca and the Académie française, Adams asserted that an American Academy would have "a happy effect" upon the new republic, for "all the states of the Union are so democratized that eloquence will become the instrument for recommending men to their fellow citizens and the principal means of advancement through the various ranks and offices of society". Prophetically he added: "English is destined to be in the next and succeeding centuries more generally the language of the world than Latin was in the last or French is in the present age. The reason of this is obvious, because the increasing population in America, and their universal connection and correspondence with all nations will . . . force their language into general use."

Adams was not alone in his conviction that isolation from Europe would result in the development of a new and vigorous language in America. Thomas Jefferson thought that the evolution of English in the United States would eventually "separate it in name as well as in power from the mother-tongue". And Noah Webster foresaw in the future "a language in North America as different from the future language of England as the modern Dutch, Danish and Swedish are from the German or from one another". Like many of his contemporaries, Webster already looked on England as a foreign nation whose language was "on the decline" and should no longer be regarded as a model. He felt that it was the duty of Americans to develop a national and independent speech of their own, free from regional dialects and attuned to standards of literary excellence. In these views Webster was staunchly supported not only by writers and educators but by statesmen who, still fearful of possible disintegration of the newly formed republic, saw clearly the importance of a uniform, national idiom as an enduring bond of union.

To this end Webster devoted his life. In 1783—just five years after his graduation from Yale—Webster brought out the first volume of his *Grammatical Institute of the English Language*. This was America's first speller, and it swiftly became a standard text in every school and household in the land, selling at the rate of one million copies a year (though the total United States' population then was barely 23 million). The second and third volumes of the *Grammatical Institute* consisted of a grammar and a reader, and these too enjoyed immediate success not only in the United States but in England. From the substantial income his trilogy produced (Webster was a canny businessman who fought for copyright enforcement), he obtained the leisure to compile his greatest work, his *American Dictionary of the English Language*. From the moment of its initial publication in 1828, Webster's *Dictionary* became the supreme arbiter of American speech.

Webster's services to the language were abetted by the schoolteacher who employed his texts in class and the Yankee pedlar who brought them to the smallest villages of the far frontier. Two other factors accelerated the growth of the national idiom: the mobility of the population and the flexibility of a social order in which the ancient class distinctions of England had been consciously erased. These developments did not go unnoticed in English literary circles. The first rumblings of disapproval were voiced even before the Revolution. As early as 1756 Dr. Samuel Johnson, in reviewing a book by an American author, denounced its "mixture of American dialect" as "a tract of corruption to which every language widely diffused must always be exposed". In 1808 several critical journals fired salvos across the Atlantic. *The Annual* excoriated "the torrent of barbarous phraseology", pouring from America, which threatened "to destroy the purity of the English language". And *The*

Edinburgh Review discovered in an American book "a great multitude of words which are radically and entirely new, and as utterly foreign as if they had been adopted from the Hebrew or Chinese".

Webster's *Dictionary* contained some 12,000 words that had not appeared in Johnson's or any other dictionary. A few months after its publication the great lexicographer was interviewed by a Scottish traveller, Captain Basil Hall, who reported later that "We had a pleasant discussion on the use of what are called Americanisms". He quoted Webster as saying that Americans not only had a right to invent new words but had been compelled to do so by the circumstances of their life in a new land.

"It is quite impossible to stop the progress of language," Webster said. "Words and expression will be forced into use, in spite of all the exertions of all the writers in the world."

"Yes," Hall said. "But surely such inventions are to be deprecated?"

"I don't know that," Webster said. "If a word becomes universally current in America, where English is spoken, why should it not take its station in the language?"

"Because," Hall said, "there are words enough already."

The voluble American populace disagreed. The national linguistic mood had been set by Jefferson, when he declared: "Certainly so great growing a population, spread over such an extent of country, must enlarge their language. . . . The new circumstances under which we are placed call for new words, new phrases, and for the transfer of old words to new objects." And so the new words came in a deluge, from every domain of American activity, from cities and farms, from industry and science, from ranching and railroading, and from the swelling streams of immigrants who converged on the new open country from all parts of Europe. The protests of purists went unheeded.

In 1832 Mrs. Frances Trollope remarked in her acidulous and sensational book *Domestic Manners of the Americans*: "I very seldom, during my whole stay in the country, heard a sentence elegantly turned and correctly pronounced from the lips of an American. There is always something either in the expression or the accent that jars the feelings and shocks the taste." A decade later Charles Dickens, while touring America, wrote to his family: "I need not tell you that the prevailing grammar is more than doubtful; that the oddest vulgarisms are received idioms."

Many of the contemporary idioms did indeed sound odd and vulgar, jarring taste and shocking the discrimination of polite British ears, for they were products of a time that never existed before or since, a free and easy time of expanding horizons and boundless promise. The national hero was Andrew Jackson, epitomized by H. L. Mencken as "the archetype of the new American—ignorant, pushful, impatient of restraint and precedent, an iconoclast, a Philistine, an Anglophobe in every fiber". The legendary heroes of the western frontier were supermen like Paul Bunyan, who could fell trees with a single blow of his double-edged axe, and John Henry, who could carry a bale of cotton under each arm and two more on his head. The frontiersmen themselves were noisy adventurers who liked to claim, each one, that he could out-drink, out-eat, out-run, out-fight, and out-talk anyone else in the woolly West. Their admiration for the big and bombastic found its verbal outlet in tall talk—in wild hyperbole, extravagant epithet, and the invention of grotesque words like *bulldoze*, *caboodle*, *cantankerous*, *catawampus*, *combobberation*, *helliferocious*, *highfalutin*, *hornswoggle*, *obfusticate*, *rambunctious*, *sockdologer*, and *spondulicks*. The taste for such bizarre and mouth-filling creations goes back to Elizabethan times. That this taste still persists, little abated today, is evidenced by the currency in recent years of such coinages as *boondoggling*, *gobbledygook*, *supercolossal*, *snollygoster* (used by President Truman in 1952), and in sports, signifying determination and drive on the part of an athletic team, *the old huckleby-buck and spizzerinkum.*

Over and above such fanciful concoctions, the frontiersmen produced some vivid and lasting phrases—metaphors and similes that have become virtually clichés of American speech. It was from their knowledge of the outdoor world that they originated expressions like to *back water*, *make a beeline*, *make tracks*, *make the fur fly*, *play possum*, *work like a beaver*, *bark up the wrong tree*, *chip on the shoulder*, *mad as a hornet*, *cross as a bear*, *settle one's hash*, and *horse sense*. And from their acquaintance with Indians came *go on the war path* and *bury the hatchet.*

In the vanguard of the frontiersmen were gold miners. Many of these were *roughnecks*, who liked to sit down to a *square meal* and get drunk at a *stag party*, but did their best to avoid a *shotgun wedding*. When things *panned out*, they *struck it rich*, whereupon they *splurged* and *painted the town red*. But sometimes things *petered out*; then they either *jumped a claim* or *pulled up stakes* and *lit out* in quest of a *boom town* where some day they might hope to *do a land-office business*. The rich vocabulary of the forty-niners, in addition to producing new words like *hoodlum* and *deadbeat*, also preserved a number of archaisms from rural English dialects, such as *gully*, *gulch*, *gumption*, and *deck* (as opposed to *pack* of cards).

Following the first wave of pioneers and prospectors came the farmers, pushing westward with their families via *covered wagon*, *prairie schooner*, *buckboard*, and *shay*. Some negotiated the first leg of their journey down the Ohio River by *flatboat* or *keelboat*. Some became *homesteaders*; others were mere *squatters* for whom home was no more than a *log cabin* and a small *lot* enclosed by a *stump fence* to confine the cow. The lucky ones who prospered in the *corn belt* or the *wheat belt* or who found good *stamping grounds* farther west could afford *hired hands*. For many the only contact with their kin back east was an occasional letter by *Pony Express*. From farflung settlements in all parts of the land a profusion of colourful farming terms soon entered the vernacular: *talk turkey*, *kick like a steer*, *fly off the handle*, *have an axe to grind*, *hold your horses*, and not worth a *hill of beans*.

It was not only on the frontier that Americans invented words. Back east the genius of their technology produced the *cotton gin*, the *telegraph* and *telephone*, the *sewing machine*, the *elevator*, the *escalator*, the *electric chair*, the *refrigerator*, and the *skyscraper* (originally an eighteenth-century nautical term applied to the topmost skysail). Individual inventors gave their names to the *Bowie knife*, the *Colt revolver*, the *Pullman car*, and the *Maxim machine gun*. Benjamin Franklin invented the *Franklin stove*.

American business has also enriched American English. From Wall Street came *boom* and *bust*, *bulls* and *bears*, *bucket shop*, *gilt-edged stock*, and *watered stock*; from industry, the *assembly line*, *payroll*, *trademark*, and *troubleshooter*; and from the turbulent annals of labour, *strike*, *sit-down strike*, *sweatshop*, *lockout*, *cooling-off period*, *take-home pay*, *goon*, *scab*, and *white-collar worker*.

Perhaps the most fertile seedbed of American word-coinage has been the field of politics. Since every nation's history lies imbedded in its native lexicon it is not surprising that many of America's political terms speak with unmistakably rustic accents. Doubtful candidates are *dark horses*, local candidates are *favourite sons*, defeated incumbents are *lame ducks*, bold campaigners stand *foursquare* on the party *platform*, cagey ones *sit on the fence*. In the big cities a politician may be backed by a *machine* or he may be a *rabble-rouser*. But all of them hope for a *landslide*.

America's political past is populated by many strange creatures—*carpetbaggers*, *mavericks*, *mugwumps*, and *scalawags*—all of complex ancestry. But of all our native political terms, none entered the American lexicon by such a devious route as the word *filibuster*. During the sixteenth century when the Dutch merchant marine dominated the seas, their word for pirate was *vrijbuiter* (from *vrij* meaning free, plus *buit* meaning booty). Their English rivals anglicized and transliterated the word to *freebooter*. The Spanish then reshaped *freebooter* into *filibustero*. During the nineteenth century the term *filibustero* or, in the United States, *filibuster* was applied to an adventurer who engaged in running arms to revolutionists in Cuba and the Central American republics. In 1853 an angry Congressman in a House debate declared that his opponents were "filibustering" against the United States government. The term caught on and since 1863 the word *filibuster* has denoted a delaying action in legislative procedure.

In the process of linguistic evolution, words rise and fall in social standing. The nineteenth century was addicted to genteelisms—euphemisms for supposedly vulgar expressions. Even before Victoria became queen in 1837, the trend toward prudery was well advanced in American polite society, owing perhaps to the dominant status and influence of women. During the 1830's words like *bitch*, *boar*, *buck*, *ram*, *sow*, and *stallion* virtually disappeared. The Biblical *ass* became a *jackass* or *donkey*; the *bull* became a *cow-creature* or *seed-ox*; and *manure* became *dressing*. In the domain of human anatomy, *belly* and *bosom* were not to be mentioned and a *leg* became a *limb*. The word *seat* was for a while more delicate than *chair*, but when it came into use as *backside*, the French *derrière* supplanted the anatomical *seat* and the *chair* returned to the parlour. A lady was *enceinte*, never *pregnant*. And one never *went to bed*, one *retired*.

When the English novelist Captain Frederick Marryat visited America in 1837, he was flabbergasted to discover that even tables and pianos had *limbs* rather than *legs*. Describing a visit to a seminary for young ladies, he wrote: "On being ushered into the reception room, conceive my astonishment at beholding a square pianoforte with four *limbs*. However, that the ladies who visited their daughters might feel in its full force the extreme delicacy of the mistress of the establishment, and her care to preserve in their utmost purity the ideas of the young ladies under her charge, she had dressed all these four limbs in modest little trousers, with frills at the bottom of them!"

The euphemism remains today one of the liveliest elements in American speech. The tendency to upgrade the prosaic and dignify the ignoble pervades virtually every area of life in the United States, and the technique by which it is accomplished is the alchemy of the public relations expert. Today most businessmen hold *positions* rather than *jobs*. When they elect to buy a house, they consult a *realtor* who shows them *ranch-style dwellings* on an *estate*. Their garbage is removed by *sanitary engineers* and their bugs are combated by *exterminating engineers*. When a death occurs in the family, a *mortician* is consulted. He takes the *loved one* or *patient* to his *funeral home*, provides a *casket* and arranges for *interment*, *entombment*, or *immurement* in a *memorial park*. If cremation is requested, the remains may be placed in a *funerary urn* in a rented niche in a *columbarium*.

Among the greatest virtuosos of the euphemism are sociologists, educators, and economists. It is, of course, a well-known fact that there are no longer any poor in America, only the *underprivileged* who happen to fall into a *low-income group*. Nor are there any poor children in the public schools, only *children unable to secure much beyond the necessities of today's world because of the modest finances of the family*. By the same token there are no bastards in the United States although some kids are *born out of wedlock*. Those who cling to the bottom of their class in school are not necessarily poor students or even lazy; they are simply *children with untapped potential* or perhaps children *with latent ability* or *underachievers*. If they fail to receive passing grades they may still qualify for *social promotion*. None of them lives in a slum, for there are no slums, although every big city has its *older, more overcrowded areas*.

In the field of economics the forbidden word is *depression*. The last *depression* was in the nineteen-thirties. Since then there have been *recessions*, but even that term is somewhat indelicate today, and there is no real necessity for retaining it. At a Congressional hearing not long ago a government economist was questioned closely as to whether he felt that a recent decline in the economy could be described as a *recession*. He replied in the negative, explaining that as he saw it, the situation was characterized simply by the *temporary absence of those affirmative forces necessary to provide the upward thrust required for the resumption of economic growth.*

Apart from euphemisms and metaphors, the process of word-making is an unending one and it continues in America today as prodigally as ever in the past. The methods used are the same as those employed by the Old English wordmakers when they combined two small words into a self-explaining compound (like *earring*), or by their successors in Middle English times who freely juggled Latin, French, and English roots and affixes to create new words or to extend meanings. Today the contemporary American vocabulary is spangled with such new but ubiquitous compounds as *aqualung*, *astronaut*, *bobby-soxer*, *double-talk*, *jukebox*, *paratrooper*, *radiogram*, *socialite*, *teenager*, *telecaster*, and *smog*. By adding suffices of varied linguistic ancestry, inventive Americans have spawned such modern hybrids as *beatnik*, *bloodmobile*, *bowlorama*, *golfitis*, *motorcade*, *payola*, *squaresville*, and *talkathon*.

As Shakespeare so often did, Americans casually convert nouns into verbs (*to audition*, *to park*, *to service*, *to orbit*); verbs into nouns (*a dump*, *a strike*, *a probe*, *a drive*); nouns into adjectives (*air tragedy*, *cover girl*, *disk jockey*, *glamor puss*, *rat race*, *skin diver*, *space age*, *summit meeting*); adjectives into nouns (*basics*, *briefs*, *compacts*, *wets*, and *drys*); and verbs into adjectives (*prowl car*, *squawk box*, and *speakeasy*). A favourite trick is to combine a verb and an adverb to obtain such combinations as *checkup*, *countdown*, *drive-in*, *feedback*, and *pushover*). On occasion words are shortened by cropping syllables either from the beginning or the end. Among examples of front-clipping, Americans have derived *phone* from *telephone*, *coon* from *raccoon*, *plane* from *airplane*, and *pop* from *soda pop*. By the process of back-clipping, there are *ad* from *advertisement*, *gas* from *gasoline*, *memo* from *memorandum*, *movie* from *moving picture*, and *photo* from *photograph*.

It is clear that the English language in America today differs from that of the past primarily with respect to its vocabulary. Its underlying architecture remains the same, and its mechanisms of invention and expansion have not changed. Only the youngest and newest of the words are different. Yet throughout the long history of the English tongue the challenge of new concepts and experiences has repeatedly forced new words into being. And doubtless the unimaginable events of the future will continue to do so. For the life of a great language is rather like that of some giant tree in the evergreen rain forests of the tropics. It knows no seasons. Around the year, random leaves detach themselves and flutter to the forest floor, and as they fall new ones appear. So in English, words useful in the past lie forgotten now amid the yellowing incunabula of ancient archives. But, continually drawn forth by changing needs, new words unfold and pulsate in human speech.

The contrasts between English and American idiom that so distressed the critics of the eighteenth and nineteenth centuries are slowly being erased by all the manifold agencies of modern communication. One of the most notable characteristics of the American language since the days of Adams and Webster has been its constant striving for national uniformity. Even so tart a critic as Captain Marryat, who felt that in America his tongue had been "debased", had to admit that "you may travel through all the United States and find less difficulty in understanding or in being understood than in some of the counties of England, such as Cornwall, Devonshire, Lancashire and Suffolk". Today in Britain as well as in America there has been a steady trend toward inter-regional speech.

Of larger importance is the fact that as the distances of the planet shrink, and as transatlantic channels of radio and television clear their throats, the intonations of English and American voices will increasingly converge. Already numerous American idioms and inflexions have entered British speech. At the same time many educated Americans now speak with neutral accents free from identifying state or regional shadings.

The trained ear can detect class differences and doubtless always will. Yet even today cultivated American speech is often mistaken for English English by casual auditors both in the United States and in Britain. Thomas Jefferson's conjecture that some day the language of the United States would no longer be English, even in name, was delusive, for no one could foresee in his day the growing international character of the American civilization. Today, overleaping national boundaries, spoken and understood on every continent, the mother tongue of England and America carries the heritage of a common culture and of common ideas around the world. Within its unity there is still diversity. But in time the force of unity will undoubtedly prove the stronger.

2.

Next to the United States, the vast subcontinent of India is the oldest outpost of the English language on earth. It was in 1640 that the first permanent agency of the British East India Company was opened on a site that ultimately became the city of Madras. The paradox of India today is that although English is the language of the government, of education and business, the Constitution specifically states that Hindi shall be the official language of the land. The Constitution, however, is written in English which, despite efforts to get rid of it, remains the "associate official language" by necessity and popular demand.

Language difficulties have racked India since the first millennium B.C. Today its 440 million people are dispersed linguistically among 845 languages and dialects, of which the most important are Hindi, Urdu, Bengali, Tamil, and Malayalam. Within this enormous polyglot land, English provides a common bridge, as it does in Pakistan and Ceylon. Krishna Menon, a native of Calicut where the local tongue is Malayalam, conducted his political campaigns in English. When Nehru addressed Congress he spoke first in Hindi, then repeated in English for the benefit of legislators representing the sixty per cent of the nation to whom Hindi is unknown.

It is curious that few English words have worked their way into any of the Indian languages. Among those which have been borrowed are: *apīl* (appeal), *gīlas* (glass), *ghārīal* (rail), *rasīd* (receipt), *simkin* (champagne), and *tumlet* (tumbler). But the reverse process has been of quite a different order. *The Oxford English Dictionary* lists nine hundred basic words derived from India, plus thousands of derivatives, reflecting more than three centuries of Anglo-Indian communication.

Many Indian words entered the English lexicon indirectly, long before the advent of British rule. For India's relations with the West go back to antiquity, when Greek and Roman traders ventured overland through Asia Minor and Persia in quest of ivory, spices, and precious stones. From this ancient trade, European craftsmen and merchants came to know *beryl*, *camphor*, *emerald*, *ginger*, *musk*, *opal*, *pepper*, *rice*, *sandal*, and *sugar*. Later, during the high tide of Moslem expansion, Arab traders brought back a yellow herb, *saffron*, for medicinal purposes, and the recipe for an Indian rice dish known as *kedgeree*; from Malay boatmen they learned the word *junk*, meaning ship.

In 1510 the Portuguese occupied Goa and became the dominant traders in the East throughout the following century. A Portuguese-Indian lingua franca evolved along the sea-coast. From it a number of native words passed through various mutations into the English lexicon, among them: *copra* (from Malayalam *koppara*, coconut kernel), *catamaran* (from Tamil *kaṯṯu*, binding, plus *maram*, wood; hence a raft), *curry* (from Tamil *kari*, sauce), *mandarin* (from Hindi *mantrī*, counsellor or minister of state, later adopted in Chinese), *mango* (from Tamil *mān-kāy*, fruit of the *mān* tree), *monsoon* (adopted in India from Arabic *mausim*, season), *pagoda* (from Tamil (*pagavadi*, temple), *teak* from Malayalam *tēkka*), and *veranda* (from Hindi *baraṇḍā*, a portico). In addition to these loan words from India via the Portuguese, a number of Portuguese words entered the Indian vernacular whence they were later appropriated by the English: *caste* (from Portuguese *casta*, meaning unmixed race), *cobra* (from Portuguese *cobra de capello*, hooded serpent), and *tank* (from Portuguese *tanque*, a pool or reservoir).

On New Year's Eve, 1600, Queen Elizabeth I granted a charter to the East India Company, an institution that would dominate India in ever greater degree until 1773 when Parliament passed the Regulating Act asserting its control over the company and thereby indirectly over India itself. During the seventeenth century the principal concern of the British in India—despite the romantic emanations of raja's rubies and rare aromatic spices—was textiles. From Calicut came *calico*, a white cloth so important in the trade that for a while its name became a generic term connoting all cotton fabrics from the East. A stained or painted calico called *chīnṭ* in Hindi, was exported and marketed as *chintz* as early as 1614; and by 1619 the trade name *gunny* (from Sanskrit *gonī*, a sack), had become attached to a type of sack manufactured from *jute* (Sanskrit *jūṭa*, fibrous root). During the eighteenth and nineteenth centuries New England provided a good market, trading apples and ice for these fabrics as well as for *seersucker* (Hindi, *śīrśakar*) and *bandanna* (Hindi, *bāndhnū*) handkerchiefs. In the nineteenth century a coarse and heavy type of cotton known as *dungaree* (from Hindi, *dungrī*) became popular as a material for trousers.

As the East India Company expanded along the coast, establishing new factories and trading posts, the resident English agents adapted happily to the customs of the land. They lived in *bungalows* (from Bengali *bānglā*, house), drank *punch* (from Sanskrit *pañca*, five ingredients) and *toddy* (from Hindi *tāṛī*, juice of the palmyra tree), smoked *cheroots*, encased their midriffs in *cummerbunds*, and bought their Indian girl friends *saris* and *bangles*. Some became addicted to *hashish*. Others, with the true Englishman's love of nature, observed the landscape and wrote letters home describing strange trees like the *banyan* and *lilac*, curious animals like the *cheetah* and *mongoose*, and huge snakes like the *anaconda* (Tamil, the crusher). Occasionally they found time to visit atolls where they collected *cowrie* shells. Noting the different social strata of India, they learned the varying status of *maharaja* and *raja*, *maharani* and *rani*, and of *Brahmin*, *nabob* (from Hindi *navāb*, governor of a province), *Rajput*, *pundit* (from Sanskrit *paṇḍita*, a learned man), *sahib*, *lascar* (a sailor), *fakir* (a mendicant), *pariah* (one of low caste, but not an outcast), and *coolie* (hired labourer), From India to England the *rupee* (from Hindi *rūpiyah*) became a symbol of Eastern wealth. The Tamil coin *kāśu* was transmuted, via the Portuguese *caixa*, into the general English term *cash*.

Midway in the eighteenth century, Britain's purely commercial interest in India was superseded by full military and administrative control. These exigencies of police activity, local wars, and the training of an Indian army brought new terms into common use in the press and in Parliament, e.g. *sepoy* (a native soldier in English uniform), *loot* (from Hindi *lūt*, a body of native irregulars whose chief object was plunder), and, later, *khaki* (from Persian *khāk*, dust), *mufti*, *puttees*, and *tattoo*. They also brought back such exotic gifts as *shawls* from *Cashmere*, *pyjamas* (from Hindi *paijāmā*, a leg-garment) made of fine *muslin*, and platters and bowls aglitter with *lac* (now lacquer). They told tales of strange customs like *suttee* and *purdah*, and the joys of tiger hunts in the *jungle*, when they shot their prey from the security of *howdahs* on the backs of elephants guided by trusty *mahouts*. They augmented the English menu with spicy fare like *chutney* and *mulligatawny* soup (Tamil for pepper water). When they had their hair washed, they called the performance a *shampoo* (from Hindi *cāpo*, a massage). When they dismissed a subject brusquely, they said, "I don't care a dam"—a *dām* being an Indian coin of very small value.

One of the most precious exports transmitted by the British to the West was a knowledge of Indian philosophy and metaphysics. An employee in the Bengali division of the East India Company translated the great Hindu epic the *Bhagavad-Gita*, in 1785. The *Upanishads* and the *Ramayana* were translated in the first decade of the nineteenth century. These towering works exerted a profound influence on Kant, Schopenhauer, and Schiller in Germany, and later upon Emerson, Whittier, and Thoreau in America. As the Western world awakened to the deep complexities of *Buddhism* and *Hinduism*, specialized terms like *Brahma*, *guru*, *karma*, *mahatma*, *nirvana*, *swami*, *Vedanta*, and *yoga* came into widening use; and their diffusion continues at an accelerating tempo today with the growing appeal of Oriental mysticism to the people of a troubled time.

For three centuries the currents of historic interchange between India and the English-speaking nations of the West have coursed along an alternating circuit. India has enriched the Occident—materially in many ways with the products of its ancient civilization, linguistically with a colourful spectrum of words, and metaphysically with its heritage of centuries of meditation on man and his role in the unfathomable cosmos. Among its bequests has been the concept of non-violence, developed by Gandhi and adopted by American Negroes as one of the most powerful implements of moral suasion that ever rebuked the Christian conscience; in Britain it has also been used to militant purpose by members of the Campaign for Nuclear Disarmament.

Alternatively, the influence of England on India has been enormous. Much of it stems from a crucial decision made in 1835 to enthrone English as the official language of government and law, the medium of higher education, and, hence, "the key to all improvements". As a consequence, there arose from the polyglot multitudes of the subcontinent a small cadre of intellectuals who, by virtue of their mutual adopted tongue, could communicate with each other and with the Western world. Inspired by English literature, by English philosophers like Locke and Mill, and English political liberalism, they formed an educated élite whose descendants of the fifth generation ultimately led India to independence in the twentieth century. If India stands forth as the leader of the newborn Asian-African nations today, it is because its leaders speak English as though it were their native tongue. The poet Edmund Waller little knew in 1658 the import of his prescient line of verse: "Under the tropic is our language spoke."

3.

Of all the dominions, Australia speaks with a breezier and more vivid idiom than any other member of the British Commonwealth. Several factors contributed to its development. One was distance: the enormous arc of ocean miles that stretch between Australia and England. Another was the nature of the land itself. For upon the great empty island continent, unique forms of life had dwelt for incomputable aeons of time in a biological vacuum, engendering a world such as Western man had never dreamed of, a world that had to be classified and named.

The initial settlers gazed with astonished eyes upon their new antipodean home in the austral summer of 1788, more than a century and a half after the establishment of the first English colonies in America and India. Although merchantmen of the Dutch East Indies fleet had often skirted Australia en route to Java and Sumatra in the seventeenth century, its treacherous northern coastline had not tempted them to pause or colonize. And so the continent remained unexplored, unmapped, and uninhabited save by the Aborigines—living fossils from the Old Stone Age—until a celestial happening supervened. In 1768 astronomers of the Royal Society persuaded the government of King George III to sponsor an expedition to the South Pacific to observe the transit of Venus across the sun.

The commander of the expedition was Captain James Cook, a surveyor trained in the Royal Navy, who, after completing the astronomical observations, sailed around New Zealand and then twelve hundred miles westward to Australia. Cook made two more voyages in the next decade, during which he claimed Australia and New Zealand in His Majesty's name, charted sections of coastline, and brought back detailed descriptions of both lands. His reports held more than scientific interest, for they arrived at a time when the government was baffled by a domestic problem that had arisen as a by-product of the American revolution. In the past, England had deported its long-term convicts to America; but now, with that repository closed, English jails were filled to overflowing with sick and dying prisoners. Captain Cook's explorations suggested a solution. On January 26, 1788, a flotilla of prison ships carrying 717 English convicts—197 of them women—dropped anchor in Botany Bay, so named by Sir Joseph Banks, the great naturalist who had accompanied Cook on his initial voyage. The first Australians disembarked and shortly thereafter settled on the shores of Sydney Harbour.

The predicament of these involuntary pilgrims was, from the outset, precarious. Although their talents were diversified—some were forgers, poachers, thieves, some Irish rebels and political offenders of varying degrees—they seemed hardly adapted for their historic role as founders of a nation and perilously ill-equipped to cope with the vicissitudes of pioneering in one of the least-known territories on earth. "The convict barracks of New South Wales," wrote one of the first Australian governors, "remind me of the monasteries of Spain. They contain a population of consumers who produce nothing." Producers, however, were not long in arriving. The discovery of rich pasture land lured numbers of sheep farmers to the empty continent in the 1820's; and the discovery of gold in 1851 swelled the migratory wave of fortune-hunters to a flood. The swift growth of population, the incredible prosperity of the wool trade, and fantastically soaring land values all combined to create a vigorous new nation, which, with astonishing speed, developed an economy, a culture, and an idiom—uniquely its own.

The idiom was, from the first, predominantly Cockney—a fact about which Australians remain a little touchy to this day, although as early as 1841 free settlers outnumbered the convict population by a ratio of four to one. Yet it was not only the convicts who vociferated the vowel sounds of London. For those who followed in their wake included a motley collection of adventurers, gamblers, speculators, wanderers, and assorted expatriates—few from the upper strata of society. With the Londoners there came émigrés from the Midlands, Scotland, Ireland, and Wales, and they too added their regional accents to the linguistic mélange.

As in America, the Australian lexicon began to grow around an initial nucleus of words suggested by and suggesting the character of the country itself, its plant and animal populations, and those activities unique to the new domain. "It is probably not too much to say," a nineteenth-century lexicographer observed, "that there never was an instance in history when so many new words were needed, and that there never will be again, for never did settlers come, nor can they ever come again, upon flora and fauna so completely different from anything seen by them before."[1] As the American colonists had done, the Australian pioneers drew their words from two fonts—one the language of the native tribesmen, the other their own English tongue applied with modifications and extrapolations to the antipodal scene. Some of their borrowings and mintings have pervaded the English language beyond Australia, some have not, and some have other meanings in other parts of the English-speaking world.

Two loan words from the Aborigines that have passed into general use the world around are *kangaroo* and *boomerang*. In his journal on June 24, 1770, Captain Cook described his first glimpse of a long-tailed, high-jumping animal and noted that the natives called it by a name that sounded something like *kangaroo*. His perceptions were accurate, for in the aboriginal tongue, *kanga* means "jump" and *roo* means "animal" or "quad-

[1] E. E. Morris: *Austral English: A Dictionary of Australian Words, Phrases and Usages* (London: 1898), p. xii.

ruped". The word *boomerang* has enjoyed an extension of meaning in English, so that today it is both a verb and a noun, and in either form it has a symbolic connotation: e.g. an action, idea, or statement can boomerang or be a boomerang. Aboriginal terms have been retained and generally used to denote the unique Australian fauna. Best known among the animals are: the *dingo*, or wild dog; the *koala*, or native "teddy bear"; the *cuscus*, the *wallaby*, and the *wombat*. Among the native birds there are: the *budgerigar* (literally "good cockatoo"), the *kookaburra* (sometimes called the "laughing jackass" or just plain "jackass"), the *bulla bulla*, and the *currawong*. And among fish there are: the *barramundi*, *nannygai*, *tabbigaw*, and *wobbegong*. Other borrowings from the Aborigines, include: *billabong* (a silted pool in a river-bend, from *billa*, water, plus *bong*, dead); "*Cooee*" or "*Cooey*" (a signal cry used by the Aborigines and adopted by the colonists, meaning, "Here I am"; one is within *cooee* of home when a short distance away); *corroboree* (a tribal dancing ceremony, hence party or get-together); *dillybag* (a bag made of grass or fur, from *dhilla*, bag); *gibber* (a stone); *humpy* (a small hut or building); *jumbuck* (a sheep); *parametta* (a light dress fabric); and to *yacker* (to work).

For other lexical requirements, the early settlers resorted to English, adapting familiar words to things bearing some real or fancied resemblance to their prototypes at home. Thus in Australia one may come upon an *oak*, a *beech*, or a *magpie* quite unlike, and biologically unrelated to, their English namesakes. Many coinages manifest considerable perceptive and often poetic imagination, as in the case of the *lyrebird* (named for the shape of its extended tail), the *whipbird* (named for the sound of its call), the *bowerbird*, *friarbird*, *frogmouth*, *ground lark*, and *honey eater*; and, in the plant kingdom, *hedge laurel*, *ironheart*, *sugar grass* and *thousand-jacket*.

Much of the Australian language, not unexpectedly, focuses on the land itself, and especially the great blank heart of the interior. The hinterland in general is known as *The Outback*, and the remotest fastnesses of The Outback—"back of beyond"—as *The Never Never*. The vast, forbidding reaches of stony desert that recurrently blotch and scar the sandy desert are called *gibber plains*. Wooded or scrubby country—or more broadly any rural area—is referred to simply as *bush*. To get lost or confused is *to be bushed*; *to go bush* is to disappear. The gold rush of 1851 enriched the vocabulary with such words as *digger* (originally a miner, now an Australian soldier), *to fossick* (originally to hunt gold, now to rummage for anything), and *mullock* (mining debris). The life of the *boundary rider* and the *jackeroo* (ranch hand) on the lonely sheep and cattle *stations* (ranches) of the frontier, produced, among other terms: *to bullock* (to work hard), *clearskin* (originally unbranded cattle, now also a politician with a clean record), *duffer* (equivalent to American rustler), *joey* (a young kangaroo), *poddy* (a motherless calf or lamb), *ringer* (expert sheep shearer), *ropeable* (violently angry, needing to be restrained), *sundowner* (a tramp or itinerant worker who turns up at sundown), *swag* (a tramp's bundle of possessions), *tucker* (food), *to waltz Matilda* (to lead the life of a tramp), and *willy-willy* (a cyclonic storm of local intensity).

Other striking Australian words and phrases include: *to barrack* (cheer, originally to jeer), *bushranger* (escaped convict living in the bush), *dinkum* (authentic, the real McCoy), *grafter* (a hard worker), *grouse* (good, excellent), *to jack up* (to abandon, reject), *larrikin* (a young tough, hoodlum, punk), *picnic* (a real mess), *plonk* (cheap wine), *plink* (cheaper wine), *Send her down, Hughie!* ("Please, Lord, let it rain!"), *shakedown* (a makeshift bed, a pad), *Sheila* (a girl, any girl), *to winge* (to complain), *wog* (a germ, virus, or the disease caused by same), *wowser* (a strait-laced, puritanical killjoy).

In Australia, as everywhere in the English-speaking world, the formal or literary language—the language of novelists, playwrights, journalists, and of radio and television announcers—is structurally Standard English. But the colour, variety, and versatility of its vocabulary lend sanction to the classification of the "Australian language", along with the "American language" as a distinct subdivision of English. It would be difficult to assert a similar distinction for either New Zealand or Canadian English. New Zealand, youngest of the dominions, is often described as "The Britain of the South". And the English of Canada has necessarily been strongly influenced by American English not only through proximity, but by reason of its historical antecedents: in a sense the English language was brought to Canada by Americans. For after the Revolutionary War some sixty thousand American Loyalists left the United States and entered

Canada rather than live under the new republic. It was they who founded the English-speaking provinces of Ontario and New Brunswick. The stream of migration continued after the War of 1812; hence, until the third or fourth decade of the nineteenth century the English-speaking population of Canada was predominantly of American origin. Later arrivals from Scotland, Ireland, and Lancaster added certain distinctive tones to the timbre of Canadian speech. Today Canadians are sometimes amiably described as people who are invariably mistaken for Englishmen in the United States and for Americans in England.

Whatever effect the swiftly multiplying and aggressively nationalistic French minority in Canada (now representing about thirty per cent of the total population) may exert on the political future of the Dominion, it is likely that English will retain its linguistic ascendancy for a good many years to come. No such prediction can be made for South Africa. There, in the last half-century, English has fallen from a position of overwhelming dominance to the status of a minority tongue. South Africa is indeed the only place in the world where English is quantitatively[1] on the decline. Its decline is not fortuitous, but the consequence of a quiet but obdurate campaign of attrition.

For more than a century following Great Britain's acquisition of the Cape Colony from the Dutch in 1814, English remained the official language of South Africa. And there—as in America, India, and Australia—the English-speaking colonists borrowed freely from the languages they found about them. From the native African tongues they appropriated *chimpanzee*, *gnu*, *tsetse*, and *voodoo*. From the Boers who characteristically adhered to Dutch rather than borrow words from the black tribesmen whom they disdained, the British adopted: *aardvark*, *veld*, *spoor*, *trek*, *kraal*, *eland*, *hartebeest*, *wildebeest*, and *springbok*. Whether on frontier farms or in the growing cities which they shared with the British, the Boers preserved their language and

[1] The word "quantitatively" is important. Qualitatively, though not numerically, the language has deteriorated in certain parts of southeast Asia and elsewhere where resident English teachers and other professional people have had to depart amid the turmoil of war and revolution.

their folk-ways. As Winston Churchill observed in his *History of the English-Speaking Peoples*, "No race has ever clung more tenaciously to its own culture and institutions than the Dutch."

Contemplating the position of the English language in South Africa, A. G. Hooper, professor of English at the University of Stellenbosch, wrote more than a decade ago: "At the turn of the century the Victoria College of Stellenbosch had many English-speaking members of staff and probably most classes were given in English. The student magazines sounded like their counterparts at many a British school. A first impression is that it was just another little outpost of Empire. In 1950 the University of Stellenbosch had an almost exclusively Afrikaans-speaking staff, and in May of the same year the Stellenbosch University Debating Society with an overwhelming majority carried the motion that 'The English language has no chance of survival'."[1]

The motion was more than the expression of a hope; it was the recognition of a trend. Today, although schools in the larger towns and cities of South Africa remain nominally bilingual, most teachers—even teachers of English to English-speaking children—are Afrikaners for whom English is a second language. On English-language radio programmes, the accents of announcers, newscasters, and actors are often freighted with the tones of Afrikaans. "It may be only coincidence," Mr. Hooper concluded in his prescient essay, "that almost the only South African writers in English who have achieved any reputation have been people who were either born overseas, or who were born here but have lived largely overseas. On the other hand, with their tradition of servants, plenty of manual labour, and a wonderful climate, there are very few South Africans beyond the first generation who retain any cultural interests, and very many ready to swallow the digests and surrender to all passive forms of entertainment."[2]

[1] Quoted by Eric Partridge and John W. Clark in *British and American English Since 1900* (London: Andrew Dakers Limited; 1951), p. 80.
[2] Ibid. p. 84.

6

THE FUTURE OF THE ENGLISH LANGUAGE WITH PARTICULAR REFERENCE TO THE U.S.A.

Here will be an old abusing of God's patience and the king's English.

WILLIAM SHAKESPEARE (1564–1616)
The Merry Wives of Windsor

"... There's glory for you!"

"I don't know what you mean by 'glory'," Alice said.

Humpty-Dumpty smiled contemptuously. "Of course you don't—till I tell you. I meant, 'There's a nice knock-down argument for you!' "

"But 'glory' doesn't mean 'a nice knock-down argument'," Alice objected.

"When *I* use a word," Humpty-Dumpty said in rather a scornful tone, "it means just what I choose it to mean, neither more nor less."

"The question is," said Alice, "whether you *can* make words mean so many different things."

"The question is," said Humpty-Dumpty, "which is to be Master—that's all."

LEWIS CARROLL, *Through the Looking Glass*

In this playful dialogue Carroll prophetically defined an issue that a century later would involve teachers, writers, lexicographers, linguisticians, and plain lovers of the English language in a bitter and protracted conflict. Warfare came into the open in the autumn of 1961 with the appearance of *Webster's Third New International Dictionary*. But for several decades prior to World War II, hostilities had simmered in academic communities and in journals of literary and social comment.

In a casual view, the battle could be seen merely as a continuation of the unending debate between grammarians and antigrammarians, purists and "progressives", conservatives who cherish tradition and form in language and free-talkers who believe that linguistic evolution should not be impeded by the past. There have always been protectors of the native tongue in every civilized land, ranging themselves against the forces of vulgarity and verbicide. Their current alarm over the despoiling of English speech may appear to differ only in intensity from that of other generations. But there is a new note. For today they find themselves not only arrayed against the perennial legions of illiteracy (centred in the electronic citadels of the Age of Noise), but also engaged in another quarter by a far more formidable host conscripted from those who have been, supposedly, custodians of the English language in America.

Rather unobtrusively, so far as the lay public is concerned, the teaching of English in American schools and the training of English teachers have become increasingly actuated by the discipline known variously as Structural Linguistics, Descriptive Linguistics, or Modern Linguistic Science. Its precepts, which grew out of studies of North American Indian tongues, sound innocuous: (1) language changes constantly; (2) change is normal; (3) spoken language is *the* language; (4) correctness rests upon usage; (5) all usage is relative. But harmless as these ideas seem individually, their total effect in practice has been the annihilation of traditional rules of grammar, the denial of any standards of "right" and "wrong" in speech or writing, and an anarchical philosophy of usage summed up by one of its exponents as: "Any word means whatever its users make it mean". Humpty-Dumpty hardly put it more baldly. And it is this Humpty-Dumpty philosophy—"Every student his own egg-head"—which governs English teaching in many levels of the United States academic edifice today.

1.

Not since the early years of the eighteenth century has such concern been expressed over the decline of literacy and the deterioration of the English tongue. But the reasons for anxiety two centuries ago were notably different from those of today. In the so-called Augustan age of England (*c.* 1700–50), reflective men of letters were clamouring for a kind of language authority that did not yet exist. The anatomy of the English tongue had never been analysed and defined in precepts of formal grammar. There was no definitive English dictionary, and there were no set rules of spelling. The brilliance of the Elizabethan poets and playwrights in the previous century had brought the English language to its fullest flower, enriching its lexicon in an outburst of linguistic creativity never equalled before or since. But now to their heirs—essayists and critics like Dryden, Addison, Defoe, Swift, and Johnson—it appeared that the national tongue had entered upon a period of blight and decay.

The question whether or not English—as opposed to Latin—was a fit medium for serious and scholarly disquisition had been resolved in the preceding half-century. Nevertheless, all serious writers of the day venerated Latin as the model for both language and literature. They could all write Latin; they knew its rules of grammar and syntax; and the rules left no middle ground between correct and incorrect usage. English, on the other hand, had never been dissected; it had no rules, no standards by which an educated speaker or writer could distinguish good from bad, right from wrong in use of the mother tongue. Shakespeare's blithe, free-ranging disregard of word function and parts of speech was all very well for poetic flights and histrionic declamation, but not for the precise essayists and philosophers of the Age of Reason who had caught a glimpse through Newton's eyes of the orderly progression of the celestial spheres overhead and the laws of mechanics and motion here on earth.

The revolution in scientific thought kindled by the publication of Newton's *Principia* in 1687 had led literary leaders to inquire if there were not some laws of language, akin to the laws of nature that so harmoniously governed the physical universe, which could be formulated to fix, regulate, and standardize usage in speech and writing. As early as 1693 John Dryden, who became poet laureate barely half a century after Shakespeare's death, complained that "we have yet no prosodia, not so much as a tolerable dictionary or a grammar, so that our language is in a manner barbarous". He confessed that he often found it necessary to phrase his thoughts in Latin before he could express them precisely in English. Jonathan Swift reiterated Dryden's lament for the absence of fixed standards, but added his melancholy opinion that the state of the language was not only bad, but getting worse all the time. In *A Proposal for Correcting, Improving and Ascertaining the English Tongue*, written in 1712, Swift glumly traced the course of linguistic decay: "The period wherein the English tongue received most improvement I take to commence with the beginning of Queen Elizabeth's reign, and to conclude with the great rebellion in 1642. From the Civil War to this present time I am apt to doubt whether the corruptions in our language have not at least equalled the refinements in it; and these corruptions very few of the best authors in our age have wholly escaped. During [Oliver Cromwell's] usurpation, such an infusion of enthusiastic[1] jargon prevailed in every writing, as was not shaken off in many years after. To this succeeded the licentiousness which entered with the Restoration, and from infecting our religion and morals fell to corrupt our language."

The chief source of corruption, according to the Augustan critics, was the new wave of French influence which inundated England with the Restoration. Charles II and his court had lived in exile in France during Cromwell's protectorate. Upon his return, the French language rose swiftly to a pinnacle of prestige it had not enjoyed since Norman times; it became *de rigueur* in the court and among the aristocracy in London and throughout the realm. French fashions were supreme then, as now; and smart conversation, when conducted in English, was sprinkled with French idioms pronounced preferably with a proper Parisian accent. As a consequence of the new French invasion, the structure of the English sentence underwent a change: it relaxed into more concise and fluid patterns, shedding the stately, contrapuntal, and often unwieldy arpeggios of Elizabethan prose. But the main impact was on vocabulary. Many old English words fell into disuse, and as cross-channel traffic revived—stimulated by the discovery (among the upper classes at least) that travel is an ingredient of education—a host of borrowed French words entered the English lexicon between

[1] In Swift's time, "enthusiastic"—from the Greek ἐνθουσιάξειν, to be possessed by a god—meant frenzied, unbridled, or, as we would say, "jazzed-up".

1650 and 1800 and have continued to dwell there as permanent and hard-working residents. Among them were: *ballet*, *boulevard*, *brunette*, *canteen*, *cartoon*, *champagne*, *chenille*, *cohesion*, *coiffure*, *connoisseur*, *coquette*, *coterie*, *dentist*, *negligee*, *publicity*, *patrol*, *pique*, *routine*, *soubrette*, *syndicate*.

As middle-class Anglo-Saxons, the literary men of London regarded the use of French words and idioms by the upper classes as an offensive status-seeking affectation. Dryden snorted: "We meet daily with those fops who value themselves on their travelling, and pretend that they cannot express their meaning in English, because they would put us off with some French phrase of the last edition; without considering that, for aught they know, we have a better of our own. But these are not the men who are to refine us; their talent is to prescribe fashions, not words." A few years later Daniel Defoe complained that "an Englishman has his mouth full of borrow'd phrases . . . He is always borrowing other men's languages . . . I cannot but think the using and introducing foreign terms of art or foreign words into speech while our language labours under no penury or scarcity of words is an intolerable grievance." Even the amiable Addison, writing in *The Spectator* in 1711, declared: "I have often wished . . . that certain men might be set apart as superintendents of our language to hinder any words of a foreign coin from passing among us; and in particular to prohibit any French phrases from becoming current in this kingdom, when those of our own stamp are altogether as valuable."

The Augustans took particular exception to the tendency, current and fashionable among coffee-house wits and other groups of the élite, to foreshorten words by cropping off trailing syllables. They inveighed against such neologisms as *extra* for *extraordinary*, *rep* for *reputation*, and *incog* for *incognito*—all of which survived despite their diatribes. Just as modern English and American fast-talkers say "*It's super*", so in eighteenth-century slang one said "*It's ult*", in order to bestow the ultimate accolade. And when someone was regarded as stuffily hypercritical, the withering phrase was "*He's hyper*". The contraction that outraged Swift above all others was the word *mob*. During the civil war, many resounding orations contained the Latin expression *mobile vulgus*, meaning "fickle populace". Repetition and familiarity eventually reduced it to *mob*, and as such it has lived on for ever after, despite Swift's ferocious campaign to expunge it from the English vocabulary and his bitter lament on losing his battle that he had been "borne down by Numbers, and betrayed by those who promised to assist me".[1]

As a lover of full syllabic values, Swift also resented the gradual wasting of the *-ed* ending in the past tense of verbs, a process that had begun in the preceding century when Shakespeare and other poets began writing *welcom'd* for *welcomed*, or *inform'd* for *informed* when it suited their metrical needs. The elision crept into popular usage and especially outraged Swift in monosyllabic verbs such as *trudg'd*, *delv'd*, *fledg'd*. To him the imbalance of consonants created "a jarring sound, and so difficult to utter, that I have often wondered how it could obtain", since English was already "overstocked with monosyllables—the disgrace of our language". Over and above foreign importations, foreshortenings, contractions, and monosyllables, Swift looked with a bilious eye on all fads of usage, all recent coinages tainted with novelty, cant, or affectation. Three contemporary words which he detested almost as violently as he loathed *mob* were *banter*, *sham*, and *bamboozle*. The origins of *banter* are unknown; etymologists can only say that it came into colloquial use at this time and has remained in use ever since with its original meaning. The word *sham* was apparently elevated from a regional English dialectal version of *shame* and endowed with its present meaning of "fraudulent trick" or "imposture", presumably causing shame. The word *bamboozle* is thought to be an imperfect hybrid of *baffle* and the Greek *bambaluzein*, meaning to "chatter with cold" or "stammer". Whatever its origins Swift regarded *bamboozle* as an obscene deviate; probably "invented by some pretty fellows".

Swift had allies who joined him in expressing their dislikes, sometimes capricious and personal, sometimes stemming from principles of logic that ultimately succumbed to the brute forces of popular usage. The critic and essayist George Harris, writing in 1751, argued in vain against such irrational, physical images as *handling a subject*, *driving a bargain*, and *bolstering up an argument*.

[1] Many Latin and Greek affixes now lead independent lives. People who hail a *taxi* seldom are aware that in 1907 the proper term for this vehicle was *taximeter cab* (from the Greek *taxis*, arrangements; plus the Greek *metron*, measure; plus *cab* from the French *cabriolet*).

Repelled by the term *subject-matter*, Harris virtually retched: "In the name of everything that's disgusting and detestable, what is it? Is it one or two ugly words? What's the meaning of it? Confound me if I ever could guess. Yet one dares hardly ever peep into a Preface, for fear of being stared in the face with this nasty Subject-Matter."

Two decades later another conservative critic, George Campbell, called attention to the illogic of terming certain types of vessels a *man of war* or a *merchantman* when sailors commonly referred to their ships as *she*. "I think this gibberish", he wrote, "ought to be left entirely to mariners; amongst whom, I suppose, it hath originated."

Opposed as they were to innovations and convinced that English, already vulgarized and contaminated to a serious degree, was in danger of losing its identity, the Augustan critics sought ways (1) to purify and refine the language and (2) to fix and standardize it in a permanent and ideal form. To this end, Swift and his associates decided to crusade for the establishment of an English Academy modelled after the Italian Accademia della Crusca, founded in 1582, and the Académie française, inaugurated by Cardinal Richelieu in 1635. Out of the Italian Accademia had come a dictionary, *Vocabulario degli Accademici della Crusca*, which appeared in 1612 and went through subsequent editions in the next century, expanding to six folio volumes in the fourth edition of 1729. The dictionary of the Académie française appeared in 1694, the product of the labours of forty lexicographers working arduously for many years.

The notion that English was changing at a rate that would render it unintelligible to readers a few generations hence had occurred to other writers before Swift. As early as 1623, Sir Francis Bacon, who wrote fluently in both English and Latin, routinely provided Latin translations of his English works, explaining that "These modern languages will at one time or other, play the bankrupts with books". And the poet Edmund Waller, writing shortly after the Restoration, had declared:

> Poets that Lasting Marble seek,
> Must carve in Latin or in Greek.
> We write in Sand . . .

Swift described his projected English Academy in a letter to the Earl of Oxford, Lord Treasurer of England, and published it in 1712 under the title *A Proposal for Correcting, Improving and Ascertaining the English Tongue*. Citing the example of the Académie française, Swift urged the appointment of a group of experts "generally allowed to be best qualified for such a work", who would meet regularly to "observe gross improprieties [of language], which however authorized by practice and grown familiar, ought to be discarded. They will find many words that deserve to be utterly thrown out of our language, many more to be corrected, and perhaps not a few long since antiquated, which ought to be restored on account of their energy and sound." He concluded by warning the Earl that "if genius and learning be not encouraged under your Lordship's administration, you are the most inexcusable person alive".

Although Swift's proposal was supported by many influential men of letters, the enterprise never truly took wing. When his most important sponsor, Queen Anne, died in 1714, the proposed Academy died with her, never to be revived. Among many factors contributing to its demise was a growing burden of doubt among men of letters as to the possibility of ever fixing any language in permanent form. One hostile critic, John Oldmixon, compared Swift's dream to such ancient chimeras as perpetual motion, the Grand Elixir of the alchemists, and the Fountain of Youth. But underlying all contemporary objections was the historic Anglo-Saxon dislike of absolute regulation in any area of human affairs; just as Englishmen never saw fit to frame a written constitution, so were they not prepared to fetter their tongue, which had so splendidly shown its capacity for free flight in the soaring stanzas of the Elizabethan poets, and commit it to a council of Academicians.

In lieu of an academy, however, the English language got a dictionary, compiled by Dr. Samuel Johnson after seven years of solitary and dedicated effort and published in two folio volumes in 1755. Although Johnson had never openly opposed Swift's campaign for an academy, he had expressed scepticism, remarking that "sounds are too volatile and subtile for legal restraints; to enchain syllables and to lash the wind are equally the undertakings of pride". Yet as he assumed his tasks as a lexicographer he also stepped unabashedly into the role of a one-man academy. In the preface to his Dictionary he declared: "Every language . . . has its improprieties and absurdities which it is the duty of the lexicographer to correct or proscribe . . . This is my idea of an English Dictionary; a dictionary by which the pronunciation of our language may be fixed, and its attainment facilitated; by which its purity may be preserved, its use ascertained, and its duration lengthened."

Upon the publication of Johnson's Dictionary, his contemporaries were quick to recognize his great achievement. The actor David Garrick composed a couplet comparing Johnson's single-handed labours with the collaborative product of the Académie française:

> And Johnson, well arm'd like a hero of yore,
> Has beat forty French and will beat forty more.

The playwright Richard Brinsley Sheridan wrote: "If our language should ever be fixed, he must be considered by all posterity as the founder, and his dictionary as the cornerstone." And James Boswell hailed his hero as "the man who conferred stability on the language of his country".

Despite its well-known flaws—its prejudices (e.g. Johnson's famous definition of oats as "a grain, which in England is generally given to horses, but in Scotland supports the people"); its pedantry ("Cough: a convulsion of the lungs, vellicated by some sharp serosity"); and its inclusion of outlandish inkhorn words (*ariolation*, *ataraxy*, *clancular*, *comminuible*, *cubiculary*, *deuteroscopy*, *digladiation*, *dignotion*, *incompossible*)—the publication of Johnson's Dictionary represented a turning point in the history of the English language. For it was, after all, the first original and comprehensive English dictionary; and in garnering the rich vocabulary of eighteenth-century England, it fulfilled a great scholarly ideal of the age. There had been other dictionaries, one as early as 1538,[1] but they were for the most part

[1] The first good Latin-English dictionary was produced in 1538 by Sir Thomas Elyot (1490–1548), scholar, philosopher, poet, moralist, and Henry VIII's ambassador to the court of the Emperor Charles V. After going through several editions, it was enlarged by Thomas Cooper, Bishop of Winchester, under the title of *Cooper's Thesaurus* and became one of the best-known Elizabethan reference books. Scholars have speculated that Shakespeare probably used it.

either bilingual—Latin-English, French-English, Italian-English—or else compilations of hard words. Most of them were interrelated by plagiarism. It was not until 1721, when Nathaniel Bailey put out an etymological dictionary, that any lexicographer attempted to list all English words in a single volume. Although Johnson had these earlier sources at hand, he assembled his great work primarily from the wellsprings of his own gigantic erudition.

The other great need of the eighteenth-century men of letters was for a grammar, and this was filled in 1761 by that remarkably versatile scientist and philosopher, Joseph Priestley, best known as the discoverer of oxygen. Though disquisitions on English grammar had appeared during the sixteenth century, their objectives, as in the case of the early dictionaries, were either to instruct foreigners or to assist in the study of Latin. But Priestley's excellent pioneering work, *The Rudiments of English Grammar*, was designed for English readers. It not only marked the dawn of interest in English grammar as a study for scholarly consideration, but it enunciated vigorously the quite modern thesis that language is a fluid, ever-changing entity, and hence that general usage should be the arbiter of speech. Within the next two years, three other grammars appeared, and in 1776 George Campbell published his influential *Philosophy of Rhetoric*, dealing with questions of taste and style. From the combined efforts of these eighteenth-century grammarians, many firm precepts of modern usage evolved. To them we owe the clear specification of the difference between *lie* and *lay*; the propriety of *different from* (as opposed to *different than*); the sins of *between you and I*, *it is me*, *who is it for?*, *this here*, *that there*, *you was*; the error of using comparatives like *more* and *most* with incomparable adjectives like *perfect*, *unique*, *chief*, *circular*; and the separate and distinct uses of *between* and *among*, and *shall* and *will*.

In formulating their rules, the eighteenth-century grammarians relied to a large extent on the precedents of Latin and Greek. But against this traditional view, a counterpoint began to emerge. In his *Philosophy of Rhetoric*, Campbell declared: "It is not the business of grammar to give law to the fashions which regulate our speech . . . Modes of fashion no sooner obtain and become general than they are the laws of the language, and the grammarian's only business is to note, collect and methodize them." From this premise Campbell went on to define the concept of *usage*, to which he and Priestley accorded final authority, as "present, national and reputable use". By *reputable use* Campbell meant "whatever modes of speech are authorized as good by the writings of a great number, if not the majority, of celebrated authors". Campbell's definition of *usage* was the accepted one on both sides of the Atlantic throughout the nineteenth century and, indeed, until a very short time ago.

Points of divergence between American and British usage have lain mostly in the domain of vocabulary and pronunciation—the spoken word. The literary language has remained more or less uniform throughout the English-speaking world. And Noah Webster helped to make it so. For though he believed (as did Jefferson) that his country would in time evolve a national speech of its own, independent of England, he was equally determined that the American language must eliminate regional dialects and attune itself to a uniform standard of literary excellence. In 1789 he wrote: "The two points therefore which I conceive to be the basis of a standard in speaking, are these: *universal undisputed practice*, and the *principle of analogy*. [In its eighteenth-century context, *analogy* meant reason, logic, or consistency.] *Universal practice* is generally, perhaps always, a rule of propriety; and in disputed points, where people differ in opinion and practice, *analogy* should always decide the controversy." Supported by these precepts, and sustained by a national consensus of the educated and those who aspire to education, the American language evolved in an orderly fashion—sweeping words into its lexicon from all the varied stores of its polyglot clientele, striking off new coinage, transmuting dusty meanings into bright ones, wielding its resources with daring and gusto—but still preserving its links with the past.

2.

What then has interrupted this ordered evolutionary process? What has plunged the American language into a state of chaos? Sounds of alarm rang from coast to coast upon publication of the third edition of *Webster's New International Dictionary*. Never in modern America has an event of scholarly or intellectual significance been met by such an explosion of outrage and dismay. Seldom have American newspapers and magazines (save for certain arcane academic journals) expressed themselves with such unanimity and vehemence. *The New Yorker* accused it of "an incredible massacre" (of 250,000 words in Webster II which had been dropped from Webster III). *Life* ran a scathing editorial, damning it as "monstrous", "abominable", and a "non-word deluge". *The New York Times* laid down a double barrage, first in a sarcastic editorial charging that "the publication of a say-as-you-go dictionary can only accelerate the deterioration of the mother tongue", and later in the Sunday Book Review section, where its columnist, J. Donald Adams, termed the huge $47.50 volume "a gigantic flop", adding scornfully, "you may decide for yourself whether the use of that word as a descriptive term is slang or a colloquialism".

The undergirding reason for all the anger and contumely was that the nation's critics saw in the philosophical stance of Webster III a betrayal of trust, an abdication of responsibility for the treasure of our tongue, and a surrender to all the flabby, flaccid forces of permissiveness, formlessness, and mindlessness that have fogbound the arts, paralysed education, and nurtured what the late James Thurber called "our oral culture of pure babble". In its capitulation, they perceived the collapse of a last great bastion of the nation's literacy. For in the absence of an academy like that of France or Italy, the English language in America has been preserved and protected, as in England, by a tradition of literacy—a tradition upheld by an unorganized consensus of professional writers, critics, journalists, teachers, and scholars who ever turned in their extremities of doubt to *Webster's Dictionary* I or II. The defection of the editors of Webster III loomed, therefore, as the final rout in a long series of retreats from the former strongholds of literacy in many desolated sectors of contemporary American culture. To some observers it held ominous auguries for the future. For the state of the language reflects the state of the culture, and the decay of a language is both a symptom and a cause of the decay of institutions; its degeneration abets and accelerates theirs.

. . .

Prior to the dropping of the great lexicographical bomb, in what areas did indications of declining literacy and linguistic blight clearly appear? Most pervasively, perhaps, in the air. We live in the epoch of the Spoken Word; and the discovery of the transistor, for which three Bell Telephone physicists won the Nobel Prize in 1956, has now made it possible for anyone to get The Word, electronically amplified and packaged in a plastic case no bigger than a book, wherever he may be—in the desert or at sea, aboard a plane or on a mountaintop, or deep in some distant forest solitude. The question is: What does it say?

Quite possibly it may say, "Let us help you to accessorize your kitchen," or "Eat peanut brittle, like when you were little." But one must not confuse the medium with its content. The vast complex of electronic communication is one of the wonders of the world, even though it has been misused, like our language. By extending the range of the Spoken Word over barriers of space and time, electronics has nurtured man's indolent proclivity for talk rather than writing. The Spoken Word comes naturally, but it requires both discipline and a set purpose to reduce a welter of blubbery thought to lean and sinewy prose. For writing starts and ends with thinking, and thinking is work for which the primate musculature and sympathetic nervous system were never made. It is much easier for a businessman to put through a long-distance call, dictate long and loosely to a tape recorder, attend a conference or committee meeting, down Martinis at a company lunch or creative cocktail hour, and bustle around the clock from appointment to appointment in a whirl of ritual that affords a sensation of activity if not work. Recoil from the kind of mental activity which involves committing ideas to writing is not, however, a prejudice peculiar to men of affairs. Professional writers suffer from it too, and often more violently than any one else. Dr. Johnson once declared that "Nobody but a fool ever wrote except for money." And in Hollywood it is an old cliché that every story conference ends in uneasy silence, broken finally by the question, "Now who's going to do the paper work?" Yet the paper work does get done, and in quantities measurless to man. And on every page of it there appear those visual symbols of sound called "words"—all written by somebody, somewhere.

• •

Any look at the state of literacy in the United States should no doubt begin with the largest single category of reading matter: the comic book. It is perhaps not generally known that the total number of comic books printed in the United States each year approximates the combined annual output of all American book publishers, including producers of textbooks, technical books, reference books, and the Bible. The comic books struck their bonanza during World War II, when they became the almost unchallenged reading staple of America's armed forces. To this day the comics have retained their hold on the juvenile reading audience, a category ranging from pre-school levels to middle age.[1]

The influence of comic books on school children is a subject that has been vehemently debated everywhere for almost twenty years, without either theoretical resolution or concrete results. It goes without saying that all exponents of traditional disciplines in education—i.e. hard work and intellectual substance—would happily see all comic books burned. However, many educational theorists and child psychologists defend comic books on the grounds that (1) it is better for the children to read comics than nothing at all; (2) a child who begins by reading comic books sometimes develops a taste for the printed word and goes on to tackle real book-type books; and (3) bloodshed, violence, and gore in the so-called "horror" comics sublimate the child's subconscious feelings of aggression (This venerable postulate has in recent years been adopted and reiterated with renewed vigour by those who profit from sex and slaughter on television.)

As for the language of comic books, it must be said that the authors of many of the "quality" comics (those endorsed by various educational organizations or *Parents' Magazine*) restrict themselves scrupulously to standard usage. But countless others —whether "animal" or "horror" types—are shot through with sound effects—POW! WHAM! BONG!—denoting impact, as well as the drab spectrum of phatic monosyllables—*Huh? Duh. Blaa! Whee! Yikes! Ug! Glub! Wha?*—with which much of teenage America informs the world of its state of being.

For all their enormous circulation—some 600 million a year

[1] **Surveys have shown that among "senior citizens" (old folks) addiction to the comics, for some reason, tapers off.**

—comic books probably exert no more influence on the use of English in this country than the editorials in the *New York Daily News*, America's largest newspaper, exercise on political thought. As Jacques Barzun has observed: "The ignorance of the unlettered takes no scrutiny to establish. What we need to plumb is the ignorance of the educated and the anti-intellectualism of the intellectual."

In purely quantitative terms of verbal output—words, words, words—the most profuse source and proliferous disseminator is the great sprawling complex of advertising. Around the clock, through its various media, its relentless logorrhoea assails the ears and eyes of everyone in the land, though the eyes be glazed and the ears unwilling. And here we do indeed find a corrupting influence on the national tongue and one, moreover, that is consciously designed and ingeniously employed to corrupt. That usually amiable and urbane essayist, E. B. White, wrote caustically of advertising jargon not long ago: "With its deliberate infractions of grammatical rules and its cross-breeding of the parts of speech, it profoundly influences the tongues and pens of children and adults . . . It is the language of mutilation."

The English Department at Princeton University keeps a watchful eye on the advertising idiom and maintains a bulletin board to which it regularly affixes choice specimens labelled variously "No-English", "Doublespeak", "Overthink", "Minitrue", and the like. Some recent cullings: *Contact-less lenses—comfort-contoured to your cornea curvature* . . . *Ready-to-eat Protein for Ready-to-eat People* . . . *Laughter-light girdles* . . . *White Sale: Bamberger's bring you a riot of bright colors* . . . *Scotch me lightly* . . . *Quicker than instant* . . . *Perfume your psyche.*

The significant fact about the linguistic abuses and misuses of advertising is that they are not the slapdash errors of unlettered hacks, but the carefully conceived creations of educated writers and editors. Their grammatical distortions are conscious devices, gimmicks to catch attention—like the patch over the eye of the shirt model or the tattoo on the hand of the Marlboro smoker. It is a credo of the "advertising psychologists" retained by all the big agencies that colloquialism and vulgar usages establish a rapport with the mass audience.

From time to time, advertisers are summoned before a Congressional committee to justify their language. In a recent inquiry, spokesmen for certain food packagers were asked to explain their use of such expressions as *jumbo* and *full quart* (as opposed to *quart*), and in particular the classification of olives and prunes as *giant*, *colossal*, and *mammoth* rather than *small*, *medium*, and *large*. One witness, a "motivational research consultant" for the olive and prune packers, provided an answer rich with the idiom of his expertise. "Our entire social structure," he proclaimed, "depends on the mass production of psychologically satisfying products as much as the individual depends on these products in fulfilling his emotional needs." Words like *colossal* and *mammoth* are "more meaningful" than *large* or even *very large*, he said, adding, "Customers do not want 'small' prunes at any price".

Another great abattoir of language is the arena of politics, as it has ever been throughout history. Somewhat more than twenty-three centuries ago the resumption of peaceful relations between Athens and Sparta at the end of the Peloponnesian War was frustrated by the inability of the warring Greeks to understand each other after three decades of hostilities. "The meaning of words had no longer the same relations to things," the historian Thucydides related, "but was changed by men as they thought proper." In our own epoch the distortion of meaning for dialectical ends has been so common a practice, especially in totalitarian states, that any cautious reader or auditor of the news automatically takes pains to select the proper referent when he encounters such terms as *democracy*, *freedom*, *justice*, *patriotism*, *law*, *people*, *republic*, *reactionary* and the like. And the disease spreads continually, affecting new concepts, new countries. Just recently a Western diplomat in Africa complained to an American reporter: "The Communists have expropriated all the good words—anti-colonialism, African personality, Pan-Africanism. How are we supposed to beat that?"

Verbicide (as the murder of a word was termed by C. S. Lewis) is only one of many methods by which politics mounts an assault on language. In addition to small-scale guerrilla operations against individual words, politicians and their accessories, the bureaucrats, wage a kind of slow-poison warfare against the whole corpus of the language by stuffing it full of indigestible, fatty, polysyllabic verbiage. Although defenders of literacy grace in England complain of the "Officialese" dispensed from Whitehall,[1] the British product seldom compares with the suety offerings exuded from the political steam tables in Washington, as well as from the various state capitals and municipal council chambers throughout the nation. "The grossest thing in our gross national product today is our language", James Reston, distinguished columnist of *The New York Times*, wrote recently. "It is suffering from inflation."

Reston's criticism applied to the language in both its spoken and written forms. For samples of the former, one need look no farther than the transcripts of any of the new-style Washington press conferences (dating from 1952) in which touchy questions, formerly quashed with a brusque and presumably undemocratic "no comment" are often met squarely with a torrent of unintelligibility. (The strategy, of course, was not invented in 1952. As Oscar Wilde once wrote, "Nowadays to be intelligible is to be found out".) The written variety of Officialese is equally distended, but usually for another purpose: the wish of the author to magnify the importance of a trivial utterance by grandiloquent terminology. Specimens of Officialese can be exhumed by the thousands from the catacombs of any branch of the government. The creative techniques involved can best be illustrated, however, by translating a simple statement into what virtuosos of Officialese term a "directive". Suppose a member of the Federal Housing Authority scribbles a memo saying, "People who live in glasshouses shouldn't throw stones", and drops it in his out-going basket. After processing, it emerges from the government printing office in full verbal flower, thus:

Lease-holders, sub-tenants, heads of families and other persons currently in occupancy of residential units assembled from prefabricated vitreous modules are advised herewith that participation in activities involving the projection by manual or mechanical means

[1] In *The Reader Over Your Shoulder*, Robert Graves and Alan Hodge characterize Whitehallese thus: "The official style is at once humble, polite, curt and disagreeable; it derives partly from that used in Byzantine times by the eunuch slave-secretariat, writing stiffly in the name of His Sacred Majesty."

of mineralogical or geological specimens represents a violation of Article VI, Paragraph 279, of the Maintenance Code of the Federal Housing Act (USHER 2289) and offenders are subject to prosecution by order of . . .

No less stupefying than this form of verbal dropsy is another, quite different malady of Officialese induced apparently by some odd notion of conserving language through the use of abbreviations and acronyms. The practice began to flourish during the New Deal with the advent of FCC (Federal Communications Commission), NLRB (National Labour Relations Board), WPA (Works Progress Administration), and the other so-called alphabetical agencies. They continued to proliferate in ensuing years—most exuberantly perhaps in the mazes of the Pentagon. Today most newspaper readers can translate SAC (Strategic Air Command), and perhaps even DEW Line (Distant Early Warning Line), and BMEWS (Ballistic Missile Early Warning System). But probably few outside the armed forces are aware that FAGTRANS stands for "first available government transportation" or that SODTICIOAP means "special ordnance depot tool identification, classification, inventory and obsolescence analysis programme".

The deadening influence that official jargon can exert upon thought was a topic that preoccupied the late George Orwell. In his novel *1984* he recounted dramatically how a government in total control of all media of communication can and will so degrade language that words are drained of meaning, the process of thinking becomes impossible, and there is no truth save what those in power define. He developed the same thesis further in an essay *Politics and the English Language* shortly before he died. Citing the downward spiral of the alcoholic who drinks because he feels himself a failure and then fails more dismally still because he drinks, Orwell observes: "It becomes ugly and inaccurate because our thoughts are foolish, but the slovenliness of our language makes it easier for us to have foolish thoughts. . . . The great enemy of clear language is insincerity. When there is a gap between one's real and one's declared aims, one turns as it were instinctively to long words and exhausted idioms, like a cuttle-fish squirting out ink . . . But if thought corrupts language, language can also corrupt thought."

• • •

Officialese, or the jargon of government, however, flows limpid as a mountain stream beside the jargon of pedantry, or Academese. Where the author of Officialese wishes most of all to sound important, the author of Academese most often seeks hegemony in some restricted field which he regards as his private preserve. Cherishing his exclusivity, he affects a private language bristling with esoteric terminology and barricaded against comprehension by the amateur. Actually little talent is required to write jargon,[1] for it demands neither grace nor clarity, and these are the most difficult qualities for a writer to achieve. The chief requisite of Academese is the rumble *de profundis*, as I discovered a few years ago when I assisted in compiling the findings produced by one of those portentous projects on "The National Purpose" which the big foundations like to put their money into from time to time. My work involved collating mountains of papers, treatises and transscripts of symposia, and distilling them into summaries of reasonable size. The task was arduous, and I was distressed after some weeks to discover that my reports were being rewritten—at far greater length—by the editor in charge, a professor of political science at Harvard. He explained, when I questioned him, that my reports had been too compressed, had "packed too much material into too little space". I replied that I had always considered a ratio of maximum content to minimum space an objective of good writing. He said: "Well, my impression is that you've been straining for lucidity."

Academese pervades every area of scholarship—psychology, sociology, education, anthropology, economics, engineering. Each has its own arcane idiom, but the final effect is the same: opacity. Consider the following specimens from three fields. Although they happen to be travesties, they are brief and illustrate the genre. (1) Legal jargon. In a lecture at Cambridge University Sir Arthur Quiller-Couch demonstrated how Hamlet's soliloquy might be rendered in a courtroom brief: "To be, or the contrary. Whether the former or the latter be preferable would seem to admit of some difference of opinion." (2) Technological jargon. In a recent issue of *Product Engineering*

[1] *Jargon:* "The technical, esoteric, or secret vocabulary of a science, art, trade, sect, profession, or other special groups"—from an old, beat-up *Webster's Dictionary.*

there appeared an up-to-date version of "And God said: Let there be light, and there was light", as it would be reported by a modern systems engineer: "In response to a verbal stimulus for luminosity, initiated by the Master Control, a complete spectrum of visible radiation occurred." (3) Psychiatric jargon. According to Lionel Trilling the simple statement, "They fell in love and married", would be expressed by any self-respecting practitioner of the Freudian school of psychoanalysis as: "Their libidinal impulses being reciprocal, they activated their individual erotic drives and integrated them within the same frame of reference."

The headwaters of the great turgid stream of Academese lie somewhere back in the caves of nineteenth-century German scholarship, where no philosopher was worthy of the name unless he evolved his own System, Method, and Lexicon. But a major tributary now flows along the frontiers of modern science. For developments in physical thought during the twentieth century revealed a gulf between the coarse-grained world of men's immediate perceptions and the invisible cosmos of the atom. To interpret events within the microcosm, as well as those in the outer universe, physicists had to resort to increasingly abstract concepts and increasingly complex mathematical techniques. Watching the towering edifice of natural science rise, the social scientists aspired to a higher status too. They had long recognized and deplored and amorphous texture of their materials, the subjective character of their research techniques—in short their lack of true scientific rigour. Apophthegms such as "Sociology is just philosophy masquerading as a science" cut them to the quick. Thus challenged, they began to adopt the inductive methods of natural science: they built "laboratories"; evolved new formats for surveys and tests of every kind; minted new vocabularies; invented new concepts, units, and functions; and, above all, plunged into the great baroque sea of mathematics with unbridled passion. Today books and papers in every branch of the social sciences are not only adorned with strange and occult terminology but riddled with mathematical symbols, and cross-hatched and hemstitched with probability tables, sine curves, and other picturesque fashions in charts and graphs.

• • •

A distinguished scholar, bothered by the buzz of Academese about him, has remarked dourly that, in the world of education today, "communication occurs by good luck". For it is not only in the realms of science and social science that the jargon of pedantry prevails. Its accents dominate the discourse of the arts and the humanities, the language of literary, aesthetic, and musical criticism. One need not explore every compartment of criticism, for the same curtains of cumulo-nimbus rhetoric enshroud them all. I submit as an archtype of the modern critical mode this brief review of an exhibition by a young American painter which appeared in a recent issue of *Art News*:

> In these she has mostly turned to forms more hard-edged than usual to convey her poetry of growth and form; since many of these forms are discontinuous, her themes of concentricity and incrementation are carried by striping and surfing their edges to make archipelagoes which lift and sway like cobras across the often burnished surface, as in *Three Towards Four*, with its gleaming gold Rapunzel ambience and diffident organic calligraphy. But these larger pictures are transitional. More certain, solid and (as usual) beautiful are the smaller works with their earth-gem colors and cycloid, gyring, oculomotility and explicitness of generative warmth. . . . In any case there is something very American about the intense inner plasticity of her reach and vision.

The fundamental principles of critical jargon are: (1) avoidance of the explicit, and (2) concealment of the absence of thought by means of pretentious, technical, impenetrable verbiage. In the passage cited above, the reader must hack his way through such thickets as "poetry of growth and form", "diffident organic calligraphy", and "intense inner plasticity of her reach and vision". These are garlands of Academese in purest form. But elsewhere in the passage there are phrases evocative of a different but still distinctly contemporary American style. I refer to "archipelagoes which lift and sway like cobras" and "gleaming gold Rapunzel ambience". These have the timbre of Pure Creative Writing.

If one is searching for springs of language undefiled by pedantry, politics, or motivational vector analysis, in what more likely place can one look than the domain of belles-lettres? For is it not reasonable to assume that poets and novelists—craftsmen who employ the English language for aesthetic ends—must cherish its form and harmonies, respect its structure and traditions, and employ its rich, orchestral resources with veneration and care? But somehow a funny thing happened to creative writers on their way to 1966. In poetry two tendencies appeared. One derived from T. S. Eliot, whose erudition and use of symbolism, multiple imagery, and masked allusions—as manifested most strikingly in *The Waste Land*—engendered what has been termed the Footnote or Cryptographic School of poetry, which has to be decoded rather than read. Its offerings are characterized, as a rule, by scrupulous adherence to the classical disciplines of metre and rhyme on the one hand, and on the other by utter inscrutability. Here is a typical example:

QUI PRIMUS AB ORIS

We live extenuating circumstance
And husk our hearts in chowders of the night.
The blade of morning shears ambivalence
And circumcises seams of citrous light.
The paring of the eye to vestal vision
Prefixes young Persephone to bone,
Recording the ineffable incision
That pinks the agate image from the stone.
Sere spring derides fecundities of season,
The young autumnal ego alters pride,
Until the sterile will impregnates reason
With seed the seven senses atrophied.
Who graves the granite graduates from grieving—
The pale pomegranate shrivels past deceiving.

In exegesis I can only offer the obvious information that from the standpoint of prosody this curious specimen is a virtually flawless Shakespearian sonnet, adorned with a good deal of alliteration, and that its title comes from the opening line of Virgil's *Aeneid* and means literally, "Who first from the shores". Apart from these small details, all is darkness.

The second main tendency in modern poetry flows toward the opposite pole. Here the objective is to cast off the restraints of traditional poetic forms and to sing with unpremeditated ecstasy. The evolution of free verse from Whitman, down through Sandburg and the poets of the twenties and thirties, is a familiar chapter of literary history and it is relevant here only with respect to its denouement in the hands of the beatniks. For along with the ad writers and pedants, the beatniks are enemies of language. The cult of slovenliness which they display in their dress is also the controller of their speech. They have no organized speech. For the most part they are determinedly anti-verbal, communicating by grunts, grimaces, and interjections. Their use of "man" and "like" may be somewhat equivalent to the average person's occasional "er", a species of stammer—e.g. "So we came to this big town like and all the streets were like crazy, man". However, a perceptive observation on the beatnik's use of "like" has been adduced by Walker Gibson, poet and Professor of English at New York University, in a recent essay: "The beats, in their crude and sloppy way, have surrounded much of their language with a metaphorical blur by using . . . the simple device of 'like'. They suggest with this blur their conviction of the impossibility of anybody else's doing any better with words. Only squares believe you can speak 'precisely'."

In accordance with their doctrine of unorganized expression, much of the beatniks' "poetry" is extemporized on the spur of the moment before an audience and recorded, if at all, on tape. Occasionally, however, their inspirations find their way on to a printed page. The following lines from an avant-garde quarterly suggest the mode:

HELLO POEM

Hello wife, hello world, hello God,
I love you; hello certain monsters,
Ghosts, office buildings, I love you. Dog,
Dog-dogs, cat, cat-cats, I love you. . . .
Hello Things-in-Themselves, Things Not Quite
In Themselves (but trying), I love you . . .

The IRT,
The BMT; the London subway
(Yes, yes, pedants, the Underground)
System; the Moscow subway system,
All subway systems except the

Chicago subway system. Ah yes,
I love you, the Chicago El-

Evated. Sexual intercourse.
Hello, hello.
Love, I love you; Death,
I love you. . . . .

A similar free flux of words characterizes the prose of the beat school of novelists. Their prototype, of course, is Jack Kerouac, and a passage in the opening chapter of his first novel, *On the Road*, not only illustrates the style but provides a revealing insight into the beatnik writer's *modus operandi*:

As far as my work was concerned he said, "Go ahead, everything you do is great." He watched over my shoulder as I wrote stories, yelling, "Yes! That's right! Wow! Man" and "Phew!" and wiped his face with his handkerchief. "Man, wow, there's so many things to do, so many things to write! How to even *begin* to get it all down and without modified restraints and all hung-up on like literary inhibitions and grammatical fears. . . ."

I personally have never had the experience of writing with an audience, even of one, hanging over my shoulder and yelling, "Wow", or "Phew" (or even "Boo!") as the little black letters appeared on the big white page. For all I know, this may be one of life's more exotic experiences that, somehow, I have missed. But the testimony of most writers suggests that the act of writing is generally a solitary effect for which applause, if any, is long deferred. It is not, I think, one of the performing arts.

Quite apart from the watcher by the writing machine, the phrases "literary inhibitions" and "grammatical fears" are revealing, for they epitomize the thinking of one school of writing (and of teachers of composition) today. The underlying premise is that the aspirant writer, the future poet or novelist, must express himself freely; that his talent will atrophy if he gets "hung up" on rules of grammar and syntax. This notion derives from a wedding of modern educational theories (of which more later) with the literary precedent of James Joyce. Endowed with neither the erudition nor the poetic genius of Joyce, exponents of the "free-write" school have found in his works (if they ever read them) chiefly the demise of sentence structure and a sanction for unintelligibility. One would think that in *Finnegan's Wake* Joyce has extended his genre to its ultimate limit. But no. We have today a new technique of "writing" that is analogous to the *collage* in the fields of painting, photography, and the cinema. It was described in a recent issue of the *Transatlantic Review* by William Burroughs, whose novels have been praised by many critics (most notably by the astute and acidulous Mary McCarthy):

Pages of text are cut and rearranged to form new combinations of word and image—In writing my last two novels, Nova Express and The Ticket That Exploded, i [*sic*] have used an extension of the cut up method i call the "fold in method"—A page of text—my own or some one elses—is folded down the middle and placed on another page—The composite text is then read across half one text and half the other—The fold in method extends to writing the flash back used in films, enabling the writer to move backwards and forewards on his time track—For example i take page one and fold it into page one hundred—I insert the resulting composite as page ten—When the reader reads page ten he is flashing forwards in time to page one hundred and back in time to page one. . . .

What does any writer do but choose, edit and rearrange material at his disposal?—The fold in method gives the writer literally infinite extension of choice. . . . The method could also lead to a collaboration between writers on an unprecedented scale to produce works that were the composite effort of any number of writers living and dead—This happens in fact as soon as any writer starts using the fold in method—I have made and used fold ins from Shakespeare, Rimbaud, from newspapers, magazines, conversations and letters so that the novels i have written using this method are in fact composites of many writers—

He then provides a specimen of the technique, a fold-in of lecture notes, texts from several writers, and newspaper articles. Here is one fragment:

On reflection we can discover cross references scrawled by some boy with scars—The last invisible shadow caught and the future fumbles for transitory progress in the arts—Flutes of Ali in the door of panic leaves not a wrack of that God of whom i was a part—The future fumbles in dogs of unfamiliar dust—Hurry up—Page summons composite mutterings flashing forward in your moments i could describe—The deja vue boatman smiles with such memory orders. . . .

What does one find in this progression from the early experiments of Joyce and Gertrude Stein in the 1920's to the fold-in *collage* of the 1960's? First, it is evident that what began as an attempt to achieve new fluencies of expression and mood by renouncing certain traditional forms and disciplines has culminated in the abandonment of all form, all discipline—and all meaning. The same flight from order has been noted, of course, in other varieties of artistic expression—in atonal music, the unstructured dance, amorphous sculpture and, most familiarly, in the abstract expressionist or drip-dry school of painting. Yet there is a difference. For where the musical scale and the colours of the spectrum impinge directly on the senses and evoke an immediate emotional response, language is merely a system of arbitrary symbols and any effect it may produce—in conveying an idea, image, or emotion—is achieved indirectly and is entirely dependent on its substantive content. However one may feel about dissonance in music or abstract expressionism as opposed to the melodies of Mozart or the representational art of the past, there is a case to be made for both of them. Atonal music can produce powerful dramatic effects; and many abstract expressionist paintings awaken, purely through the interplay of form and colour, a range of the same sensations of pleasure induced by striking designs in wallpaper or upholstery. But words do nothing if they are emptied of meaning. Language is wholly cerebral: it is an artificial medium of communication, far subtler than wavelengths of light or harmonic frequencies, which are found in nature. Language was devised by man, it is unique to man, and it works only when men agree on what its components mean.

Far more than the retreat from form, it is the retreat from content that has most seriously disturbed many critics of contemporary writing. In his provocative book, *The House of Intellect*, Jacques Barzun points out that for several generations the trend in all art forms has been away from common experience and common understanding and in the direction of "the singular and indefinable". The notion has spread that aesthetic experience is not only private but incompatible with explicit thought or precise articulation. To *feel* is the important thing. And this liking for the ambiguous and mystical, Barzun contends "is, at bottom, a love of confusion—confusion sought as a release from responsibility".[1]

In their assault on precision of language and precision of thought, the avant-garde writers have not been without allies. They have been "met halfway", Barzun observes, "by a public turning aside from words and greedy for speechless art. The new pastimes of the educated amateur are the arts of non-articulate expression"—e.g. Sunday painting, quartet playing, ceramics, wood-carving, and similar "creative" hobbies. "Everywhere pictures and sound crowd out text. The Word is in disfavour, not to say in disrepute—which is indeed one way of abolishing the problem of communication. . . . The revulsion from words, syntax and coherence accounts for the widespread anarchy in the handling of the mother tongue." A vivid manifestation of the recoil from words may be observed in the popularity of a new type of phonograph record which revives the most memorable song hits of the thirties and forties with the original lyrics excised and supplanted by animalic grunts (oh! ah! oo! dum! do!) to the rhythms of rock 'n roll.

3.

The war against the English language is thus a many-pronged offensive, waged amid jungles of jargon, over oceans of Officialese, prairies of pedantry, and mountains of mish-mash, while the air oscillates with electronic frenzy. The common bond that unites the foe is utter disdain for the reader. Each saboteur at the typewriter keyboard is preoccupied solely with his own objectives. Whether for reasons of indifference, incapacity, or indolence, they all ignore Dr. Johnson's crucial precept: "What is written without effort is in general read without pleasure."

[1] The current fad for Zen Buddhism reflects these tendencies. For the concepts of Zen, like those of most Oriental philosophies, lie enshrouded in veils of cosmic mist. A characteristic statement of aesthetic purpose by a Zen-minded composer, John Cage, was quoted recently in the *Saturday Review:* "I have nothing to say and I am saying it, and that is poetry as I need it." To which a Zen-minded reviewer added approvingly: "The poetry of silence is endless; the purpose of purposelessness is union. This is most ancient wisdom."

Writers of the past respected this opinion and sometimes rephrased it in other ways, as did Yeats, for example, who wrote:

> A line will take us hours maybe,
> Yet if it does not seem a moment's thought,
> Our stitching and unstitching has been naught.

Anatole France expressed it thus: "*Caressez longtemps votre phrase, elle finira par sourire.*"

Signs of disintegration of the language might have gone unnoticed by the American public for several years—despite skirmishing, infiltration, and the fall of isolated redoubts—had it not been for the collapse of two major bastions of the mother tongue: The Bible and The Dictionary. Early in 1961, the New Testament section of *The New English Bible* appeared, the latest of modern translations (its most recent predecessor being the Revised Standard Version of 1952). Since the King James Version and the works of Shakespeare have generally been ranked together as the noblest monuments of the English language, many laymen wondered why the majestic seventeenth-century translation could not be left alone. For of all the Bibles in Christendom it is only the English Bible that is regarded as a great work of literature. And as Dwight Macdonald has observed, the rest of the world might think us fortunate that our greatest prose work is also, by virtue of religious veneration, the most widely read book in the English tongue. The intent of the translators of the new version was twofold: to correct textual errors in the King James Version revealed by recent discoveries of new manuscripts, and by rendering it in "frankly contemporary English" (changing *thou* and *thee* to *you*, for example), to make it as "readable" as any other book. Unfortunately, a good many readers have felt that although the objectives of scholarship may have been fulfilled, the new version has simply stripped away the beauty and splendour of the old without any notable addition to understanding. Even such an upholder of the contemporary idiom as Bergen Evans (who has staunchly defended Webster III against its critics) confessed to being repelled by its style. Remarking that most of the changes seemed to him "unnecessary and even harmful . . . mere busywork", Evans wrote in *The New York Times* Magazine: "In achieving the blandness of contemporary expository prose, the inoffensive language of a commercial civilization, the translators have been dismayingly successful. . . . Maybe the Bible can't really be translated into contemporary prose. The poetic archaism of the King James Version—with its majesty, its stupendous music, its moving eloquence, its wildness and passion—may be ideally suited to its subject. Can Ecclesiastes, for instance, really be stated in the idiom of Rotary? Does the Book of Job lend itself to the language of *The Reader's Digest* or Isaiah to the speech of the tabloids?" On the other side of the Atlantic, T. S. Eliot dismissed the new version as "a combination of the vulgar, the trivial and the pedantic".

The reaction to *The New English Bible* seemed but a murmur, however, in comparison to the explosion touched off by the publication a few months later of *Webster's Third New International Dictionary*. Critics who viewed the rewriting of the King James Version as a misdemeanour, somewhat akin to the defacing of a public edifice, saw in the transmutation of the Dictionary by Dr. Philip B. Gove and his staff a sack of the uttermost citadel and sanctuary of the English language in America by the very people charged with its preservation. It was as though the Secretary of the Treasury had helped himself to the gold stores at Fort Knox in order to play the horses. In brief, the editors of Webster III were charged with abrogating their responsibility as custodians of the language by: (1) blurring to the point of obliteration the traditional criteria for distinguishing levels of usage—e.g. they had dropped completely such warning labels as *colloquial*, *erroneous*, *illiterate*, and employed the terms *non-standard* and *slang* with a caution amounting to reluctance; (2) including hundreds of transitory and dubious expressions as standard; (3) expunging a quarter of a million words from the literary past, with the cut-off date arbitrarily set at 1755; (4) discarding illustrative citations from the classics in favour of contemporary utterances by, among others, Bob Hope, Jimmy Durante, Art Linkletter, and Ethel Merman; (5) compounding misunderstanding by refusing to discriminate between words often confused (such as *semi-monthly* and *bi-monthly*, *depreciate* and *deprecate*, *forceful* and *forcible*). This bill of particulars, considered in toto, thus accused the editors of Webster III of degrading the language by refusing to acknowledge there is any difference between good and bad, correct and incorrect usage. And, indeed, Dr. Gove did not repudiate the charges. On the contrary, he made it clear that in his view verbal usage is simply a matter of social usage, an aspect of etiquette. A dictionary, he declared, "should have no traffic with . . . artificial notions of correctness or superiority. It must be descriptive, not prescriptive."[1]

Dr. Gove's viewpoint—and his dictionary—have had their defenders as well as their detractors, and it is revealing to discern how the opposing forces line up. Arrayed overwhelmingly, almost unanimously against Webster III were professional writers, journalists, critics, professors of literature and the humanities, and lovers of the language in general. On the other hand it was widely approved by educational theorists, many English teachers, and all apostles and exponents of Structural Linguistics (of which Dr. Gove is one). As the adversaries clashed violently, in print and on the air, the public became dimly aware of certain developments that faculty members in liberal arts colleges and universities and other observers of trends in education have known for a long time—namely, that the teaching of English in America has undergone a revolution in the last three decades, and that this revolution has, as Dwight Macdonald wrote in a scathing review of Webster III in *The New Yorker*, "meshed gears with a trend toward permissiveness in the name of democracy, that is debasing our language by rendering it less precise and thus less effective as literature and less effective as communication".

For some years before the issues burst into the open, however, businessmen, lawyers, editors, personnel managers of corporations, and deans of admission of professional schools had been complaining that today's college graduates (to say nothing of high-school graduates) cannot spell, punctuate, or organize their thoughts in coherent verbal form. From various quarters some disquieting communiqués made their way into public view. For example:

[1] Commenting on Dr. Gove's statement, E. B. White has written: "This approach struck many people as chaotic and degenerative, and that's the way it strikes me. . . . Unless someone is willing to entertain notions of superiority, the English language disintegrates, just as a home disintegrates unless someone in the family sets standards of good taste, good conduct and simple justice."

• A report entitled *The National Interest and the Teaching of English*, published by the National Council of Teachers of English in 1961, disclosed that some four million school children in the United States have "reading disabilities", that approximately 150,000 students failed college entrance examinations in English in 1960; and that seventy per cent of American colleges and universities find it necessary to offer remedial work in English.

• Dean Erwin N. Griswold of the Harvard Law School reported that numbers of applicants to his school, otherwise apparently acceptable, offered college records showing no courses in literature or language (nor for that matter in mathematics, science, or philosophy), but consisting wholly of such subjects as Principles of Advertising Media, Office Management, Principles of Retailing, Stage and Costume Design, and Methods in Minor Sports.

• The United States Department of State has initiated a course in English composition for its officers and staff men who often cannot understand one another's memoranda.

• Washington University, in St. Louis, announced in 1963 a special project, budgeted at $136,000, to translate the jargon of social scientists into English.

• A newspaper editor, admonishing the deans and faculties of American schools of journalism, declared in 1963: "I know you are weary of hearing that your graduates are deficient in spelling and in basic grammar, but I assure you all—or almost all—of the college graduates we have got in recent years, whether journalism graduates or not, are below the better grammar school graduates of 30 years ago in spelling and grammar."

If democracy depends on literacy, then one finds here some cause for alarm. What produced this sorry state of affairs? In an address before the Modern Language Association of America at the end of 1963, Dr. Francis Keppel, United States Commissioner of Education and former dean of the Harvard University faculty of education, pointed squarely at the English teachers of the nation's schools and colleges. "The situation in the teaching of English at all levels of American education is grave", Dr. Keppel declared—so grave indeed as to threaten the foundations of the whole educational system. He noted the unequal apportioning of Federal funds for education—the force-feeding of science and technology at the expense of the starving humanities. But at the same time he looked askance at the qualifications of the teachers themselves, pointing out that a recent survey of high-school English teachers had disclosed that, out of a polling sample of nearly 7,500, only 50.5 per cent had majored in English in college. The survey also showed that the teachers placed a rather low evaluation on their own competency. Nearly one-half rated themselves as poorly prepared to teach literature, two-thirds assessed themselves as poorly prepared to teach composition and speech, and 90 per cent acknowledged that they were poorly prepared to teach reading. At the college level, Dr. Keppel reported, the situation was "equally disturbing". Ten years ago 20 per cent of college English professors held the degree of Doctor of Philosophy; only 12.6 per cent have Ph.D.'s today.

In 1961 the National Council of Teachers of English issued an extensive report on the problem, confessing with some understatement that "neither informed laymen nor leading teachers of English are satisfied with the results of present-day English teaching". To the extent of 140 pages (complete with charts and tables), the authors of the report set forth their analysis of the situation. First and foremost, they declared, many English teachers are inadequately educated for their calling; and secondly—and surprisingly—many state departments of education could hardly care less. After some illuminating statistics, the report proceeded to swing wildly in all directions, seeking targets, and finding, among other reasons for the low estate of English teaching today, such factors as: crowded classrooms, overloaded schedules, and inadequate library facilities (doubtless legitimate complaints); poorly planned buildings; lack of coordination among states in the absence of national standards; lack of proper supervision; lack of articulation in English curricula from grade to grade; lack of tape recorders, record players, and other mechanical aids; and lack of "basic pedagogical research and experimental planning".

The report also included some recommendations: "If the teaching of English is to be improved throughout the United States, bold and direct action must be undertaken nationally."

This would involve "large-scale programmes supported by Congressional appropriations or massive co-ordinated programmes sponsored by independent educational foundations". And what would these large-scale, massive co-ordinated programmes include? Well, among other things: "Development of national institute programmes to provide training in the essential content and methods of English . . . Establishment of regional centres for study and demonstration of sequential, articulated programmes in English . . . Assistance to architects and administrators in planning ideal facilities for English instruction . . . Experimentation in using electronic, audio-visual, and other aids to improve English teaching . . ." etc., etc.

As one caustic advocate of old-fashioned teaching methods observed after studying this report, "It seems to have been written from the moon".[1] For, as might be expected, it uttered not a single word about the factors that almost everyone outside the cloisters of pedagogy (including an increasingly voluble number of parents) holds responsible for the prevalence of student illiteracy today. To many it seems obvious that the reasons Johnny can't read and College John can't write lie not in any need for sequential, articulated programmes or electronic, audio-visual aids, but in the theories and practices of American education as they have luxuriated in the past thirty years. John Dewey has absorbed much of the blame for the deterioration of educational rigour, the emphasis on adjustment rather than achievement, the supplanting of competition by conformity and the substitution of discussion for study. But it was rather his apostles and exegetes, who diverted the course of education away from the pursuit of knowledge and toward the cloudy goal of "preparation for life".

Thus today teachers no longer teach subjects, they "teach the whole child". Indeed, the old familiar subjects can no longer be discerned; they have been melted down, and transfused into viscid amalgams called "Earth Science", "Language Arts", "Social Studies", and "Human Relations". The very

[1] Of an earlier report by the same organization, Jacques Barzun once declared: "The volume is one long demonstration of the authors' unfitness to tell anybody anything about English."

word "study", is outmoded. For, recognizing that concentration—the difficult art of paying attention to a sequence of thought—is arduous and distasteful to a well-adjusted child, the educationists have invented a whole range of "activities" to while away the classroom day and lull the restless spirit—"research projects", "living predicaments", "panoramas", and "junior town meetings".

The bill of particulars against modern pedagogy is a lengthy one and has been well articulated elsewhere. But with respect specifically to the teaching of English and the promotion of literacy, the most violent storms centre upon the "whole-word" or "look-say" method of reading instruction, the contrivance known as "vocabulary control", the prevalence of fatuous readers and reading lists, and the universal employment of multiple-choice or punch-card examinations.

Under the look-say reading system, a pupil is taught to identify words as homogeneous units, instead of perceiving their components through knowledge of the alphabet and syllabification. Although the traditional phonic system, which was standard until the educational revolution of the thirties, is returning to some schools, others do not expect a child to know what a syllable is until the third grade (about 9 years old) or to know the order of the alphabet until junior high (15 or 16 years old). According to a recent study by the Council for Basic Education, a child taught by the "look-say" method generally commands a vocabulary of some 1,300 words by the end of the third grade, while a child taught by the phonic method has a vocabulary twice that size by the end of the first grade. As a matter of fact, the great Italian educator Maria Montessori showed more than half a century ago that children learn to read best by learning to write—by translating familiar sounds into visual symbols, rather than the reverse. But in modern education writing is considered a secondary and even peripheral skill.

Equally controversial and, it would seem, even less defensible, is the strange device known as "vocabulary control", which is expressly designed to hold down the number of words a child may learn at any given time. Under the assumption that gulping too many new words at a sitting may give the tender young reader a case of verbal indigestion, writers of textbooks confine themselves to rigidly restricted word lists, which are let out an inch or so at a time from grade to grade. Thus in the fourth grade the American school child uses a primer of some 1,800 words. The Russian child, according to a recent comparison of American and Soviet school systems, has a primer of 2,000 words in the first grade and of 10,000 words in the fourth. He is, moreover, reading Tolstoy in the first grade, while Johnny is working his way through books entitled *A Good Big Fire*, *The Blue and Yellow Boats*, and *A Funny Sled*.

Within the limits of vocabulary control and word frequency lists, the primers are bound to be dull and totally deviod of literary merit. And as the grades roll by, the texts used in English classes continue to be delimited by various paralysing restrictions. It is not only the ever-present fear of controversy, of sex, or of the American Legion and other book censors that holds down the range of permissible reading matter. The educationists have imposed a variety of controls of their own, born of the sensational discovery that knowledge of literature is useful not for its own sake, but because of the "positive values" it may impart. In his informative book, *The Schools*, Martin Mayer quotes a member of the English Department at Teachers College, Columbia University, who proclaimed authoritatively, "You can teach the same values with Edna Ferber as you can with Shakespeare". And indeed Edna Ferber ranks high on many a high-school reading list, along with Pearl Buck, Ernest Hemingway, J. D. Salinger, stories from *The Saturday Evening Post* and assorted radio and television dramas. Nowhere on the lists does one find the works of Swift, Fielding, Addison and Steele, Leigh Hunt, Boswell, Dryden, Pope, or other great writers of the Augustan Age. For, as in the case of Webster III, there has been a cut-off date. "Everything before the Nineteenth Century has almost disappeared," Mayer reports, "except for Shakespeare and the excerpts in the anthologies."

The same idiosyncrasies pervade the contemporary texts devoted to composition and grammar. Why should anyone learn to write?—To articulate thought? Tell a story, expound a theory, or reduce a poetic concept to disciplined iambics? Not at all. According to a publication of the National Council of Teachers of English, entitled *Meeting Youth's Needs Through Writing*: "Sharing ideas or experiences through writing is one way of learning to know one's self and to enrich one's personality." And the topics suggested in the composition books as essay assignments include *Getting Along With People*, *My First Date*, *No Mother Is Like My Mother*, *Teachers As They Really Are*. One professor from a conservative New England institution has declared flatly: "English composition is the sickest subject in American education today."

Another contrivance of the modern educational system, equally destructive of literacy, is the multiple-choice examination, for it demands of the student only an X on a dotted line rather than the sustained intellectual effort of marshalling his thoughts and expressing them coherently in an ordered structure of language. The reasons for its inception and universal use are well understood: there simply are not enough examiners to grade millions of essay-type questions, and computing machines are faster and cheaper. Nevertheless, many thoughtful critics of modern education look upon the multiple-choice examination with concern. For one thing, the phrasing of questions is often imprecise and ambiguous, and an intelligent student who can discern several possible answers to a question is more likely to select a wrong answer than another who has less imagination. The bright student will perceive nuances and shades of meaning; he will sense pitfalls and anticipate traps; he will want to qualify his responses. But like a witness in a courtroom, bullied by a prosecutor who demands a *Yes* or *No* answer, he will be forced to gamble all his reservations and modulations of thought upon a single X in a blank. A machine will scan it and accept no explanations—and kindly do not staple or bend, for ideas do not fit into programmed computers. The case against the multiple-choice or "objective" test has been best epitomized by Dr. Banesh Hoffman, Professor of Mathematics at Queens College. Their basic defect, he says, is that "they call for choices but not reasons for choices. . . . Defective test questions tend to turn multiple choice tests into lotteries. . . . For multiple choice tests, by their very nature, tend to favour the pickers of choices over the doers, and the superficially brilliant over the creatively profound. And the use of these tests has a baleful influence on teachers and teaching."

4.

More baleful, however, than any of the other factors conducing to the demise of literacy and the degeneration of English has been the abandonment of grammar in favour of "modern linguistic science". The enmity between upholders of traditional grammar and the exponents of Structural Linguistics runs deeper than any other conflict in the whole battleground of education. And the Structural Linguists appear to be winning. In a single generation they have driven grammar, as it was taught to everyone now over forty, out of most of the public schools of the country. They have buried Caesar, without praise, and laid Cicero to rest by his side along with the whole corpus of Latin grammar and literature. They have infiltrated the English departments of many teachers' colleges, influenced the training of student teachers and thus affected the teaching of English to children in public elementary and secondary schools. They have, as noted earlier, taken over Webster's Unabridged Dictionary. And they dominate the National Council of Teachers of English, which accounts, of course, for the fact that the Council's periodic jeremiads upon the sad state of English teaching place the blame on everything but the practice of teaching itself. A recent N.C.T.E. report clearly reflects its bias through the recurring use of such phrases as "traditional eighteenth-century Latinate grammar", "old-fashioned grammatical apparatus", "language superstitions", "substitution of a scientific attitude for eighteenth century assumptions", and "pressure of the demand for traditional grammar from the uninformed". On the other hand the report acclaims the "spectacular advances that have been made in the field of descriptive linguistics", adding that "these advances . . . constitute a breakthrough comparable to those in physics and mathematics".

What kind of breakthrough? Inasmuch as there is only the murkiest understanding of Structural Linguistics outside its own domain, it must be explained that the term involves both a method and a philosophy, or rather—since the Structural Linguists regard *philosophy* as a dirty word—a set of principles. The method has proved of enormous worth in several varied fields. It is the essential tool of cultural anthropologists concerned with studies of languages outside the Indo-European family, and especially those of primitive people without a system of writing. It is extremely useful to certain language teachers whose function it is to impart a quick, practical grasp of a second (i.e. foreign to the student) *spoken* tongue. And by virtue of its painstaking techniques of vocal sound analysis, it has greatly assisted communication engineers in the design of equipment for the transmission of speech, data-processing machines and digital-to-sound transducers.

Granted these undeniable contributions, the question remains: What does Structural Linguistics have to offer to the practice of teaching English to children born to the English tongue? Many educators in the country today believe that the methods of Structural Linguistics are, in this capacity, of dubious value at best. Some believe them downright calamitous. Yet if the dispute had involved only Method, the arguments pro and con might have been contained discreetly within the academic community. But the Structural Linguists are not—and have not been for the last quarter-century—content with a role as objective scientists, collectors of data, technicians, and taxonomists. Their approach embraces psychology, sociology, and education, and they propagate it with evangelical fervour. It is, therefore, their "basic principles" that have aroused a conflict which has spread far beyond educational circles to the nation at large. These principles have been stated most succinctly by Dr. Robert A. Hall, Jr., Professor of Linguistics at Cornell University, in his book *Linguistics and Your Language*:

There is no such thing as good and bad (or correct and incorrect, grammatical and ungrammatical, right and wrong) in language.

There is no such thing as "written language". There is speech and there is writing; and of these two, speech is basic in human life and writing is a reflection of speech. Changing the writing is not changing the language.

A dictionary or grammar is not as good an authority for your own speech as the way you yourself speak.

Words do not have any "real" meaning as opposed to other "false" meanings. Any meaning people give to a word is automatically its *real* meaning under those circumstances. [Cf. Humpty-Dumpty.]

All languages and dialects are of equal merit, each in its way.

When languages change, they do not "decay" or become "corrupted"; a later stage of a language is worth neither more nor less than an earlier stage.

Inasmuch as Structural Linguistics developed in the United States out of the quiet work of a few anthropologists engaged in the study of Athabascan, Algonquian, and other American Indian tongues, it seems astonishing that such a remote and highly specialized realm of scholarship could engender the extraordinary precepts enunciated above or exercise such a powerful effect on standards of English—the most widely used language in the world—and the methods of teaching it in schools.

Man's interest in language, as opposed to linguistic science, goes back (along with most other components of Western culture) to the ancient Greek philosophers who debated at length the question whether language inheres in the nature of things, and is hence logical, or consists merely of an arbitrary set of symbols without logic. The latter view was upheld by Socrates and is contested by no one today. From Socrates down to the nineteenth century the study of language remained a by-product of the study of history, theology, philosophy, and literature, and as such was confined to the written languages of Europe as well as Hebrew and Arabic. The age of exploration, however, disclosed that in the new, unfolding, far-off lands, exotic tongues were spoken, far outnumbering the transcribed languages of the civilized world. As trade and commerce spread, knowledge of these curious tongues grew swiftly, and in the decade between 1806 and 1817 a pair of devout and assiduous German scholars translated the Lord's Prayer into nearly 500 languages collected from all corners of the globe. Linguistics began to emerge and diverge from philology in the latter half of the nineteenth century as a consequence of the work of two German scientists: the versatile physicist Hermann von Helmholtz, who initiated research in vocal phonetics, and the physiologist Wilhelm Wundt, who first studied language within the framework of social psychology. The most important linguistic developments of the century, however, occurred in France and Russia. In Paris, a young scholar named Ferdinand de Saussure (1875–1913) conceived the idea that structure, not meaning, was the key to language analysis. In a series of lectures, which were published only after his death, he showed that language is never a mere sequence of words, like beads on a string; on the contrary each and every language in the world is a complex structure or system which can be analysed—and, most specifically, analysed *without regard to meaning*. For his contribution, de Saussure is generally regarded as the founder of modern descriptive linguistics. Of no less importance was the formulation by the Russian linguists Baudouin de Courtenay and Nikolai Kruszewski of a concept that provided the basic tool of linguistic analysis: the unit of speech known as the *phoneme*. Armed with the phoneme, linguists are able to isolate, analyse, and record the vocal sounds of any language in the world without recourse to alphabets or other existing calligraphic codes. The phoneme has been called the molecule of speech; and like the molecule of chemistry it is not a fundamental or irreducible particle but a rather complex entity with properties about which linguists do not always agree.

In the United States, the great anthropologist Franz Boas of Columbia University made extensive studies between 1897 and 1908 of the languages of various American Indian tribes, which, of course had no script, no history and had never before attracted scholarly interest. But it was not until the second and third decades of this century that Structural Linguistics came to full flower through the work of two men who are universally recognized as its American progenitors. One was Boas's brilliant student Edward Sapir (1884–1939), who divided his professional career between investigating the language and culture of the Wishram and Athabascan Indians of the northern Pacific coast, and teaching—his final academic post was the Sterling Chair of Anthropology and Linguistics at Yale. The second was Leonard Bloomfield (1887–1949) of Chicago, a behaviourist, who first worked intensively on Menominee (a branch of Central Algonquian still spoken in Wisconsin and around the Great Lakes), and in later years made a definitive study of Tagalog, the language of Luzon and now the official tongue of the Philippine Islands.

Their early studies were pursued with enormous patience in the face of enormous difficulties—for the languages they undertook to master had no written script whatever. By the tedious process of questioning native speakers day after day, week after week, they eventually began to discern distinct forms and elements in what had seemed at first an impenetrable vocal blur. Many of the sounds articulated by the Indians could not be represented by the familiar letters of the Roman alphabet. The grammar—a term defined by Bloomfield as "the meaningful arrangements of forms in a language"—was utterly different from that of English, Latin, or any of the historic tongues which had been the only concern of linguistic scholars in the past. They found, moreover, that the presumably "primitive" Indian languages were by no means primitive in the sense of being rudimentary or unevolved; on the contrary, they proved to be extremely complex and endowed with rich resources of expression and content. The linguists' most important contribution, however, transcended their first practical success in analysing the structures and recording the vocabularies of obscure and hitherto unknown tongues. More memorably, they discovered the existence of certain basic elements of human speech which the Indian languages shared in common not only with each other but with all other languages on earth. And thus they conceived a means of analysis that could be universally applied without reference to the terms and concepts of traditional grammar. From the pioneering work of Sapir and Bloomfield, the more detailed methods and principles of Structural Linguistics subsequently evolved. In the next quarter-century, many massive volumes, densely forested with phonetic symbols, mathematical equations, and occult terminology (*rephonemicization*, *suprasegmental*, *morpholexical*) were extruded by disciples of Sapir and Bloomfield in universities across the land. And as the tonnage mounted, Structural Linguistics attained maturity and status as a full-fledged, objective, quantitative, inductive, empirical, precise, positivistic, procedural branch of Science.

Amid the fog of Academese that now engulfs the subject, a few of its basic ideas and details of methodology can be distinguished. To begin with, the Structural Linguists, as noted earlier, concerned themselves only with the spoken language. The low esteem in which they hold writing derives in part from the statistic that only about 5 per cent of the world's 4,000 languages have any written form. "Language", as defined by the official publication of the Linguistic Society of America, is "a system of arbitrary vocal symbols by means of which a social group co-operates". The three words "arbitrary", "vocal", and "symbol" are all significant. Taking them in reverse, words are *symbols* because they are not identical with the objects and events they denote; they have meaning but they must not be confused with their referents. They are *vocal* because they are produced by the human voice, as opposed to other auditory symbols (sirens, bells, whistles, Morse code), visual symbols (pictures, gestures, writing), and tactile symbols (Braille). A written word, therefore, is merely a visual symbol of a vocal symbol and both are completely *arbitrary*. They are arbitrary because "it is convention alone—a kind of tacit agreement among the members of a social group—that gives any word its meaning". There is no reason other than social consensus why a quadruped of the species *Equus caballus* should be called *horse* in English, *cheval* in French, and *Pferd* in German. Even onomatopoeic words (from which, some theorists have suggested, human speech arose) vary from one language to another. Thus a dog goes *bow wow* in English, *wauwau* in German, *bubu* in Italian, *wan wan* in Japanese, and *ouâ-ouâ* in French. The English word *whisper is flüstern* in German, *chuchoter* in French, and *susurrar* in Spanish.

From this premise—that the tacit agreement of the social group gives any word its meaning—the Structural Linguists have extracted their axiom that usage is determined solely by *vox populi* and that if an "error" or "incorrect form" becomes sufficiently prevalent, then it is no longer an error and no longer incorrect, whatever purists may say. As Sapir expressed it, "The drift of a language is constituted by the unconscious selection of those individual variations that are cumulative in some special directions." Language changes constantly; it ceases to change only when it ceases to be spoken—e.g. old Egyptian. (Greek and Latin continued to change down through the Middle Ages.)

Since popular usage is the ultimate and not-to-be-disputed arbiter of language, the Structural Linguist simply describes, he does not prescribe. His *modus operandi* is to observe and study the speech of a particular social group, to ascertain its characteristic patterns, and to define and classify the arrangements and relationships of linguistic forms within the overall structure. A description of these patterns, arrangements, and relationships constitutes a description of the structure or grammar of the language.

The primary interest of the linguistician, however, is the *sound* of a language; and it is in the field of phonetics—or more specifically *phonemics*—that Structural Linguistics has erected its most elaborate methodological edifice. The starting-point and basic unit of linguistic analysis, as noted above, is the phoneme. But the curious fact is that no two Structural Linguists define it in the same way—a fact that has led some captious critics to remark that their contempt for writing doubtless stems from their inability to write. Here are a few of the attempts they and their expositors have made, over a quarter of a century, to describe the fundamental tool of their trade:

PHONEME

Leonard Bloomfield in *Language*: "A minimum unit of distinctive sound-feature."

Bernard Bloch and George L. Trager in *Outline of Linguistic Analysis*: "A class of phonetically similar sounds, contrasting and mutually exclusive with all similar classes in the language."

Simeon Potter, Baines Professor of English at the University of Liverpool, in *Language in the Modern World*: "A class or bundle of sounds of phones, no two of which can ever take each other's place in the same environment."

Colin Cherry of Imperial College, University of London, in *On Human Communication*: "A minimal list of phonetic elements with which it is possible to distinguish one word from another in the language."

Joshua Whatmough, Late Professor of Comparative Philology at Harvard University, in *Language: A Modern Synthesis*: "A grammatical abstraction to designate a class of equivalence of minimum speech sound."

John B. Carroll, Professor of Education at Harvard, in *The Study of Language*: "A unit of a culturally determined system which arouses a differential response in a member of the culture. It represents, within that system, a class of possible events (in this case *allophones*, that is, physically or phonetically, different sounds) which are equipollent with respect to the behavioural discriminations which can be observed in the users of the system." Webster III: "The smallest unit of speech that distinguishes one utterance from another in all the variations that it displays in the speech of a single person or particular dialect as the result of modifying influences."

The reason for all the lexical fog that swirls around these definitions is that the phoneme is both an entity and a composite of lesser entities. Thus the initial sounds of *pit* and *bit* are different phonemes. The initial sounds of *keep*, *cool*, and *coal*, as well as the final sound of *rock* are all varieties of the phoneme/k/, although they are physiologically and acoustically different. Such varieties of the same phoneme are called *allophones*. The possible number of allophones for a given phoneme is far greater than the untrained ear ever discerns. Consider, for example, the phoneme /t/ as it is uttered in the words *top* and *stop*. In *top* the letter *t* is articulated with a puff of air or, as the phonetician would say, it is aspirated; in *stop* it is unaspirated. In the word *net* or *cat* its emphasis wanes still further. And when it appears wedged between two other stop consonants, as in the combination *rapt dreamer*, it produces no acoustical effect whatever. Dr. John R. Pierce of the Bell Telephone Laboratories reported recently that a delicate phonetic analysis disclosed no fewer than ninety possible allophones of the phoneme /t/ as it is sounded in English speech. In any language the number of allophones is far greater than the number of phonemes, for it is a prerequisite of phonemes that they must be meaningful—a change of one phoneme changes the meaning of the word—while allophones may vary with pronunciation and regional accent. Phoneme lists for various languages fall within a narrow numerical range. Most of them allow English from 38 to 45 phonemes, about the same number found in Russian, as against 36 for French and German. Some Polynesian tongues have as few as 20, and some dialects of the Caucasus as many as 75. Out of the 40-odd phonemes in English speech have come the 400,000 words listed in Webster III, to say nothing of the 650,000 enshrined in Webster II and the *Oxford English Dictionary*'s more than 500,000 words. The vocal apparatus of man, however, is an extraordinarily versatile instrument, capable of producing hundreds of sounds, and no language has begun to utilize its full resources. Dr. Pierce has calculated that if the sounds employed in any one regional dialect of English alone were arranged in all possible combinations, the number of words of average length (short to medium) that could thus be constructed would approximate 10 billion. And if all the sounds used in all languages were put together in all possible sequences, then the possible lexicon would pass beyond terrestrial numeration.

Once the component phonemes of a language have been distinguished and classified, the next step in linguistic analysis is to discover how the phonemes are built up into *morphemes*. A morpheme is the smallest unit of lexical meaning—which is not to say that a morpheme is necessarily a *word*. In the terminology of Structural Linguistics, a morpheme is defined (by Bloch and Trager) as "any form, whether free or bound, which cannot be divided into smaller meaningful parts". The key terms here are "free" and "bound". Words like *cat*, *book*, and *home* are examples of single free morphemes. Words like *cats* and *catty*, *books* and *bookish*, *homes* and *homely* contain two morphemes, of which the secondary morphemes—*s*, *ty*, *ish*, and *ly*—are bound, for they cannot appear alone and have lexical meaning. Words that contain two free morphemes—*catlike*, *bookmark*, *homework*—are known as compound words.

The total store of morphemes in any language is its lexicon. A lexicon, in itself, however complete, tells little about a language unless it is augmented by an understanding of the meaningful arrangements of its component forms. To ascertain how morphemes are arranged in larger patterns, the linguistic analyst must listen attentively for a variety of small and subtle signals. He must cock his ear, for example, to the matter of *juncture*—the difference between *an aim* and *a name*, *I scream* and *ice cream*, a *nice house* and *an ice house*, *night rate* and *nitrate*. He must discern nuances of *stress*—as disclosed in the pronunciation of the following words:

the noun *cón vict* versus the verb *con víct*, *cón tract* versus *con tráct*,

or the phrase *black bírd* versus the compound *bláckbird*.

Some expressions are differentiated by a combination of both stress and juncture:

all togéther versus *áltogether*, *líghthouse keeper* versus *light hóusekeeper*.

Another subtlety lies in what the descriptive linguist calls "phonemic modification"; thus the compound *gentleman* differs from the phrase *gentle man*, not only in stress and juncture, but in the modification of the final morpheme. Finally, there is the question of *modulation* or *pitch*: a single free morpheme like the proper name *John* conveys different meanings when it is articulated as *John!* (John! How nice to see you! . . . John! It's time for dinner . . . John! Stop that!), or *John?* (John? Is he in town? . . . John? Is that you, dear?), or just plain *John*, (spoken with a falling pitch in answer to a question—"What's his first name? Who was that on the telephone?")

More important than these sound signals, however, is the question of *order*—the sequence of elements in a larger form. In English and most other modern Indo-European languages, order is all-important, for (to lapse into the vocabulary of classical grammar) they share in common the basic sequential pattern of subject-verb-predicate. For example, the description of an event is reversed completely if one says *Man bites dog* instead of *Dog bites man.*[1] Both statements are grammatical, but the meaning depends on the order in which the elements are spoken. Linguisticians are firm in their insistence that grammar has nothing to do with meaning—a *grammatical* statement need not be *meaningful* or significant in a semantic sense. Thus Dr. Noam Chomsky of the Massachusetts Institute of Technology, one of the younger stars in the linguistic galaxy, cites two word strings: (1) *Colourless green ideas sleep furiously* and (2) *Furiously sleep ideas green colourless*; and observes that although both series are nonsensical, the former constitutes a perfectly grammatical English sentence.

When the order of a language has been discerned, the linguistician can then identify "form-classes", which is to say the components that can fill a functional slot in a given construction. For example, in the sequence, "*The . . . was good*", the open slot can be filled with certain forms like *concert*, *food*, *skiing*, *liquor*, but not with others like *cerulean*, *argued*, or *nevertheless*. To the Structural Linguist the term "form-classes" connotes approximately what "parts of speech" means to those educated

[1] See Chapter 4, p. 72.

in the "outmoded concepts of eighteenth-century Latinate grammar". Structural Linguistics divides form-classes into two main headings, *function words* and *content words*. Function words operate largely as a means of expressing the relations of grammatical structure—the so-called "particles", "conjunctions", "prepositions", and "auxiliaries" which constitute the cement and mortar of the house of language. Content words fall into three classes: *things*, *actions*, and *qualities*—corresponding to "nouns", "verbs", and "adjectives or adverbs". To those who inquire why the old terminology had to be revised, the Structural Linguist replies that the traditional parts of speech were first defined by Greek grammarians, then adopted by the Romans, and subsequently applied to modern Indo-European languages. In English, as anyone who has ever studied traditional grammar knows, it is often difficult to distinguish adverbs from prepositions (like *up* and *before*), and many nouns and verbs are interchangeable (*slice* of ham, *slice* the ham).[1] In languages outside the Indo-European family, moreover, the classical terminology often does not work at all; their sentences do not follow the subject-verb-predicate pattern; and their lexicons contain many words that cannot be classified in the Greco-Latin framework.[2] In the South-West American Indian Hopi language, for example, events of brief duration—*lightning*, *wave*, *flame*, *meteor*, *puff of smoke*—have the character of verbs, although *cloud* and *storm*—concepts of longer duration—resemble nouns. Even such a basic concept as *word*—as the symbol of a single unitary referent—does not always fit into the structure of non-Indo-European languages. Thus in the Nootka language (spoken by the Indians of Vancouver Island) there is a "word" which denotes *I have been accustomed to eat twenty round objects* (*e.g. apples*) *while engaged in* (*doing so and so*). The idea of a *sentence* presents similar difficulties when it is applied to the analysis of languages outside the Indo-European family.

To illustrate how a language can be analysed without reference to traditional concepts, and without resort to semantics, Dr. William G. Moulton, Professor of Linguistics at Princeton, has dissected Lewis Carroll's poem *Jabberwocky* in the light of modern linguistic theory:

[1] See Chapters 2, 4, and 5, pp. 31–33, 133–4, 156.

[2] See Chapter 4, p. 72.

'Twas *brillig*, and the *slithy toves*
Did *gyre* and *gimble* in the *wabe:*
All *mimsy* were the *borogroves,*
And the *mome raths outgrabe.*

Here the italicized words are nonsense words which Caroll invented. But, in the perspective of Structural Linguistics, they are also the *content* words of the quatrain. If they are eliminated and replaced by blanks, only the essential *function* words and *function* forms (bound morphemes), remain.

'Twas . . . . . , and the . . . . .y . . . . .s
Did . . . . . and . . . . . in the . . . . :
All . . . . .y were the . . . . .s,
And the . . . . .s out. . . . . . .

It is these function words that give the verse structural meaning. The blanks are simply the slots into which content words (or nonsense words) can be inserted. Dr. Moulton then provides a third version, in which the function words and forms are eliminated and the content slots are filled with real words.

. . . . . evening, ... frisk. . dog
. . . . . play . . . . . frolic . . . . dale:
. . . . . gloom . . . . emerald frog
. . . . . solemn hare . . . . .wail.

In this final version there is content but no structure, hence no meaning. "Though the theory of function words and content words is not yet fully worked out," Dr. Moulton observes, "it has obvious implications for language teaching. Up to now we have relied largely on frequency counts in choosing the words which we want to include in an elementary course. This new theory suggests that only content words should be chosen on the basis of frequency, and that even in an elementary course all, or nearly all, of the function words should be included regardless of their frequency. Function words are the blood and bone of language; content words are fillers which can fit into particular types of slots. Children learn nearly all the function words of their native language at a very early age; they will keep on learning content words throughout their lives."

An analogous illustration of the way in which the forms of a language may be ascertained and its underlying structure perceived without any need to understand the meaning of content words is cited by C. K. Ogden and I. A. Richards in their classic work *The Meaning of Meaning*:

Suppose someone to assert, *The gostak distims the doshes*. You do not know what this means; nor do I. But if we assume that it is English, we know that *the doshes are distimmed by the gostak*. We know too that *one distimmer of doshes is a gostak*. If, moreover, the *doshes* are *galloons*, we know that some *galloons are distimmed by the gostak*. And so we may go on, and so we often do go on.

So brief an outline of modern linguistic theory cannot be said even to skim the surface of a subject that is still evolving and has fragmented into many subdivisions and specialized realms in the years since Sapir and Bloomfield first recorded the results of their research and cerebration. Among the major compartments of Structural Linguistics flourishing today in universities across the North American Continent are: Descriptive Linguistics, Historical or Comparative Linguistics, Linguistic Geography, Motor Phonetics, Acoustic Phonetics, Perceptual Phonetics, Instrumental Phonetics, Phonemics, Morphonemics, Glossematics, Metalinguistics, Exolinguistics, and Kinesics (the study of non-vocal bodily movements that play a part in communication). Not surprisingly, the terminology of this proliferating science emits a murmurous sound, as from a bee-loud glade. In addition to the fundamental *phoneme*, the *morpheme*, and the *allophone*, the modern linguistic lexicon includes the *sememe*, which is the meaning of a morpheme; the *taxeme* or smallest unit of grammatical form; the *tagmeme* or smallest meaningful unit of grammatical form; the *episeme*, which is the meaning of a *tagmeme*; and the *kimeme*, the basic unit of kinesics or gestural expression.

Some faint notion of the rarefied realms in which Structural Linguists now operate and the mode in which they write may be conveyed by random samplings of their style. The following is from *Syntactic Structures* by Dr. Chomsky: "When transformational analysis is properly formulated we find that it is essentially more powerful than description in terms of phrase structure, just as the latter is essentially more powerful than description in terms of finite state Markov processes that generate sentences from left to right." And in one of the most highly regarded of the basic texts, *Structural Linguistics*, by Zellig S. Harris of the University of Pennsylvania, the reader finds this roulade: "Another consideration is the availability of simultaneity, in addition to successivity, as a relation among linguistic elements. . . . The consideration of elements among which there obtains the relation of simultaneity involves removing the limitation to one dimension from linguistic analysis. Removal of this limitation is all the easier in view of the ease of arranging letters on paper two-dimensionally. . . ." From such passages, which march in sesquipedalian splendour through volume after volume of the expanding bibliography of Structural Linguistics, there have emerged new concepts in communication theory, in psychology, epistemology, the theory of signs, cultural anthropology, and the general philosophy of language. But the question many educators and parents are asking today is: How did the concepts of this extremely abstruse discipline come to permeate and affect American education?

From the beginning, Bloomfield himself was not content to present his analysis of linguistic structure as an intellectual insight free from social connotations. His studies of Indian tongues coincided in time with the development of egalitarian theories of education which began to flower in the thirties. Hence in his major work, *Language*, published in 1933, he set forth the idea that insistence on "correct" or "good" English is a form of social snobbery stemming from the British upper classes, perpetuated by the "fanciful doctrine" of grammarians imbued with eighteenth-century authoritarianism, and swallowed by a naïve American public eager to climb the social ladder. He observed that many Americans have a foreign background and are "easily frightened into thinking that a speech form which is natural to them is actually 'not English' ".

Although Bloomfield's observations were brief and came at the end of a lengthy scientific work, they had a profound effect on American educators, who during the depression years were eager to help the underprivileged and eliminate distinctions in the classroom. The idea that the condemnation of "incorrect" usage was undemocratic conformed perfectly to the temper of the nation and also to an educational scene where rigorous teaching methods and standards of achievement were swiftly beginning to sag. The educational theorists, impatient with rote learning, drills, and memory work, were looking for short cuts in every realm. They seized happily, therefore, on Bloomfield's conviction that "correct" English was simply upper-class English, and that to insist on the punctilios of spelling, usage, and diction was to impose harmful class, or status, distinctions on the young.

The developing conflict between the social philosophy of the Structural Linguists and the traditional precepts of grammar might have hung in uneasy balance had it not been for World War II. As the theatres of war expanded around the globe to remote and exotic lands, the government suddenly found itself in need of personnel who could speak not only the familiar languages of Europe but such esoteric tongues as Burmese, Korean, Housa, Pashto, Fanti, Tagalog, and Thai. Foreseeing this need, a group of linguists attached to the American Council of Learned Societies instituted early in 1941 an intensive programme of analysis of little-known tongues. After Pearl Harbour the government called on the Council for help. By the summer of 1942, courses in some twenty-six languages were set up at universities around the country, under the supervision of trained linguistic scientists. Before the war ended, the number of foreign tongues taught under various army programmes totalled fifty. Although various methods were employed, the contribution of the linguisticians became widely known, and the success of the programmes attracted enormous acclaim. Newspaper and magazine articles spoke of the "miraculous" results achieved and gave much of the credit to the new linguistic science. At the same time, the first notes of disparagement began to be heard concerning traditional methods of language teaching in schools. So the issue between old and new methods was now truly joined. Many progressive schools and colleges began to experiment with the techniques used during the war and to introduce some features of the Army's training programme—among them the extensive use of mechanical aids and the procedures of linguistic analysis. In so doing, they turned increasingly away from the literary and cultural objectives of language teaching and toward exclusive emphasis on the spoken word.

The apostles of Structural Linguistics might still have confined their interest to the teaching of foreign languages had it not been for the extremely influential work of Professor Charles Carpenter Fries, of the University of Michigan, a prolific writer who in 1940 published "a scientifically oriented description of actual usage". Entitled *American English Grammar*, it was based on an examination of three thousand letters written to the United States War Department in 1918 dealing with the subject of pension money, and classified according to the social status of the writers. In 1945 Fries brought forth another book called *Teaching and Learning English as a Foreign Language*. Applying the principles of Structural Linguistics to English, Fries also embraced Bloomfield's antagonisms toward criteria of speech. He quoted Bloomfield in his preface: "Our schools are conducted by persons who, from professors of education down to teachers in the classroom, know nothing of the results of linguistic science, not even the relation of writing to speech or of standard language to dialect. In short, they do not know what language is, and yet must teach it, and in consequence waste years of every child's life and reach a poor result." To this Fries added: "The views of language that prevail in the schools and among even the 'educated' public still perpetuate the authoritarian attitude of the second half of the eighteenth century and serve to create a huge market for cheap dictionaries and unscholarly handbooks of 'correctness'."

The principles of Bloomfield, Fries and their disciples swept the educational field. Borne on the turbulent and chaotic currents of modern pedagogic theory, the teaching of English grammar followed the teaching of Latin into the Dead Sea of abandoned subjects. And as it sank beneath the surface, the linguisticians continued their warfare against all standards of usage anywhere. From Cornell University, Dr. Robert A. Hall declared:

> It can be just as much of a *faux pas* to say *I saw him*, where your hearer expects and wants *I seen him*, as the other way around. One friend of mine found that, when he went to work in a Houston shipyard during the Second World War, he was regarded as a snob for saying *these things* instead of *them things*, and he did not get full cooperation from his fellow workers until he started to say *them* things. . . . What is it that makes some forms "incorrect" and others not? . . . It all boils down really to a question of acceptability. . . . "Correct"

can only mean 'socially acceptable' and apart from this has no meaning as applied to language.

And from Harvard came an "Amen" from Professor John B. Carroll:

I agree with Hall in rejecting the undemocratic and socially immature attitudes whereby variant and substandard language patterns are condemned; I would go further and say that pupils should be taught under what circumstances such language patterns can be used appropriately and effectively. Overinsistence on rigid standards of usage may be detrimental to the development of personal styles of oral and written communication.

5.

To almost everyone who cherishes the English language for its grace and beauty, its combination of precision and flexibility, the social philosophy of the Structural Linguists seems past comprehension—epitomizing indeed the "anti-intellectualism of the intellectual". Among all the forces of cultural vandalism at work in the country, their influence has been, perhaps, the most insidious. The vulgarities of advertising and mudflows of jargon can be shovelled aside. But the impact of the Structural Linguists is like that of slow atomic fallout: through their influence on teachers' colleges and teachers, hence on the schools and the pupils within them, they are incapacitating the coming generation. And the paradoxical aspect of their assault on the English language is that they claim to be motivated only by the purest democratic principles. Recoiling from what they consider the "socio-ethnic snobbery" of graceful speech, they are actually abetting an utterly undemocratic freezing of caste. For if good and correct English is regarded as a sign of status, like good manners or good clothes, then to commit a language student for ever to his own level of speech is surely as undemocratic as denying him the hope of any kind of social or economic advancement. Again and again in the writings of the linguistic philosophers, there appears the *leit-motif* that language should not be corrected or refined, that everybody should continue to talk the way his parents did, and that any teacher who attempts to improve a student's language is undermining his psyche and morale. Commenting on this strange doctrine in a recent article, Joseph Wood Krutch observed:

"Social mobility" is supposed to be one of the glories of our civilization. What becomes of it if the school undertakes to confine every pupil to his own social level? . . . If the purpose of classes in English is not to encourage pupils to speak and write in some fashion different from that which they bring into the classroom with them, then what are these classrooms for? You don't need to go to school to use language in the way your parents and your "group" uses it.

Another blind spot of the Structural Linguists and their academic exponents distorts their whole outlook on language as the prime implement of human communication: they deny the importance of writing and the written word. In their preoccupation with the sounds of speech, they painstakingly listen for nuances of pharyngeal resonance, voiced fricatives, and subglottal closure, while professing indifference to questions of phrasing and style, to say nothing of spelling and punctuation. Some of their spokesmen have indeed stated flatly that writing is a "secondary skill", and that time devoted to spelling and punctuation not only irritates teachers and students but contributes nothing to life-adjustment in the modern world. Why the spoken word, which can be employed with felicity only by the exceptionally gifted (the late Winston Churchill, Charles de Gaulle, for example), should academically outrank the written word is difficult to explain. (The inadequacies of oral discourse are apparent to anyone who has ever listened to a taped recording, to an extemporized address or read the transcript of a press conference.) Although no one denies that *Homo sapiens* developed speech before writing, the advent of writing marked the advent of civilization and of history. And writing has been the medium by which culture—the accumulated experience of the past—has been transmitted down through five millennia since the Sumerians first began to scratch cuneiform symbols on clay tablets in their walled cities on the Tigris-Euphrates plain.

In their attacks on the rigid attitudes of "purists" and "hidebound grammarians", the linguisticians are, in a sense, tilting at windmills. For not even the most rigorous defender of good usage, not even the most contemptuous critic of the huge dictionary that has become the hostage of Structural Linguistics, has ever contended that the English language is static or will ever be. Every lover of the language knows that its glory resides in the recurring infusions of new elements it has received from all the nations on earth, and that change is constant, continual, and will never cease. But the written word is the brake on the spoken word. The written word is the link between the past and the future. It demands precision if it is to be the carrier and container of all that is precious in human thought. And along with precision it can be invested with elegance and felicity of style.

Precision and style, however, require premeditation, and premeditation is exactly what is lacking in many current modes of self-expression or "creativity"—whether in Greenwich Village or a high-school English class. It is indeed a distaste for premeditation that unites in fellowship the modern educationist and the exponents of drip-dry painting, say-as-you-go poetry, free-write fiction, scriptless cinematography, improvised play-acting ("happenings"), and hardware-store orchestration. Whatever the medium, there can be no preliminary cerebration; the motive is not to communicate but to "feel" and emit—on a one-way channel. And the question in the mind of the practising genius is not "What do I wish to convey?" but "How do I feel?"—a question that neither requires nor expects an answer. The auditor, observer, or reader is optional. For the important function of "creativity" is to get it out, get it on canvas, get it on film, get it on tape, and (to reprise Kerouac) "get it all down without modified restraints and all hung-up on like literary inhibitions and grammatical fears". But creativity aside, the need for two-way and multiple communication of complex ideas, facts, principles, and interpretive exposition has never been greater than it is today in a fragmented world jangling with crises on every meridian. And that is why one can only regard as malign a philosophy of language and language-teaching whose apostles disdain the written word, decry good usage as social affectation, and in their classrooms subordinate the rigours of premeditated recitation and composition to unpremeditated "open discussions" which amount to nothing more than an exchange of ignorance.

In their depreciation of writing and good usage, the Structural Linguists and their disciples in the educational establishment ignore the relationship between language and thought. Yet thought and language are inextricably entwined. The entity called the mind can conjure up visual images and other sensory memories, and be aware of the turbulence called emotion, but it cannot crystallize an idea without words. Psychologists from the earliest days of experimental psychology in the nineteenth century have repeatedly asked: Can thought precede its formulation into words, or is the process of verbalization a prerequisite of thought? The consensus today is that without language there seems to be nothing like explicit thought whatever; any incipient thought remains vague in the thinker's mind until it has been expressed either to himself or to other.[1] Some psychologists insist that thought is nothing more than silent speech. It is well known that certain individuals move their lips when reading or thinking. But experimental evidence has shown that, quite apart from such visible action, the thinking process is always accompanied by implicit language activity in the form of minute changes of tension in the organs of the vocal apparatus, duplicating those involved in audible speech—delicate, abortive motions of the tongue, lips, glottis, and often of the hands and eyes. "Thinking", therefore, appears to be symbiotically linked with speech movements performed on a very small scale, and substituted for the overt acts.

The process of isolating and articulating a thought recapitulates the development of language in a child. In the beginning the infant emits plain noise, meaningless babblings, and emotive sounds akin to those of any young animal indicating his desires or state of being. Then slowly, through a long sequence of trial and error, he acquires a rudimentary vocabulary useful to him in attaining his ends. As years pass, his vocabulary expands, he acquires a knowledge of grammatical relationships, ways of expressing abstract and symbolic concepts, and a sense of the structure and higher functions of language. In much the same way, within an imperceptible time scale, an idea evolves in the adult mind. At first it is nebulous, without form or substance. And it remains so until the thinker, drawing on his linguistic memory, the vast, slumbering repository of his unique and private lexicon, congeals and solidifies his thought in the architecture of words, either inwardly or to others via exophasic speech or writing. No subtle or abstract thought, no intricate or

[1] Interior, non-vocal verbalization is known as *endophasic* speech as opposed to vocal, audible or *exophasic* speech.

coherent train of reasoning can exist without the scaffold of language by which it is sustained. And the more complicated the thought, the greater the need for its accurate expression in words. As Colin Cherry of the University of London has pointed out, "The rules we call grammar and syntax are not inviolate, but the more we break them the lower are our chances of successful communication."[1] Hence, when teachers of English who have been indoctrinated by the precepts of Structural Linguistics condone slovenly speech and slovenly writing, they are simultaneously condoning slovenly thinking, which would seem to subvert the educational process.

One of the ironies of man's predicament as a talking animal is that his organs of speech work faster than his mind. His complex and versatile apparatus is capable of producing an enormous number of words in a very short time. His ability both to speak and hear exceeds the speed of thought. Expressing himself on the subject of glibness, Niels Bohr once said: "I must never speak more clearly than I think." Human communication is thus subject to mental rather than physical limitations. The pages of newspapers and news magazines, to say nothing of the airwaves, are cluttered with words that outstripped thought. But conversely the pages of history are embellished with words that have survived the centuries. It is notable that the most dynamic periods of American history coincided with presidents who wrote and spoke with superb mastery of the language—Jefferson, Lincoln, Wilson, and both Roosevelts. And the world will never forget the words of Winston Churchill, which kindled the English-speaking people of both hemispheres in the blackest night of World War II. For some two thousand years—since Plato, Demosthenes, Cicero, Paul of Tarsus—men of eloquence have used language to reach, inspire, and enlist the minds of their fellow men. For language is not only a vehicle of thought but a catalyst of thought and an implement of incalculable power. To use it well is surely more than a social grace. And it is difficult to see why precision in language should be thought any more undemocratic than precision in mathematics or seismology.

Such considerations are, of course, self-evident to professional

[1] Colin Cherry: *On Human Communication* (New York: Science Editions, Inc.; 1961), p. 19.

men in government, law and diplomacy, who know what hazards and disasters can devolve from the careless use of language.[1] In these realms the relationship between a word and its referent may be crucial, requiring painstaking scrutiny and analysis. If this were not true, there would be no surrogates' courts to determine how the construction of a subordinate clause or the position of a comma should affect the disposition of a legacy to competing heirs. Nor would there be the necessity of a Supreme Court to interpret the intent of the authors of the Constitution and the interrelationship of its wording with that of state laws or new acts of Congress.

Quite apart from its domestic applications, the English language has been proliferating around the planet at a dizzying tempo since World War II. It has become in effect an international language, a lingua franca of travel and commerce, of science and diplomacy, in both hemispheres. The future of mankind may depend on a consensus of thought that can only be achieved by a precise use of English words and a reciprocal comprehension of what they mean. For there can be no communication without comprehension. The mechanical media of communication have evolved at a rate which presages the day, not far off, when nations will be able to transmit live television programmes daily over the poles and across the seas. If the electronic highways of the air are to serve any useful purpose, however, the content of their signals—the ideas they transmit at the velocity of light—must be garbed in lucid and felicitous language. If English is allowed to degenerate into a babel of regional dialects, social stratifications, vulgarities, jargon, and juvenile slang, the hope of true understanding among the millions of English-speaking people around the earth is commen-

[1] There is evidence that an error in translation of a message sent by the Japanese government in the closing hours of World War II might have been responsible for the holocaust of Hiroshima. Had the translator rendered one word differently, the atomic bomb might never have been released. The word *mokusatsu,* used by the Japanese Cabinet in their reply to the Potsdam surrender ultimatum, was given out by the Domei news agency as "ignore" rather than correctly, as "withholding comment [pending decision]". Unaware that the Japanese were still considering the ultimatum, believing indeed that it had been rejected, the Allies proceeded to open the atomic age. See "The Great *Mokusatsu* Mistake" by William J. Coughlin, in *Harper's Magazine*, March, 1953.

surately dimmed. In the health of the English language, the health of Western civilization may well reside.

It is difficult to believe that, after 2,500 years of an intellectual tradition illumined by the light of ancient Greece, there should be any need to make a case for clarity of thought and precision of expression. Yet amid the massive onslaught upon intellect and language, waged on so many fronts, it may be worth recalling certain precepts from the past. In the first century A.D., the Roman rhetorician Quintilian set a standard for precision of language when he declared: "One should not aim at being possible to understand, but at being impossible to misunderstand." And more than five centuries earlier the great Chinese philosopher-statesman Confucius expressed his views on the relationship between language and government. Asked what he would undertake to do first, were he called upon to rule a nation, Confucius replied: "To correct language. . . . If language is not correct, then what is said is not what is meant; if what is said is not what is meant, then what ought to be done remains undone; if this remains undone, morals and art will deteriorate; if morals and art deteriorate, justice will go astray; if justice goes astray, the people will stand about in helpless confusion. Hence there must be no arbitrariness in what is said. This matters above everything."

BIBLIOGRAPHY

General Works

Baugh, Albert C., *A History of the English Language*. London: Routledge & Kegan Paul; 1951.

Baugh, Albert C. (ed.), *A Literary History of England*. London: Routledge & Kegan Paul; 1950.

Bloomfield, Leonard, *Language*. London: George Allen & Unwin; 1935.

Churchill, Winston S., *A History of the English-Speaking Peoples*. London; Cassell & Company; 1956–8.

Darwin, Charles, *The Origin of Species & The Descent of Man*. London: J. M. Dent & Sons, Everyman Series.

Frazer, Sir James G., *The Golden Bough*. London: Macmillan & Company; 1922.

Green, J. R., *A Short History of the English People*. London: J. M. Dent & Sons, Everyman Series. First published 1877.

James, William, *Psychology*. Greenwich, Conn.: Fawcett Books; 1964. First published 1920.

Jespersen, Otto, *Growth and Structure of the English Language*. Ninth edition. Oxford: Basil Blackwell & Mott; 1948. First published 1905.

Krapp, George P., *The English Language in America*. Two volumes. New York: Frederick Ungar Publishing Co.; 1960.

Marckwardt, Albert H., *American English*. New York: Oxford University Press; 1958.

Mencken, H. L., *The American Language*. Fourth edition and Two Supplements. London: Routledge & Kegan Paul; 1919, 1945, 1948.

Ogden, C. K. and Richards, I. A., *The Meaning of Meaning*. Second edition. London: Routledge & Kegan Paul; 1944.

Partridge, Eric, *Origins. A Short Etymological Dictionary of Modern English*. London: Routledge & Kegan Paul; 1959.

Partridge, Eric and Clark, John W., *British and American English Since 1900*. London: Andrew Dakers; 1951.

Pei, Mario, *The Story of English*. London: George Allen & Unwin; 1953.

Pei, Mario, *The Story of Language*. London: George Allen & Unwin; 1950.

Potter, Simeon, *Language in the Modern World*. Harmondsworth, Middx.: Penguin Books; 1960.

Potter, Simeon, *Our Language*. Harmondsworth, Middx.: Penguin Books; 1950.

Sapir, Edward, *Culture, Language and Personality*. University of California Press; 1956.

Sapir, Edward, *Language An Introduction to the Study of Speech*. New York: Harcourt, Brace & Company; 1949.

Schlauch, Margaret, *The Gift of Language*. New York: Dover Publications; 1955. (Revised edition of *The Gift of Tongues*; London: George Allen & Unwin; 1943.)

Trevelyan, George Macaulay, *History of England*. London: Longmans, Green & Company; 1941.

Chapter 1

Partridge, Eric, *A Charm of Words*. London: Hamish Hamilton; 1960.

Partridge, Eric, *Here, There and Everywhere. Essays Upon Language*. Second edition. London: Hamish Hamilton; 1950.

Pei, Mario, *Language For Everybody*. New York: Devin-Adair Company; 1956.

Report of the Official Language Commission. New Delhi: Government of India Press; 1956.

Rundle, Stanley, *Language as a Social and Political Factor in Europe*. London: Faber and Faber; 1946.

Chapter 2

Bodmer, Frederick and Hogben, Lancelot, *The Loom of Language*. London: George Allen & Unwin; 1944.

Lewis, C. S., *Studies in Words*. Cambridge University Press; 1960.

Moore, John, *You English Words*. London: William Collins, Sons & Co.; 1961.

Ogden, C. K., *The System of Basic English*. Second edition. London: Routledge & Kegan Paul; 1944.

Partridge, Eric, *A Charm of Words*. London: Hamish Hamilton; 1960.

Partridge, Eric, *Here, There and Everywhere. Essays Upon Language*. Second edition. London: Routledge & Kegan Paul; 1959.

Pei, Mario, *Language For Everybody*. New York: Devin-Adair Company; 1956.

Serjeantson, Mary S., *History of Foreign Words in English*. London: Routledge & Kegan Paul; 1961.

Smith, Logan Pearsall, *The English Language*. Oxford University Press; 1952.

Tucker, Susie I., *English Examined*. Cambridge University Press; 1961.

Weekley, Ernest, *The Romance of Words*. London: Guild Books; 1949.

Chapter 3

Appel, Fredric C., "The Intellectual Mammal". *The Saturday Evening Post*, Vol. 237, No. 1 (January 4, 1964).

Boas, Franz, *The Mind of Primitive Man*. New York: The Macmillan Company; 1948.

Brown, Roger, *Words and Things*. Glencoe, Ill.: The Free Press; 1958.

Bryant, Margaret M. and Aiken, Janet Rankin, *Psychology of English*. Second edition. New York: Frederick Ungar Publishing Co.; 1962.

Cherry, Colin, *On Human Communication*. New York: Science Editions; 1962.

Childe, V. Gordon, *Man Makes Himself*. London: C. A. Watts & Co., Thinkers' Library; 1941.

Childe, Gordon, *What Happened in History*. Harmondsworth, Middx.: Penguin Books; 1942.

Coon, Carleton S., *The History of Man*. London: Jonathan Cape; 1955.

Coon, Carleton S., *The Origin of Races*. Second edition. London: Jonathan Cape; 1963.

Dart, Raymond A. and Craig, D., *Adventures with the Missing Link*. London: Hamish Hamilton; 1959.

Diamond, A. S., *The History and Origin of Language*. London: Methuen & Co.; 1959.

Diringer, David, *The Story of the Aleph Beth*. London: Thomas Yoseloff, Popular Jewish Library; 1958.

Eiseley, Loren, *The Immense Journey*. London: Victor Gollancz; 1958.

Frankfort, Henri; Frankfort, Mrs. Henri; Wilson, John A. and Jacobsen, Thorkild, *Before Philosophy*. Harmondsworth, Middx.: Penguin Books; 1951.

Frings, Hubert and Mable, "The Language of Crows". *Scientific American*, Vol. 201, No. 5 (November 1959).

Goodall, Jane, "My Life Among Wild Chimpanzees". *National Geographic*, Vol. 124, No. 2 (August 1963).

Greenough, James Bradstreet and Kittredge, George Lyman, *Words and Their Ways in English Speech*. Second edition. New York: The Macmillan Company; 1962.

Hockett, Charles F., "The Origin of Speech". *Scientific American*, Vol. 203, No. 3 (September 1960).

Hogben, Lancelot, *From Cave Painting to Comic Strip. A Kaleidoscope of Human Communication*. London: Max Parrish; 1949.

Jespersen, Otto, *Language, Its Nature, Development, and Origin*. London: George Allen & Unwin; 1922.

Kellogg, Winthrop N., "Dolphins and Hearing". *Natural History* (February 1960).

Koenigswald, G. H. R. Von, *Meeting Prehistoric Man*. London: Thames & Hudson and Constable & Company; 1956.

Labarre, Weston, *The Human Animal*. The University of Chicago Press; 1954.

Langer, Susanne K., *Philosophy in a New Key*. Cambridge, Mass.: Harvard University Press; 1951.

Leakey, Louis S. B., "Adventures in the Search for Man". *National Geographic*, Vol. 123, No. 1 (January 1963).

Lorenz, Konrad, *King Solomon's Ring*. London: Methuen & Co.; 1952.

Lorenz, Konrad, *Man Meets Dog*. London: Methuen & Co.; 1955.

Moore, Ruth, *Man, Time and Fossils*. Second edition. London: Jonathan Cape; 1962.

Murphy, Gardner, *Historical Introduction to Modern Psychology*. Fifth edition. London: Routledge & Kegan Paul; 1949.

Pfeiffer, John E., "The Apish Origins of Human Tension". *Harper's Magazine*, Vol. 227, No. 1358 (July 1963).

Pierce, John R. and David, Edward E., Jr., *Man's World of Sound*. Garden City, N.Y.: Doubleday & Company; 1958.

Schaller, George B., "Mountain Gorilla Displays". *Natural History*, Vol. LXXII, No. 7 (August–September 1963).

Tinbergen, N., "The Evolution of Behavior in Gulls". *Scientific American*, Vol. 203, No. 6 (December 1960).

Washburn, S. L. and Vore, I. De, "The Social Life of Baboons". *Scientific American*, Vol. 204, No. 6 (June 1961).

Chapter 4

Adams, J. Donald, *The Magic and Mystery of Words*. New York: Holt, Rinehart & Winston; 1963.

Charlesworth, M. P., *The Heritage of Early Britain*. London: G. Bell; 1952.

Clark, John W., *Early English. A Study of Old and Middle English*. London: André Deutsch; 1957.

Coulton, G. G. G., *Chaucer and His England*. Eighth edition. London: Methuen & Co.; 1950.

Greenough, James Bradstreet and Kittredge, George Lyman, *Words and Their Ways in English Speech*. Second edition. New York: The Macmillan Company; 1962.

Haskins, Charles H., *The Normans in European History*. London: Constable & Company; 1959.

Magoun, Francis P., Jr., *Anglo-Saxon Poems*. Cambridge, Mass.: Department of English, Harvard University; 1956.

McAdam, E. L., Jr., and Milne, George (ed.), *Johnson's Dictionary. A Modern Selection*. New York: Pantheon Books; 1963.

Morrison, Theodore, *The Portable Chaucer* (Introduction). New York: The Viking Press; 1958.

Poole, Austin Lane, *From Doomsday Book to Magna Carta, 1087–1216*. Oxford: The Clarendon Press; 1955.

Quirk, Randolph and Wrenn, C. L., *An Old English Grammar*. London: Methuen & Co.; 1958.

Serjeantson, Mary S., *History of Foreign Words in English*. London: Routledge & Kegan Paul; 1961.

Smith, Logan Pearsall, *The English Language*. Oxford University Press; 1952.

Spaeth, J. Duncan, *Old English Poetry*. Oxford University Press; 1927.

Theme, Paul, "The Indo-European Language". *Scientific American*, Vol. 199, No. 4 (October 1958).

Trevelyan, George Macaulay, *Illustrated English Social History*. Four volumes. London: Longmans, Green & Company; 1949–52.

Weekley, Ernest, *The Romance of Words*. London: Guild Books; 1949.

Wrenn, C. L., *Beowulf with the Finnesburg Fragment*. Second edition. London: George G. Harrap & Co.; 1953.

Wyld, Henry C., *A History of Modern Colloquial English*. Third edition. Oxford: Basil Blackwell & Mott; 1936.

Chapter 5

Baker, Sidney J., *The Australian Language*. Sydney: Angus & Robertson; 1945.

Brown, W. Norman, *The United States and India and Pakistan*. Cambridge, Mass.: Harvard University Press; 1953.

Edwards, Michael, *A History of India*. London: Thames & Hudson; 1961.

Garratt, Geoffrey T. *The Legacy of India.* Oxford: The Clarendon Press; 1937.

Horwill, Herbert W., *An Anglo-American Interpreter.* Oxford: The Clarendon Press; 1939.

Kurath, Hans and McDavid, Raven I., Jr., *The Pronunciation of English in the Atlantic States.* University of Michigan Press; 1961.

MacPherson, Margaret, *I Heard the Anzacs Singing.* Toronto: McClelland & Stewart; 1942.

Mallery, Richard D., *Our American Language.* New York: Halcyon House; 1947.

Mathews, Mitford M., *American Words.* New York: The World Publishing Company; 1959.

McLeod, Mitford, *A Dictionary of Americanisms.* The University of Chicago Press; 1951.

Nevins, Allan (edited and compiled by), *America Through British Eyes.* New York: Oxford University Press; 1948.

O'Malley, L. S. S., *Modern India and the West.* Oxford University Press; 1941.

Pyles, Thomas, *Words and Ways of American English.* London: Andrew Melrose; 1954.

Rao, G. Subba, *Indian Words in English.* Oxford: The Clarendon Press; 1954.

Report of the Official Language Commission. New Delhi: Government of India Press; 1956.

Wentworth, Harold and Flexner, Stuart Berg, *Dictionary of American Slang.* London: George G. Harrap & Co.; 1960.

Chapter 6

Adams, J. Donald, *The Magic and Mystery of Words.* New York: Holt, Rinehart & Winston; 1963.

Barzun, Jacques, *The House of Intellect.* London: Martin Secker & Warburg; 1960.

Barzun, Jacques, "What Is A Dictionary?" *The American Scholar,* Vol. 32, No. 2 (Spring 1963).

Bell, Laird, "Admit and Flunk". *Atlantic Monthly*, Vol. 210, No. 4 (October 1962).

Bernstein, Theodore M., *Watch Your Language*. Great Neck, N.Y.: Channel Press; 1958.

Bernstein, Theodore M., *More Language That Needs Watching*. Manhasset, N.Y.: Channel Press; 1962.

Bloch, Bernard and Trager, George L., *Outline of Linguistic Analysis*. Baltimore: The Linguistic Society of America at the Waverly Press; 1942.

Carroll, John B., *The Study of Language*. Cambridge, Mass.: Harvard University Press; 1959.

Cherry, Colin, *On Human Communication*. New York: Science Editions; 1962.

Chomsky, Noah, *Syntactic Structures*. The Hague: Mouton & Company; 1962.

Coughlin, William J., "The Great *Mokusatsu* Mistake". *Harper's Magazine*, Vol. 206, No. 1234 (March 1953).

Crowther, Sir Geoffrey, "English and American Education". *Atlantic Monthly*, Vol. 205, No. 4 (April 1960).

Dewey, John, *Experience and Education*. New York: Collier Books; 1963.

Evans, Bergen, "Grammar For Today". *Atlantic Monthly*, Vol. 205, No. 3 (March 1960).

Evans, Bergen, "But What's A Dictionary For?" *Atlantic Monthly*, Vol. 209, No. 5 (May 1962).

Follett, Wilson, "Grammar Is Obsolete". *Atlantic Monthly*, Vol. 205, No. 2 (February 1960).

Follet, Wilson, "Sabotage In Springfield". *Atlantic Monthly*, Vol. 209, No. 1 (January 1962).

Fries, Charles C., *American and English Grammar*. New York: Appleton-Century; 1940.

Fries, Charles C., *Teaching and Learning English as a Foreign Language*. University of Michigan Press; 1946.

Gibson, Walker, *The Limits of Language*. New York: Hill & Wang, American Century Series; 1962.

Gleason, Henry Allen, *An Introduction to Descriptive Linguistics*. New York: Henry Holt & Company; 1955.

Graves, Robert and Hodge, Alan, *The Reader Over Your Shoulder*. London: Jonathan Cape; 1947.

Gray, Louis H., *Foundations of Language*. New York: The Macmillan Company; 1939.

Guetzkow, Harold, *Simulation in Social Science Readings*. Englewood Cliffs, N.J.: Prentice-Hall; 1963.

Hall, Robert A., *Linguistics and Your Language*. Garden City, N.Y.: Doubleday & Company; 1960.

Handlin, Oscar, "Are the Colleges Killing Education?" *Atlantic Monthly*, Vol. 209, No. 5 (May 1962).

Harris, Zellig S., *Structural Linguistics*. The University of Chicago Press; 1961.

Hayakawa, S. I., *Language in Thought and Action*. London: George Allen & Unwin; 1952.

Hayakawa, S. I., *The Use and Misuse of Language*. Greenwich, Conn.: Fawcett Publications; 1963.

Hockett, Charles Francis, *A Course in Modern Linguistics*. New York: The Macmillan Company; 1958.

Hodenfield, G. K. and Stinnett, T. M., *The Education of Teachers*. Englewood Cliffs, N.J.: Prentice-Hall; 1961.

Hughes, John Paul, *The Science of Language. An Introduction to Linguistics*. New York: Random House; 1961.

Koerner, James D., "How Not To Teach Teachers". *Atlantic Monthly*, Vol. 211, No. 2 (February 1963).

Krutch, Joseph Wood, "English As She Is Spoken". *Saturday Review*, Vol. 42, No. 27 (July 4, 1959).

Lamport, Felicia, "Dictionaries: Our Language Right Or Wrong". *Harper's Magazine*, Vol. 219, No. 1312 (September 1959).

Larsen, Roy E., *Communication and Education*. Boston University Press; 1960.

Lucas, F. L., *Style*. London: Cassell & Company; 1955.

MacDonald, Dwight, "The Decline and Fall of Good English". *Life International*, Vol. 32, No. 7 (April 9, 1962).

MacDonald, Dwight, "The String Untuned". *The New Yorker*, Vol. 38, No. 3 (March 10, 1962).

Mayer, Martin, *The Schools*. London: The Bodley Head; 1961.

Moulton, William G., "The New Structure of Language Learning". *Princeton* Alumni Weekly, Vol. 42, No. 22 (March 16, 1962).

National Council of Teachers of English, *The National Interest and the Teaching of English*. Champaign, Ill.: The National Council of Teachers of English; 1961.

The New English Bible. New Testament. Oxford University Press and Cambridge University Press; 1961.

Orwell, George, *Shooting an Elephant* ("Politics and the English Language"). London: Martin Secker & Warburg; 1950.

Pei, Mario, "The Dictionary as a Battlefront". *Saturday Review*, Vol. 45, No. 28 (July 21, 1962).

Pei, Mario and Gaynor, Frank, *A Dictionary of Linguistics*. London: Peter Owen; 1957.

Pierce, John R. and David, Edward E., Jr., *Man's World of Sound*. Garden City, N.Y.: Doubleday & Company; 1958.

Pike, Kenneth Lee, *Phonemics. A Technique for Reducing Languages to Writing*. University of Michigan Press; 1947.

Pooley, Robert C., *Teaching English Grammar*. New York: Appleton-Century-Crofts; 1962.

Quiller-Couch, Sir Arthur, *On the Art of Writing*. Cambridge University Press; 1950.

Roberts, Paul, *English Sentences*. New York: Harcourt, Brace & Company; 1962.

Roberts, Paul, *Understanding English*. New York: Harper and Brothers; 1958.

Sebeok, Thomas A. (ed.), *Style in Language*. New York: The Technology Press of M.I.T. and John Wiley & Sons; 1960.

Smith, Henry Lee, Jr., *Linguistic Science and the Teaching of English*. Cambridge, Mass.; Harvard University Press; 1956.

Strunk, William, Jr., and White, E. B., *The Elements of Style*. New York: The Macmillan Company; 1959.

Sturtevant, E. H., *Linguistic Change*. The University of Chicago Press; 1961.

Vallins, G. H., *The Pattern of English*. London: André Deutsch; 1956.

Vigilans (pseud.), *Usage and Abusage*. London: André Deutsch; 1952.

Whatmough, Josua, *Language. A Modern Synthesis*. London: Martin Secker & Warburg; 1956.

White, E. B., *The Points of My Compass*. London: Hamish Hamilton; 1963.

Williams, Raymond, *The Long Revolution*. London: Chatto & Windus; 1961.

INDEX